W9-BLV-361

THE YEARS OF CHALLENGE

The Commonwealth and the British Empire
1945–1958

OTHER BOOKS BY THE SAME AUTHOR

RAINBOW ON THE ZAMBESI

THE RHODESIAN

TEN STARS SOUTH OF ASIA

942.085
T

THE YEARS OF CHALLENGE

The Commonwealth and the British Empire
1945–1958

by

DON TAYLOR

ILLUSTRATED

Wingate College Library

FREDERICK A. PRAEGER, *PUBLISHERS*
NEW YORK

Published in the United States of America in 1960
by Frederick A. Praeger, Inc., Publishers,
64 University Place, New York 3, N.Y.

All rights reserved

Library of Congress catalog card number 60–8368

© Don Taylor 1959

Printed in Great Britain

To
D. B.

CONTENTS

13712

ILLUSTRATIONS

AUTHOR'S NOTE

THE PURPOSE of this book is to detail the major events in the years between 1945 and 1958 bearing on the development of the Commonwealth and the British Empire. In those thirteen remarkable years, the evolution of British colonial policy was decisive, and successful completion of the Nigerian Independence Conference in 1958 marked the beginning of the final stages.

How fared the Commonwealth itself whilst the Colonies were progressing so dramatically? That story, too, I have tried to trace. It has been my conviction that during this period, the ultimate fate of the Commonwealth as a whole has been decided. What has been achieved must now be built on, or lost. Whether the Commonwealth will survive as a decisive force in the world, or whether it will be marked down in history as a great experiment which failed, will depend on the positive efforts of all its members, and not on Britain alone.

A great many people have given me invaluable assistance and encouragement in writing this book. I would particularly like to mention the Earl of Home, Secretary of State for Commonwealth Relations, and Mr Alan Lennox-Boyd, Secretary of State for the Colonies; the staffs of the Commonwealth Relations and the Colonial Offices; the offices of the Commonwealth High Commissioners and Colonial Commissioners and Representatives in London; the correspondents and staff of *New Commonwealth* and the former *Crown Colonist*; Mrs Diana Jagoda and Mrs Ann Kean. I am also indebted to the directors of Tothill Press Ltd for permission to reproduce the maps in this book.

CHAPTER I

OUT OF THE DARKNESS

ON AUGUST 30, 1945, a strong British naval force under Admiral C. H. J. Harcourt steamed into the port of Hong Kong. Such a symbol of British power had not been seen in those waters since Christmas Day of 1941, when the heavily outnumbered garrison of the Colony had been overwhelmed, submerged by the flood of Japanese military might bent on establishing the Greater Asia Co-Prosperity Sphere.

"Life begins again for Hong Kong after 44 months of nightmare like an entombment", cabled *The Times* correspondent. He added, in a cry from the heart, "We have been forgotten folk and have undergone severe hardship."

But now was the time of redemption. The bitter humiliation of 1941 was erased by the sight of the naval landing-parties surging shorewards, by the small and impassive Japanese envoy, still in his rumpled uniform and incongruously carrying a briefcase, boarding the Rear-Admiral's cruiser in abject surrender. That same day, Mr F. C. Gimson, the Colonial Secretary, was released from prison camp and set up an administrative office. Rear-Admiral Harcourt broadcast from the Colony's radio station that Hong Kong was under British military government.

It was fitting that Hong Kong, the first of Britain's Colonies to fall to the Japanese, should be the first to be liberated. Only four days later, the Commander-in-Chief of the East Indies Fleet was at Singapore. By September 10 the Japanese forces in North Borneo had laid down their arms. In the Solomon Islands the Australians were wiping out the last, isolated pockets of enemy resistance.

His Majesty King George VI could well, with a full and thankful heart, send out a message of thanksgiving to "my peoples and the peoples under my protection in the Far East" at their deliverance. ". . . The ties which unite my peoples everywhere will now be fully restored," he wrote. "I know full well that these ties of loyalty and affection between myself and my Far Eastern peoples have never been broken. But they have been maintained in darkness and in suffering. The time has now come when their strength and permanence will again be displayed in triumph before the whole world."

Who but a few anxious prophets and confirmed cynics could doubt that the power and glory of the British Commonwealth and Empire would be restored? This extraordinary association of 500 million people, inhabiting over 11 million square miles of the earth's surface, was the proud apotheosis of the British political genius. It was designed to stand against time and circumstance. The messages of loyalty poured in, the great crowds from Nairobi to Hong Kong, from the Falklands to the Canadian Arctic, cheered the victory parades, the demobilized soldiers began to stream back, the "Thanksgiving Gifts to Britain" schemes were organized in the Colonial capitals, a rich crop of development and resettlement schemes lay ready.

The war was ended. It was as if a rich valley of busy towns and smiling villages had been overwhelmed by floodwater and tempest. But now the fury was over. What lay under the cleared sky and the receding waters?

The savage and protracted struggle for existence had not prevented Britain herself from pursuing her imperial course. Through the darkest periods of the six-year-long war the grave debates on the Colonial Empire had gone forward in Parliament, the constitutional advances for the dependent territories had been meticulously discussed and planned in Whitehall, the money for future economic development had been solemnly voted. There had been no departure from the established principles that Britain must ensure good government in her Colonies as long as she was responsible for them, and that she must train the peoples of those Colonies to finally govern themselves.

There was some difference of opinion as to how long it was going to take to teach the dependent peoples how to govern themselves. Indian, Sinhalese and Burmese "nationalist" leaders were stretching the tired tolerance of British Cabinet Ministers to the limit. But not all ordinary Members of Parliament were so inhibited. They could foresee that the curriculum might well have to be shortened. Indeed, a body of Conservative M.P.s had, early in that year of 1945, strongly recommended that Burma should be given full Dominion status within six years of the end of the war.

That sort of optimistic thinking could, however, be tempered by the cautionary opinions of older hands such as Sir Richard Windstedt, who had worked long and arduously in Malaya. In his booklet *Britain and Malaya* he warned that "These two difficulties, the aversion of the Malays from political union among themselves and the existence of a Palestinian rivalry between Malays and the immigrants into Malaya, especially the Chinese, are an insurmountable obstacle to self-government for Malaya within any time that can be foreseen."

What was the true picture of all that had taken, that was still taking place? The cost of the war to Britain, in treasure, in prestige, in suffering had been almost overwhelming. Her policies in the past had often been bitterly criticized; her position as head of the greatest Empire in human history made her a vulnerable target in a world which was dazzled by a rebirth of the idea that all peoples should be equal. Yet it remained true that the principles for which Britain had fought the longest and the hardest were those to which the United Nations Organization was to pledge itself. It remained true that the powers which Britain had opposed were evil, predatory and committed to the degradation of the human spirit.

For a bitter and desperate year of the war, she had stood alone with her Commonwealth and Empire behind her. A proud and historic year, a year which above all else put the world in her debt. That was how the British saw it. Who could blame them if they believed that they were entitled to resume their great role as the leaders and mentors of a quarter of the human race?

In 1939, after declaration of war, Herr von Ribbentrop had said: "There is no part of the world where the British flag is not waving against the will of the people in question, and where deeds of violence, robbery and lies do not mark the path of British Imperialism." This had been a lie on the magnificent scale. The answer to it had surely been given by the Colonial people themselves, and more particularly by their leaders. The Paramount Chief of Accra had summed up the matter. "If the worst comes to the worst," he had said, "I will take off my sandals and walk barefooted side by side with British soldiers right into the firing line."

The Paramount Chief may have overdrawn the bow. But, in essence, he had voiced the opinion of the Colonial leaders, of all the great paramount chiefs of British Africa, of the sultans of Malaya and the rajahs of India, of the emirs of Nigeria, of all those rulers whose power and influence had rested on the substance of British power. "Indirect Rule" it had been called. It had developed and broadened, that system of rule, but it still ensured the influence of the local rulers.

Without doubt the traditional rulers in the main were ready to resume their tutelage in 1945. But now other voices were raising themselves in the Colonies. They were the voices of men of middle or lower class who believed that their traditional rulers had sold the national birthright, had been nothing but "stooges" of the British. They indulged in the heresy that the war had never been their war, that it had been fought purely in Britain's interest. An "imperialist war" they scornfully called it, and they had never seen it in any other light than as a possible means of furthering nationalist aspirations. In India, in Burma, in Malaya some of them had openly assisted the enemy—traitors from the British point of view, patriots from their own.

To the farseeing and the realistic, these men and their like were the men who might well count for more than the traditional rulers. (Even the traditional rulers were not all that thankful for what had been done for them. Sir Philip Mitchell, the Governor of Kenya, acidly told a gathering of chiefs just before the end of the war that "some of you write as if you, out of your goodness and courage, had come to help us. That sort of talk is foolishness.... this is in the fullest sense your war. It is you who have received help. Had we been defeated you would have been cast into slavery.")

There was something strangely fitting in the fact that the very man who had introduced that system of Indirect Rule—in Nigeria—died in that year of 1945. Lord Lugard, soldier-statesman of the Colonial Empire, was a figure comparable to the great Marshal Lyautey of France. His life was an epic of Empire. He had served under Roberts in Afghanistan, taken part in the expedition that tragically failed to save Gordon at Khartoum. On behalf of the British East Africa Company he had taken over Uganda with only 50 Sudanese soldiers. He had pacified, practically built up the vast Colony of Nigeria. No man better fitted the description of "Empire builder". Yet he was wise, farseeing, a counsellor of great imagination until his death in his 88th year. He had not failed to move with the times, but it remained true that his death marked the end of an historic phase of imperial history. The new phase might not perhaps be so romantic but, in its way, it promised at least as much drama.

That year of 1945 saw just as unlooked for a change on the home political front. Despite the immense prestige of Winston Churchill, the British Conservatives were defeated at the polls and for the first time in British history a Labour Government came to power with an overall majority. The election result represented, rightly or wrongly, a revulsion from the old order of things and a powerful hope of a brave new world.

Into office as Secretary of State for the Colonies, in place of Oliver Stanley, member of one of Britain's ancient, aristocratic families, came George Hall, ex-coal-miner. Arthur Creech Jones, a prominent Fabian and back-room thinker for Labour's Colonial policy, took over as Under-Secretary of State. Whatever was hopefully said about "a joint approach to Colonial affairs" there was little doubt that the new Government would accelerate the rate of progress towards self-government, would give more attention to the views of Colonial politicians as against those of officials, and would adopt an approach to economic affairs based on Socialist doctrine.

In the Colonies themselves, there was a significant divergence of opinion about the new British Government. In the main, European communities regarded its advent with foreboding. The *Kenya Weekly News* declared: "There are certain aspects of the Labour Party's declared policy which are antipathetic to the ideas and ideals of white settlement." On the other hand, the *Gold Coast Independent* told its African readers that "we in the Colonies believe that the Labour Government will understand our point of view ... we look forward to the day when the Labour Government will break up the combines, cartels and amalgamations that have made it impossible for the people of this country to live decently, even though they produce half the world output of cocoa. We look to the Labour Government to extricate the Gold Coast from its economic and social chaos."

Whether the Labour Government liked it or not, even at this early stage it had become identified in the eyes of Colonial peoples as the party dedicated to the interests of coloured peoples, just as the Conservative Party had unfortunately got itself into the position of being regarded as the champion of white reactionaries. Time and circumstance were to demonstrate how absurdly wide of the mark were such simple and convenient labels.

Overshadowing all else there loomed the suspicion that the Socialists might well hand over ultimate control of the Colonial Empire

Wingate College Library

to the proposed United Nations Organization. Indeed, Mr Creech Jones himself, as chairman of the Fabian Colonial Bureau and before he was appointed to Government office, had issued a Report on "Colonies and International Conscience" which ended by asserting that the administration of all non-self-governing peoples should be a matter of international concern, and that machinery should be devised to make such supervision effective. Whatever the extent of the international control visualized by Mr Creech Jones, to Europeans in the Colonies, to members of the Opposition, to the officers of the Colonial Service and to a vast number of other Britons who simply thought Britain ought to run her own imperial affairs, this looked disturbingly like a retreat from greatness.

In point of fact, the San Francisco Conference in June of 1945, which preceded the inaugural assembly of the United Nations in January of 1946, had agreed on principles affecting dependent peoples which might well have been drawn in entirety from Britain's Colonial policy. "Self-government or independence", said the Conference, "should be the goal of the Colonial peoples." Britain, alone among Colonial powers, had laid down that same policy before the war had ever started. But that did not prevent her from being tainted with imperialism. In the great tidal wave of emotional idealism which heralded the end of the war, the Colonial powers were being washed up on a beach of reaction, finished, out of place in the new "common man's century" in which the riveter from Brooklyn, the peasant in the Burma paddy field, the blood and milk drinking Masai of Kenya had miraculously become the brotherly citizens of one world.

Britain could hardly have been an imperial power for three centuries without having a long and varied experience of the international pillory. She could well anticipate lasting out this latest, rising attack even though in the new state of international opinion, and with her own strength dissipated, it was more dangerous than any that had gone before. What was really alarming was that the United States, emerging as world leader, was already emphasizing her anti-imperial views.

Oliver Stanley, Britain's former Secretary of State for the Colonies and an able and idealistic man, saw very clearly the disaster which could come in the wake of such an American policy. Addressing the American Outpost in London he said that "one misconception is that Britain has been in these Colonial territories for many years, even centuries, and yet done very little". He warned his listeners,

"No 'splinterization' of the British Colonial Empire would be in-
the interests of the world." And he asked, "Would it really be an
advantage to create another 40 independent states, all small?"

One might have thought, in view of all that had happened in
Europe over the centuries, in view of the new effort even then being
made to create a federation in Europe, that the answer to Oliver
Stanley's question was clear. Unhappily, it seemed that most Ameri-
can ears were still deafened by the splash of tea-chests landing in
Boston harbour.

The British, warmed by the thought that the world of free men
owed them an immeasurable debt for their efforts during the past
six years, had by no means grown accustomed to the rôle of poor
relation let alone the prospect of departed power. But the econo-
mists, busily totting up the cost of war, were pointing out that
Britain's sterling debts were then approximately £4,000 million, that
her economy was dislocated, that she had sold many of her overseas
investments, that lend-lease had ended and that the dollar deficit
could approach £500 million in the next two years. In short, the
painful truth was that Britain was sorely in need of American
financial aid. It was a gesture of infinite faith that, deeply in debt
though she was, she passed the Colonial Development and Welfare
Bill guaranteeing £120 millions for the Colonies in the next ten
years.

Clearly, America and Britain had to continue in close alliance, but
just as clearly the Americans were in the position to make their views
predominate. It was, at the least, embarrassing not to have American recognition, let alone approval, of what Britain was trying to
do in the Colonies. And on the face of it, there was a solid section
of opinion in America which saw no value in the British Commonwealth, let alone Britain's Colonial policy, and which advocated the
ending of both the sterling area and Imperial Preference. Most Americans recognized Britain's value to the world, a few even recognized
that the Commonwealth might be an instrument for the good of
humanity, but the general belief was that this was the American
era of leadership and that the sooner old imperial concepts and out-
croppings were removed the better.

Little wonder that Oliver Stanley, now out of office, gravely
warned a Royal Empire Society audience in London that the next
few years would be among the most critical in the whole of Britan's
Colonial history. He added: "Whether or not we conduct our ad-

ministration with sympathy and act with wisdom and decision, will determine whether we alienate the people of these territories or bind them to us more closely."

What of the Dominions, those independent nations of the Commonwealth which had also borne the brunt of war with Britain? Before 1939, they had depended on the shield of British military strength; they had the assurance of British economic leadership. Now, they saw the powerful, respected leader of the Commonwealth reduced almost to beggary, exhausted by her efforts, dependent on others as they had formerly been on her.

Australia and New Zealand had seen the Americans, not the Royal Navy, turn back the dreaded tide of Japanese invasions. Canada had been steadily drawn into the American economic orbit. South Africa, where Field-Marshal Smuts held an uneasy power, looked with suspicion and fear on British policy in Africa. There was rejoicing over the common triumphs in war, there was loyalty and affection, in varying degree, for "the Old Country". But behind it all there was an uneasy thought, that the old order of things in the Commonwealth had ended, that the power at the centre had been so weakened that it might well amount to no power at all.

What, then, were the chances of meaningful survival for this British Commonwealth of Nations and this Colonial Empire? All that it stood for was suspect in the world. The leader was brought low in poverty and weakness. Nationalism was rampant, and throughout the Colonies the rising political leaders saw their mission as breaking the chains of British imperialism. Britain's major ally, the new leader of the world, viewed her aspirations without sympathy and virtually no understanding. A new government had attained power in Britain dedicated to policies which, vaguely worded as some of them were, led to the fear that a renunciation of imperial responsibilities was a distinct possibility.

It was not a picture to inspire hope. Those who thought that, despite Winston Churchill's resounding defiance, the liquidation of the British Empire would not long be delayed, and that the Commonwealth itself would inevitably disintegrate, had no lack of seeming evidence to support their views.

What was not so apparent was that it was not simply the Commonwealth that was on trial. It was the entire Humanism which had been the mainstay and the glory of the Western world. That Humanism, the uneasy marriage of Christianity and Greek-Roman culture, had been carried throughout the world by the Europeans, sweeping away, destroying the ancient, indigenous cultures. And the chief instrument of evangelism had been the British Commonwealth and Empire.

CHAPTER II

THE GATHERING CLOUDS

EVEN BEFORE 1945 had closed it was only too clear that the Empire was under considerable strain. There were problems common to all the territories as they were unshackled from the general war machine or from the grip of the enemy; the painful process of switching over to a peacetime economy; the building-up of competent administration after occupation; the complications of reintroducing returning soldiers to civilian life; the shortage of goods and equipment, inevitably coupled with rising prices.

But over and above these common difficulties there were the special problems of individual territories. Some of these were of long standing, like that of Palestine. For twenty-six years Arabs and Jews had consistently failed to co-operate for the common good of the country, or even to recognize any justice in each other's case.

True, Palestine was not a colony, but Britain held the mandate and was required both to facilitate Jewish immigration and at the same time to see that such immigration did not prejudice the position of the Arabs. It was an impossible assignment. The Jews claimed Palestine as their own because of past history and because a Jewish homeland had been promised after the First World War. The Arabs were no less sure that Palestine belonged to them, on the simple grounds that they had lived in it for a thousand years past.

In November, Ernest Bevin, Britain's Secretary of State for Foreign Affairs, announced the setting up of a Joint Anglo-American Committee of Inquiry "to examine the question of European Jewry and to make a further review of the Palestine problem in the light of that examination". For, as Bevin pointed out, Hitler's persecution of the Jews, their appalling martyrdom in Europe, had sharpened the ambition of many Jews to settle in Palestine.

B

The Foreign Secretary's intention was to make Palestine an international concern, to lift it out of the colonial sphere. "The repercussions of the conflict have spread far beyond the small land in which it has arisen," he declared. "The Zionist cause has strong supporters in the United States, in Great Britain, in the Dominions and elsewhere. On the other side, the cause of the Palestinian Arabs has been espoused by the whole Arab world, and more lately has become a matter of keen interest to their 90 million co-religionists in India."

Strikes and riots by Jews in Tel-Aviv were the answer to Mr Bevin's statement. The Arabs followed suit when the Arab League decided to boycott goods manufactured by the Jews of Palestine. Sir William Fitzgerald, the Chief Justice of Palestine, warned: "Those of us who have humbly served Palestine for several years know how near we are to an abyss, in which the many high hopes may be swallowed for generations."

The significance of the Palestine problem to the British Empire did not lie in its impact on colonial policy for, as Mr Bevin had indicated, it was soon lifted into the field of foreign affairs. What Palestine demonstrated was, firstly, the rapidity with which opposing factions were ready to take up position now that the war was ended, and, secondly, a growing belief that British power was fading and that she could no longer hold a balance when it was required of her. Above all, Palestine sadly revealed that the brotherhood of man was quite certainly not at hand. On the contrary, the passionate desire of controlled or subject peoples to settle their own future and their own quarrels if need be had rarely been more emphatically underlined. These factors were to repeat themselves time and again in imperial affairs henceforward.

It was in the East that the British Empire faced its greatest and most immediate dangers. All the Colonial powers were confronted with these same acute dangers, which sprang from a general, proud feeling over most of that great area to be done with the overlordship of Europe. It was not a new feeling. For years before the war such leaders as Mahatma Gandhi of India and Dr Sun Yat-sen of China had struggled to bring their people into the sun, to give them equality and freedom.

The success of Japanese arms in the early years of the war had given Asian nationalist leaders their great chance. At one and the same time it struck the death blow at the lingering idea of indisputable European supremacy, and created a chaos out of which national renascence could spring. Some of the nationalist leaders co-operated with the Japanese conquerors, others did not. All of them used the occupation period to advance their own patriotic ends. By the time of the Japanese surrender to the Allies many plans for independence were far forward.

Yet, running parallel to the flood of nationalism was the struggle between democracy and communism, even at this early stage. In the countries under British control, democracy had found its firmest roots. That was not so evident in those early post-war months, but it was soon to become significantly clear. In the end in Southeast Asia, the Commonwealth countries were to prove the most dependable advocates of democracy (although that by no means meant that they were the allies of the West).

It was in China that Asia's surging nationalism and the struggle between democracy and communism were most immediately manifest. In short, China was at once an inspiration and a warning to all Asia. Whichever of the two political systems triumphed would have a spectacular effect on the great mass of humanity in the surrounding lands.

Just before the end of the war, General Chiang Kai-shek's Nationalist Kuomintang government had negotiated with the Chinese Communists in a last effort to establish national unity. It was foredoomed to failure; and when the Japanese surrender came China was still divided, with the Communists under Mao Tse-tung holding the northern provinces. Before the year was out, civil war was certain.

To the south-west, in India, another massive revolution in Asian affairs was resolving itself, a struggle which was to prove a counterbalance to that in China. For here the struggle was not between communist and democrat, but against British control, and between Hindu and Muslim. Communism was not in the field in practical strength, nor was Britain entirely discredited. Subhas Chandra Bose had indeed formed an Indian National Army to fight with the Japanese, but it was also true that 28 Indians had won the Victoria Cross fighting with the British. More than 24,000 Indians were imprisoned during the war, including the Congress Party Working Committee, yet a year before the war ended Gandhi was out of gaol and in the spring of 1945 discussions were going forward to find a constitutional solution prior to India's independence. Reason and moderation had not vanished entirely.

The great hope of the new British Labour Government was that

a united India would soon become a free partner in the Commonwealth, and the most powerful bastion of democracy in Asia. But
the Simla Conference in the spring of 1945 had already blown to
the winds any idea that Hindus and Muslims would build one State
together. The Congress Party and the Muslim League nursed hopes
and policies far too wide apart for any bridging of the abyss between
them.

Though the Congress Party adopted a political programme designed by its extreme tolerance to draw the support of all sections of
the Indian population, it was becoming abundantly clear, even to
the Socialist Government in Britain which desperately desired to
launch one India into the troubled waters of the post-war world,
that partition of the sub-continent seemed the only solution. There
was still a lingering hope that the two parties could be brought together, but there also lingered Gandhi's decisive rejection of Sir
Stafford Cripps' approaches in 1942.

The irony of the situation lay in the fact that the new British
Government wanted the sub-continent to be free as quickly as possible, and that it was now the intended beneficiaries who were
putting on the brake, however reluctantly. For the major mistake
of British policy in the past, often repeated, had been to offer Indian
leaders too little, and that generally too late. In the event, a great
deal of goodwill and even more of pride of association with the
British had gone beyond retrieval.

Yet, looking back, the significance of British policy at this point
can hardly be over-estimated. For she, alone of the European colonial powers—let alone those elsewhere—was willingly renouncing her
control over India. She was in process of helping to establish a giant
democratic power—two, indeed, as it proved—in Asia before communism became an all-powerful influence. And from now on, this
sense of urgency was to inform her entire colonial policy, sometimes,
in the eyes of critics to the detriment of the free world, her own position and even the future prospects of the liberated countries.

As Britain went forward with the unswerving intention of handing over power whenever possible and practicable, the Dutch and
the French both clung to pre-war ideas of imperial responsibility. It
is easy to be over-complacent. Both the Netherlands and France had
been themselves occupied by the Germans, and their Eastern possessions taken by the Japanese. The link between ruling country and
Empire had been broken, decisively as events turned out.

French Indo-China had been administered by the Vichy France officials from 1942 until 1944, but under the iron grip of Japan. But as soon as France herself was liberated the Japanese took over direct control. In the August of 1945, after Japan's collapse, the nationalist (and Communist) leader Ho Chi Minh set up a republic. From then on, although Ho Chi Minh put on a conciliatory front in the early stages, the French position was under continued assault.

Things were worse still for the Dutch in their East Indian possessions. The Japanese, in one dying blow at the Dutch, encouraged the setting-up of a nationalist government before the actual end of the war in the East. The British, landing on the Dutch East Indies Islands to restore order after the Japanese surrender, believed that the only solution for the time being was to recognize the nationalist government until the emergencies of the situation were cleared up. For the Dutch, it was the beginning of the end. They were in no position to restore their own influence on anything like the former scale, and they found, moreover, their wartime allies either directly opposed or at the best reluctant to help them.

The war-time Prime Minister of the Netherlands, Professor P. S. Gerbrandy, wrote bitterly, some years later:[1] "For four centuries we, the people of the Netherlands, had been the protectors of the many peoples of the great chain of East Indian islands which stretches from Sumatra to New Guinea. We had maintained law and order and had established a quiet and orderly, yet unostentatious, form of prosperity. The East Indies formed part of our sovereign realm. . . .

"The United States authorities, notoriously uncertain in their conduct of diplomacy in the Far East, in effect obliged us to part with our heritage and hand over power to the clamant group who now, after their own fashion, rule over Indonesia. The Soviet representatives and those of their satellites chuckled in the corridors of the United Nations Organization, and Great Britain, after an initial spurt of misplaced energy, not only left us in the lurch but was indifferent to our fate in the Far East."

Britain herself was no better able to retrieve her position in Burma. The original tragic error was made at the outbreak of the war, when the Burmese offered to support Britain if a promise of independence was made. The offer was harshly rejected. Britain wanted no gunpoint bargains. She paid dearly when the Japanese swept across Burma in 1942. To the Burmese it was Britain's war and if she was

[1] *New Commonwealth*, September 1, 1952.

defeated perhaps they could strike a better bargain with the Japanese. As things turned out, they did not. The new rulers of the land were infinitely worse than the old. But when the land was cleared of the Japanese, Britain soon discovered a powerful Burmese nationalist sentiment which would accept nothing short of self-government. Not even a promise of Dominion status as soon as feasible was sufficient of a compromise. In truth, British policy in Burma had been, too often since 1886 when Britain took over the country, unimaginative and dilatory. Now was the time of reckoning. U Aung San, who was in command of Burma's Army during the war, fighting against and then with the British, was the new national leader. He was hardly the man to advocate a continuing link with the Commonwealth of Nations.

The same pattern might easily have been repeated in Malaya, for there, too, there were aspiring nationalist leaders who had seen the opportunity to further their aims in the chaos of war. But Malaya was a multi-racial territory of Malays, Chinese and Indians. Racial sentiment was stronger than nationalist, and the power of the Malay rulers had remained considerable despite the Japanese occupation. There had been no collaboration army as in Burma. Instead, the most effective force had been the Malay Peoples' Anti-Japanese Army, whose Chinese leaders were the most implacable enemies of the invaders.

The Japanese had encouraged racial enmity. The slogan which they adopted was "Malaya for the Malays". Accordingly, the Chinese were the victims of a terrorist campaign. The Indians, especially the Tamils, fared little better, for nearly 100,000 of these were sent to Siam to work on the infamous "death railway".

The British returned to find the jungle invading many of the rubber plantations and the tin-mine dredges rusting in the tropical sun. They returned to find human chaos where there had been settled order, the roads crowded with refugees returning from Siam or from the interior. Worst of all, they found race hatred flourishing, rioting and murder between Malays and Chinese, and suspicion and mistrust of British motives. Who could say what new force or what older but revitalized force would eventually emerge?

With that great maelstrom of events in China, how could Malaya escape the powerful impact? To the British, inauspicious altogether though the circumstances might appear, the answer was obvious. Malaya must be urged forward to nationhood. Within a few months of the Japanese defeat, a plan for an early Malayan Union was in sight of completion.

The Japanese had also engulfed the neighbouring British or British-protected territories of North Borneo, Sarawak and Brunei in the South China Sea. These territories were so far behind most of their neighbours politically that their immediate problems seemed entirely those of economic rehabilitation. But it was not quite so simple. Even here the old order could no longer hold good. Sarawak, so long ruled over by Rajahs of the remarkable Brooke family, seemed certain to come under closer Colonial Office control. And British North Borneo could hardly continue to be the last territory administered by a Chartered Company, however paternal, when all Asia was in ferment.

The East indeed was the most anxious and early consideration from the British point of view. Africa was stirring, with white settlers seeing the portents and anxiously planning to consolidate their position, whilst the new school of politically-minded black leaders sensed that their opportunity was not so far away. But Africa gave yet a little time. The East did not.

Even Hong Kong's position was dubious. Already there was talk of a Chinese demand for its return, with the possibility of American backing. This great commercial outpost situated at the very gates of China meant much to British export trade, and even more to British prestige in the East. After the havoc of war it stood sadly in need of a robust and energetic administration and there seemed to be some delay about providing one.

Only Ceylon seemed to be still following the careful and steady pattern laid down over the years of peace. That lovely island had escaped the havoc of war, though narrowly enough at that. It had been under constant threats, as the headquarters of Lord Louis Mountbatten's South-East Asia Command. The more cynical Sinhalese said that was the real reason why Britain promised them full internal civic administration as soon as possible. The end of the war would herald a different tune, they believed. But it was not so. Lord Soulbury headed a commission to work out a new constitution, and by November of 1945 this had been accepted by the Ceylon State Council.

The ambition of Ceylon's leaders, themselves strongly steeped in British traditions, was to attain Dominion status in two years. They realized Ceylon was a small island, of great strategic importance,

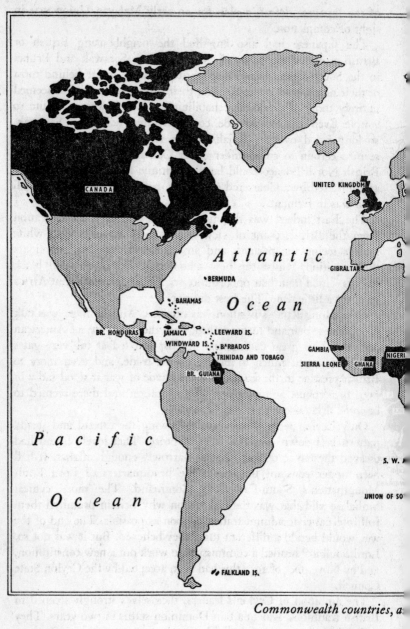

Commonwealth countries, a

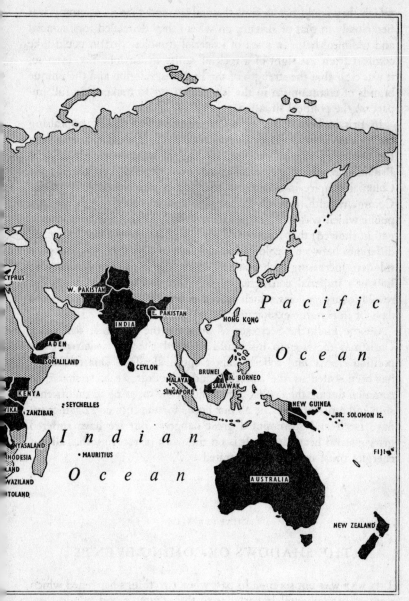

...endent territories of Britain.

which they could not defend themselves, and that its economy was tied closely to that of Britain, on whom they depended for financial and technical help. In a sea of imperial troubles, Britain could take comfort from the sight of a rock of sanity in Ceylon. Yet, even so, it was clear that the strength of the Buddhist religion and the unique brands of communism in the island had yet to make their full impact on the political situation.

In Britain herself, the new Government was rapidly appraising the difference between ideals and reality when it came to handling the affairs of a great empire. Its leaders were in no doubt that Britain's prosperity and prospects of power depended on keeping the Colonial Empire in being and merging it into a new and greater Commonwealth. But it was not very easy to bring that home to a public which was so ill-formed (as a B.B.C. listener research investigation showed) that four out of every five people did not know the difference between a colony and a dominion. Neither was it easy to sidestep increasing exhortations from the Fabian guardians of Labour's imperial conscience and various colonial newspapers for revolutionary policies which would demonstrate that "the bad old days of imperialist exploitation" had gone.

George Hall, the Secretary of State for the Colonies, sent out a Christmas message to his world-scattered charges which put the position clearly and soberly, albeit optimistically: "Our friendship has been sealed by the suffering and the effort we have shared in common during the last six years; and in the fostering of that friendship and sense of unity lie all our hopes for the future. Together we have faced and surmounted great dangers. But we have suffered grievous and heavy losses. It is on the work of recovery that all our energies must now be concentrated. . . ."

CHAPTER III

THE SHADOWS OF COMING EVENTS

THE WAR WAS not six months past when two things happened which were of fundamental importance to the economic and political development of imperial policy. Early in 1946, the Anglo-American Loan, and the Bretton Woods Agreement which was bound up with it, was accepted by the British Parliament. And at almost the same time a White Paper was issued dealing with inter-territorial organization between the three East African territories of Kenya, Uganda and Tanganyika. The first of these happenings was to bear heavily on economic co-operation with the Empire and Commonwealth; the second revealed that though Britain was leading the colonies towards independence, she was not to be stampeded into panic action either by foreign opinion or by pressure from within the colonies themselves.

The Loan from America was accepted with reluctance, even with bitterness. It seemed to many British people that America had forgotten the principle of equal sacrifice between allies and was striking a hard and ruthless bargain. For here was Britain, exhausted and in grave financial straits from the very magnitude of her efforts, forced to accept conditions which even a beaten enemy would have thought crushing.

Leopold Amery, former Secretary of State for India and all his life a passionate advocate of the British Empire, decribed the Loan itself as "a perfectly fair and reasonable business deal, equally in the interests of both parties".[1] It was the U.S. commercial policy linked with the Loan that he found iniquitous, and a large body of opinion supported him. Amery made what—in the light of later events—was a remarkable prophecy. "The real danger to the peace of the world is if two predominant economic blocs, the one practising a totalitarian economy, the other preaching the restoration of the 19th-century unregulated price economy, compete for mastery over an unorganized world of small economic units, forcing them in practice to join one side or the other."

In his view "the true interest of world peace, in the economic as in the political field, lies precisely in the formation of nation groups or families, like the Empire sterling group, which can deal on a footing of equality with either the United States or Russia, and which need not follow exactly the economic or political policies of either but can co-operate in friendly independence with both."

But to the Americans, their policy was the only real way of ensuring free world trade. If, at the same time, it undermined "Colonialism", well that too was all to the good. They had no intention of bolstering the British Empire by allowing Imperial Preference and the Sterling Area to go on any longer than need be. In any case, they

[1] American Chamber of Commerce in London Luncheon, March 1946.

intimated, they were ready to lower tariffs if Britain would consent to whittling away the Imperial Preferences which bolstered trade between the countries of the British Empire and Commonwealth. Was it not in the best interests of the world to break down the trading barriers? Yet, as Foreign Secretary Ernest Bevin said, "The United States say they want freer trade. But freer trade does not mean only the lowering of tariff barriers. It depends on the actual fact as to whether they buy goods."

Did the Loan, and all that followed it, destroy the Empire and Commonwealth as an economic unity? Was it not true that much of the Imperial Preference system had become outmoded and of little value? Would the new independent nations of the Commonwealth, yet to emerge, ever have consented to a rigid preference system? The argument goes on still—but the acceptance of the Loan did bring home the startling fact that the economic pattern was changing, that the new panacea being peddled for the world's economic ills was multilateral trade with free convertibility, however unrealistic the condition of the post-war world made such proposals.

The White Paper on East Africa simultaneously signposted the direction of British Colonial policy. It signified Britain's intention to link up, wherever possible, neighbouring Colonial territories to give them a chance of strong nationhood eventually. And—as I wrote earlier—it also demonstrated that there would be no retreat from responsibility by the Labour Government.

A great deal of further co-operation had developed during the war between the East African territories of Kenya, Uganda and Tanganyika. Transport, defence, posts and telegraphs, customs and excise, income tax, higher education—all these had been established as common services. It was only to be expected that those people who had been urging closer union between the three territories should have had high hopes. East Africa was a geographical and economic unit, they argued, and the time had come to launch it on the road towards Dominion status. These hopes were dashed by the White Paper, which made clear the British Government's intention to retain responsibility for the three territories, and also intimated that any political fusion was regarded as quite impracticable for the time being. Yet, by introducing an East African High Commission and a central legislature, the British Government seemed to nurse the hope that an East African federation would, in the future, emerge—though it cautiously emphasized that the present proposals involved neither political closer union nor the fusion of the East African governments.

The very nature of the three territories concerned made closer union extraordinarily difficult. Kenya was a colony where the European settlers exerted a powerful influence. Tanganyika was a mandated territory which Britain governed, but which she was shortly to place under the United Nations Trusteeship Council. Uganda was a protectorate where the people of the largest and most important province, Buganda, were able and ambitious, and determined to control their own land eventually.

The reaction of the Europeans in Kenya to the White Paper was immediate and hostile. Sir Alfred Vincent, Leader of the Elected Members of the Legislature, said, "We have not the slightest intention of allowing the white settlement to be liquidated today, tomorrow or at any other time." A speech in Britain on the future of Kenya by Arthur Creech Jones, the Under-Secretary of State for the Colonies, led Sir Alfred to retort that if Creech Jones was speaking for the British Government then the settlers must fight for a form of government which would give them control of their own affairs.

In Tanganyika, the Europeans were similarly agitated. They too wanted to move into closer union with Kenya and the White Paper was hardly comforting to them. They were even more apprehensive about the return of Tanganyika to international trusteeship. Would Britain be able to govern the land effectively with the United Nations putting an awkward oar in every so often? What Tanganyika's Europeans wanted was a pledge that the Amery statement of 1920 —that Tanganyika was an integral part of the British Empire—still stood intact.

Even at this early stage the Europeans in East Africa had recognized that their position in the chaotic post-war world would be under increasing challenge. They wanted, very naturally, to stabilize that position while there was yet time. They believed that their leadership was essential in East Africa as far ahead as could be seen. But they also believed that time was not on their side, particularly with a Labour Government in power in Britain. The black-white struggle in British Africa had begun.

The main and immediate problems of the British Colonial Empire were, however, in the East. Africa, the giant which had slept so long, was showing signs of being well awake, but even though the white settlers did not believe it, the Colonial Office thought there

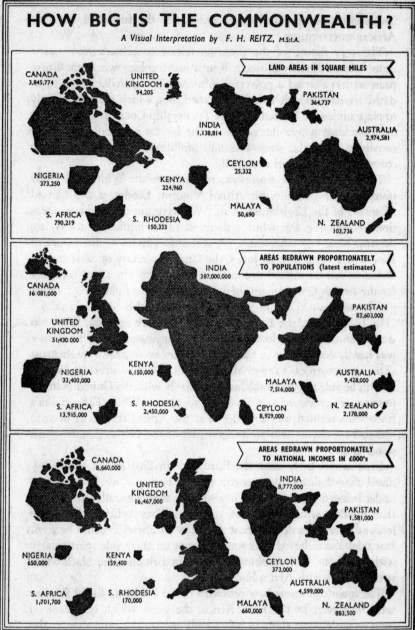

HOW BIG IS THE COMMONWEALTH?

A Visual Interpretation by F. H. REITZ, M.S.I.A.

LAND AREAS IN SQUARE MILES

CANADA
3,845,774

UNITED
KINGDOM
94,205

PAKISTAN
364,737

INDIA
1,138,814

AUSTRALIA
2,974,581

CEYLON
25,332

NIGERIA
373,250

KENYA
224,960

S. AFRICA
790,219

S. RHODESIA
150,333

MALAYA
50,690

N. ZEALAND
103,736

AREAS REDRAWN PROPORTIONATELY TO POPULATIONS (latest estimates)

INDIA
387,000,000

CANADA
16·081,000

PAKISTAN
83,603,000

UNITED
KINGDOM
51,430,000

NIGERIA
33,400,000

KENYA
6,150,000

AUSTRALIA
9,428,000

MALAYA
7,516,000

S. AFRICA
13,915,000

S. RHODESIA
2,450,000

CEYLON
8,929,000

N. ZEALAND
2,178,000

AREAS REDRAWN PROPORTIONATELY TO NATIONAL INCOMES IN £000's

CANADA
8,660,000

UNITED
KINGDOM
16,467,000

INDIA
8,777,000

PAKISTAN
1,581,000

NIGERIA
650,000

KENYA
159,400

CEYLON
373,000

AUSTRALIA
4,599,000

S. AFRICA
1,701,700

S. RHODESIA
170,000

MALAYA
660,000

N. ZEALAND
883,500

was still time and space for manœuvre in that great continent. There was clearly no time to be lost in the clamorous, demanding East, where the fury of war had unleashed powerful forces which somehow had to be guided into channels that would prevent a further relapse into chaos.

Malaya needed urgent attention. Hitherto it had been divided into three main parts—the Straits Settlements, the Federated Malay States and the Unfederated States. For long, a Union of Malaya had been regarded as a most desirable goal, both by the British and by the educated people of Malaya. Before the war Malaya had been like Britain in its attitude to the outsider. It welcomed them into the land, adapted them to its use, and provided an atmosphere of tolerant hospitality. The Malays themselves were remarkably accommodating hosts. Chinese and Indians, in particular, found peace and prosperity in the Malay Peninsula and contributed greatly to development. Before the war, Malaya was an almost unique example of a multiracial area where differences of religion and tradition did not prevent harmony.

The war had changed that state of affairs to a disastrous degree. The British proposals for Union, unhappily, changed it still further. It is plain now that the Malayan Union proposals were too hastily devised and, worse still, that they aroused suspicion and mistrust. The various rulers of the Malay States were induced to conclude fresh agreements with Britain, to clear the way for a single government and legislature at the centre. The rulers were to be left with Advisory Councils in their own States and were to form a Central Advisory Council under the chairmanship of the Governor of the Union, to exercise functions relating to the Mohammedan religion and other delegated subjects. Each State and Settlement was also to have its own council for purely local affairs.

Such a move was long overdue if Malaya was ever to be united. But linked with it was a proposal for a common Malayan citizenship (this also applied to the great entrepôt of Singapore, which was excluded from the Union for the time being). This too was clearly a necessary step. But, together, the two proposals induced something near to panic among the Malays. At the same time as the power and influence of their rulers was being reduced, here were the Chinese and Indians, who had already a stranglehold on commerce, being given full citizenship rights, including the right to enter the higher Administrative Service. This, to the Malays, was selling their birthright. The rulers, who had relied on Britain knowing what was best, had bitter second thoughts about treaty revisions. They had only asked the British to advise and protect them in the first place. That their friends and guardians should now open the way to foreign settlers to govern Malaya—for this was how they saw "common citizenship" developing—was as near betrayal as made no odds.

It is necessary to remember that Malaya was still suffering intensely from the aftermath of war. Food was still desperately short, malnutrition and disease were painfully apparent, labour unrest and violent crime seemed to have become permanent features in erstwhile happy Malaya. The Sultan of Selangor publicly stated "that the relations between these two races (the Malays and Chinese) had deteriorated suddenly as a result of the Japanese occupation". Terror gangs flourished in the remoter areas, whilst the black market, extortion rackets and strikes were rampant in the towns. It was not the most propitious time to rush through vital and controversial changes in government.

As the reaction to the British Government's proposals grew more bitter in Malaya, the Communists—who had a remarkable record of resistance to the Japanese during the occupation—showed their hand. They called a general strike in Singapore and Johore, bringing normal life to a standstill. Chinese were killed in various demonstrations which turned into riots. The term "subversive elements" began to be used increasingly. Malaya had started off on a long and bloody road, and no man could see where it was leading. The British Government, overwhelmed by the weight of criticism both in Britain and Malaya, delayed the issue of the Order dealing with the new constitution, lamely explaining that it was never intended to be anything more than "a flexible framework". More discussions and consultations were necessary, Mr Creech Jones intimated.

The damage had been done. Many Malays felt that the British— or at least the reigning Government—were no longer to be trusted as guardians of their political, religious and cultural future (and that was precisely what the British had been in the past). Now, it seemed that the British were determined to impose on them a system which sprang entirely from Western civilization, which threatened to destroy a way of life which was precious indeed to them.

The Malays, deeply perturbed over British policy, saw their suspicions strengthened by what was happening in neighbouring Sarawak. This independent state, ruled by a Rajah of the famous Brooke family, had treaty relations with Britain, which also conducted its external affairs. Certainly it was an anachronism and possibly vexatious to a tidy, bureaucratic eye, but there was no disputing that the Brooke family had ruled with great imagination and liberality. Now, the British Government wished to tighten its control over Sarawak's affairs, in short to take over the territory.

At the best, it could be said that Colonial Office policy for Malaya and Sarawak revealed a tidy-minded passion for coherence. It might even have been claimed that the urgency of the position in South-East Asia made haste a virtue, even at the expense of tact. Unfortunately, to the people most closely concerned, it looked uncommonly like a rigid doctrine put into effect without regard to natural feelings.

George Hall, the Secretary of State for the Colonies, had the unpalatable task of explaining what appeared to be little less than a whitewashed annexation of Sarawak. He pointed out that the Rajah, who had not been in the territory since 1941, had declared that the time had arrived for Sarawak to be ceded to the King of Britain. It was only too clear that neither Mr Hall nor the Rajah had any idea what the people of Sarawak thought about it all. In short, they had not been asked. And there were sound reasons to believe that if they were—these Chinese, Malays, Dyaks and other jungle tribes —they would resist the new and firm control suggested by Britain.

Sarawak is only a 50,000 square-mile coastal strip of the island of Borneo, but that did not make it any the less important. At a moment when Britain had reaffirmed her intention of guiding her charges towards self-government, whilst bearing in mind the wishes of those charges, she was demonstrably breaking both pledges. Finally, 13 out of 24 members of the Sarawak State Council opposed cession, and a majority of two in favour was only obtained because of the four European members supporting the proposal.

Sarawak became a colony. It is possible to look back now and see that this cynical sacrifice of principle in favour of expediency had a far-reaching effect on Britain's reputation in the East, and in the wider world. And reputation was increasingly to be Britain's major card in transforming the old Empire into the new Commonwealth. She could not afford to tarnish it.

CHAPTER IV

AFRICA: THE SHAPING PATTERN

IF BRITAIN WAS fumbling in the Far East, it certainly proved no bar to her going ahead with the same extraordinary speed in other dependent territories. Spring had only just begun when it was announced that the two major colonies in West Africa, the Gold Coast and Nigeria, were to be given new constitutions. In each case there was to be a large African membership of the legislature, an unofficial majority and introduction or widening of the elective principle.

Clearly, the British were determined to be ahead of events where possible, in those territories not overrun by the war. That was nothing new. It had been the lasting lesson of the American War of Independence. There were periods when the lesson was forgotten, but 1946 was not a year when such folly was possible. Indeed, one of the more famous and individual of Colonial Governors had been known to say that he had two guiding principles: always to be one step ahead of the people he governed, and never to have concessions wrung from him because he was besieged by the populace in Government House.

It was the Gold Coast's peaceful progress that brought the greater comfort and satisfaction to Whitehall. For this was known as "the Model Colony". It had advanced smoothly for over 70 years under British rule, although the state chiefs had, in large measure, tended to become more and more remote from their own people through the part they played in that rule. To the small but vigorous African intellectual and middle class, the chiefs were merely the tools of the British.

But the new constitution introduced by the Governor, Sir Alan Burns, proposed a measure of real self-government never known before. Of the 30 members of the new Legislative Council, 18 were to be elected, six were to be officials and six were to be nominated. There were very few people inside the Gold Coast who thought the proposals anything less than generous.

There were plenty of people outside the Gold Coast, particularly the Europeans of Africa, who thought British liberalism was running wild. They pointed out that, at the very time when the African was being given such a powerful say in government in West Africa, the infamous Leopard Men of Calabar were busily engaged in murdering and mutilating their victims, whilst the notorious "Ju-Ju Murderers" of Kibi, in the Gold Coast, still awaited sentence.

There was one citizen of the Gold Coast, however, who thought that the Burns Constitution was the reverse of generous. He was in London, writing that colonial rule spelt nothing but deliberate economic and political exploitation. His main study was how to bring about the end of colonial rule, beginning in the Gold Coast, by revolution and efficient organization. He was a 37-year-old Akan of the Nzima tribe called Kwame Nkrumah. But he was almost alone in his condemnation of the Burns Constitution. He certainly did not speak for the new members of the Legislative Council—the great paramount chiefs, the clergymen, the middle-class men who had achieved their ambition of sharing in the government of their country. There was talent and prestige there, sober judgement and long experience, backed by education. Relinquishing her indirect rule through the chiefs, Britain had the gratification of seeing her plan working smoothly. For there was no denying that the African members of the new Council seemed to be those best fitted, by qualification and training, to be there.

In the heart of Africa, European leaders were watching what was happening in the territories round the Gulf of Guinea with alarm. They had foreseen it all, but it had come much earlier than they had thought possible. Those who backed the idea of amalgamating Northern and Southern Rhodesia under white leadership pushed forward with their plans. Roy Welensky, that extraordinary son of a Dutch Afrikaner mother and a Swedish-Jew father, who had emerged as a Northern Rhodesia political leader after a colourful career as a trade union leader and a professional boxer, announced that he would press for amalgamation in London.

In truth, he and the shrewd Prime Minister of Southern Rhodesia, Sir Godfrey Huggins, had laid the broad plans for their amalgamation campaign long before the war had ended. The advent of a Socialist Government in Britain, which they firmly believed to be anti-white, the policies which they saw being implemented in West Africa, had simply stiffened their resolution to unite. (Welensky himself was a symbol of the dramatic change which had taken place in the African scene since the turn of the century. For his father was in the siege of Bulawayo by the warrior Matabele. Strangely enough, one of the African members of the Gold Coast's new Legislative Council, Dr F. V. Nanka Bruce, had gone through the historic siege of Kumasi Fort in 1900.)

The trend of European opinion in Southern Africa, the clear indication that as the black men advanced in other parts of the continent, so must the white men consolidate, was further significantly revealed by the High Commissioner for South Africa in London, Mr Heaton Nichols. At a luncheon in honour of the retiring Southern Rhodesian representative in London, he envisaged not only a new Dominion of Central Africa—comprising the two Rhodesias and Nyasaland— but a federation of that Dominion with the Union of South Africa.

South Africa itself did not present a very comforting picture. Field-Marshal Jan Smuts, the revered elder statesman of the Commonwealth, was beginning to lose considerable ground. Towering though his reputation was in the great world beyond, there were many to criticize him in his own country, many who thought that the Field-Marshal ought to be back home looking after his own troublesome parish. Smuts' chief opponent, a former predikant of the Dutch Reformed Church, Dr Daniel Malan, was indubitably gaining ground as fast as Smuts lost it. He was a fanatical believer in the *apartheid* policy, in its most extreme form, the form which spelt eternal white supremacy over the black.

It was not that Smuts did not also believe in *apartheid*. But he was a man of wide and tolerant mind, a world statesman who saw outside the borders of his native land and knew that its policies could not develop in isolation without danger. He was, too, a fervent believer in the value of the British Commonwealth of Nations as a force for world stability. To him, it represented a potentially decisive political instrument. His opponents were, at the best, lukewarm in their feelings about the Commonwealth. It was the old imperialism writ large. Their heart's desire was a South African republic steeped in the old Boer tradition.

The dissolution of colonial power in the East so largely held the world stage that it was easy, at that time, to think that the eventual African pattern would be long in appearing. But one can look back now and see that the old order ended before the guns had ceased firing. It began to die when black soldiers fought, beside white men, against yellow soldiers, when African workers found that they could not only work in the white man's industry, but halt it. The old tribal traditions and loyalties no longer provided a discipline for the young men who had been caught up in the European way of life. In 1946 these things seemed sporadic, unconnected, the natural reactions of a return to peace, just as had happened after the 1914-1918 war. They proved, this time, to be something far different. They were the early indications that a new generation of Africans had arisen whose leaders saw that circumstance would give them the chance to challenge the white man's position. Few of these leaders held any official power. They were, indeed, few in number—such men as Harry Nkumbula of Northern Rhodesia, Jomo Kenyatta of Kenya, Nnamdi Azikiwe of Nigeria—but without doubt they carried considerable influence among their own people. The returning ex-soldiers, the land-hungry peasants, the rapidly-increasing class of urbanized Africans found their new prophets in such men.

Reflect that in the Northern Rhodesia Copperbelt many thousands of Africans were gathered together in an industrial belt which was as far removed from the traditional tribal scene as could be imagined. In a matter of twelve years that urbanized army was to grow to something approaching a quarter of a million, including the women and children. And more and more of these people became permanent dwellers in the Copperbelt, what the villagers called a *muchona*, "a lost one". The average age of the Africans in the mining towns steadily fell (today there are few over 50).

Here, then, was the raw material for the new type of African leaders to work on. They were losing old faiths, they lacked direction, they were caught up in the European money economy which made willing prisoners of them. The African rural life in which they had spent their childhood, a full and communal life which bore a resemblance to the medieval country life of England, was itself weakening.

It would not be true to claim that a spirit of pan-Africanism was arising throughout the continent—or even that there is now. What was beginning to assert itself was the spirit of Africanism, the growing desire of Africans to play a more purposeful and positive rôle in the development of Africa. A means of communication between the diverse, indigenous peoples of the continent had arisen—the printed word. There was a striking example of this when Creech Jones, the Under-Secretary of State for the Colonies, visited East Africa. When he held a press conference in Nairobi, eleven African editors attended, most of them representing publications which had arisen in the twelve months since the end of the war. Ignorance of the printed word held millions of Africans in darkness, but a generation was arising which could overcome that darkness. That was a fact of the most towering importance in the years to come.

Looking at Africa in the context of the Commonwealth, it was already clear that here, even more than in Asia, the principles on which the Commonwealth was based would be put to the most severe test. Long though the white man had been overlord in Asia, he had not, generally, been a settler there. In Africa, there were many white men who regarded themselves as much natives of that continent as the black man. And with good reason, for their remote forefathers had lived and died there.

The overwhelming majority of these white men believed that they could only survive as worthy representatives of their race by assuming leadership, by keeping their race intact. In the Union of South Africa that feeling was infinitely stronger than elsewhere, but it prevailed in the greater part of the continent whenever the races were in contact. How could Britain reconcile this with the idea of a multi-racial Commonwealth in which all, eventually, would be equal?

CHAPTER V

THE ELDER BRETHREN

As BRITAIN STROVE to preserve the ideal of Commonwealth in a bewildering world, to unravel the many problems of the Colonial Empire whilst at the same time launching a social and economic revolution within her own borders, how were the post-war views of the "elder brethren" of the Commonwealth developing? How did the independent members see the future of the great human experiment of which they were a part?

In April and May of 1946, a meeting of the Prime Ministers was held in London. It was a white man's conference, with Britain, Canada, Australia, New Zealand and South Africa represented. If one looked at the official communiqué, it was a Whitehall masterpiece of the innocuous. The delegates had covered a broad field of discussion which had "contributed greatly to the elucidation of many problems and to a mutual understanding of the issues involved". The subjects discussed included draft peace treaties, the future of Germany, economic and welfare co-operation in South-East Asia and the South Pacific.

The real significance of this conference was that Britain no longer presided as the real and overwhelming power behind the organization, with her economic and military strength providing its material potential. The discussions, let alone the painful evidence of national austerity all around them, brought home to the delegates that though Britain had won imperishable honour she was unlikely ever again to play her old dominant rôle in the world. And that meant that the British Commonwealth and Empire itself could not be so powerful a factor in world affairs, unless its independent members began to do something about it. But it was early days for such a thought to really strike home.

The outlook of each of the independent members had been deeply affected by the war and its outcome. And their attitude to the Commonwealth had correspondingly changed.

Canada, the senior Dominion, had for long under her Liberal Government been pleasantly satisfied with the Commonwealth as almost her own creation in its present form. The Liberal Government saw the Commonwealth as a most useful and praiseworthy instrument in helping Canada to exercise influence in world affairs. But that Government was also clearly looking to the new United Nations Organization primarily. It was true that the French element provided a seemingly strong reason why Canada should be equivocal in her approach to Commonwealth affairs. But this, as time went on, was contradictory, for French-Canadians became increasingly Commonwealth-minded in the post-war years, if only because they fervently desired a counter to the growing American influence on Canada. That, in fact, was the chief element in Canada's approach to the Commonwealth in 1946—the extent to which the Dominion had been drawn into the American economic and political orbit during the war. That great neighbour to the south had emerged indisputably as the leader of the Western world. When one adds to this the fact that the Canadians had largely and understandably adopted an American way of life, it is easy to see how irresistible was the impulse to look increasingly to America.

Naturally, it had always been a basic concept of Canadian policy that the Dominion must always act as an honest broker between Britain and the United States. Any quarrel between those two nations would have the most disastrous impact on Canada, and so it was that the "North Atlantic triangle" became the most important theme in Canadian foreign policy.

Yet it was at that point of time, in the spring of 1946, when a positive assertion of Canada's stake in the Commonwealth was most necessary. If the British Empire were ever to avoid the fate of all other empires in human history, then the Commonwealth into which it had grown must develop a dynamic of its own. That meant that its senior independent members must take a positive share of responsibility for its survival, must show signs of sharing the leadership with Britain at some future stage. Canada did not show those signs in any clear degree. She was a good spokesman for the value of the Commonwealth, a strong defender of Britain's Colonial policy. It was not enough. It was too negative. It seemed to indicate that Canada believed in the Commonwealth as a worthy association of well-wishers, and that she saw British colonial policy as a sort of finishing school in self-government, not as the means of establishing a multi-racial organization which could prove a decisive instrument in preserving the freedom of men.

Australia, although far distant from the United States, had none-theless emerged from the war deeply conscious of the power of that nation. It was the Americans who had won the decisive sea battles which saved Australia from Japanese invasion. A great gathering of American men and materials of war had left a lasting impact. Con-trariwise, the fall of Singapore, the presence of Japanese submarines in Australian waters had indicated that the shield of the Royal Navy was no longer enough.

Yet this reluctant recognition of the new order of things battled in the Australian mind with an abiding loyalty to Britain herself, and to the Commonwealth and Empire as Britain's creation. To the Australians, there were certain things beyond dispute—a dependence, a partnership with Britain, and a passionate loyalty to the Crown. The thought that Britain could no longer sustain them was almost heresy, but it had to be faced, though with anguish and bewilder-ment. How could these conflicting ideas be resolved? There was also the further complication, so dimly realized as yet, that Australia was no longer the furthest bastion of Empire, but that she was in some way caught up in the revolution of Asia.

The idea began to develop that somehow Britain, America and the Commonwealth must be balanced. It led, later, to a dawning conception that Australia had an important part to play in reconciling all three. But, in those early days, that conception was befogged by still another idea, fathered by Dr H. V. Evatt, that Australia should be the spokesman of the smaller nations in the United Nations. But behind all was the dominant factor that, emotionally, almost every Australian saw himself as a distant citizen of Britain.

The New Zealanders were even more British. Prime Minister Fraser, in 1939, had said that "Where Britain goes, we go; where she stands, we stand." And so they had. In 1946, almost no New Zealanders would have altered Mr Fraser's declaration. Their country had never been in such grave and immediate danger from the Japs as Australia. They had not seen such powerful evidence of American might. Always, in the past, they had known that their influence in the world, small though it was, had been immeasurably increased by membership of the Commonwealth. To New Zealand, the Commonwealth meant Britain and their delegates came to London in 1946 with the same deep trust and loyalty as ever. For if Britain were no longer to count in the world, what sort of future could New Zealand look to?

There is a strange irony in the fact that the country whose Commonwealth loyalties were most suspect was led by the man whose positive concept of it was far the most dynamic. Field-Marshal Smuts' idea of the Commonwealth was expressed by the word "holism", which meant that the whole was greater than the sum of the parts. Strongly and faithfully led, he believed it could be of decisive importance to mankind. There were few in his own land who caught even the merest glimpse of the Field-Marshal's vision. As I have written previously, the Commonwealth was a suspect British invention to his opponents, and even his supporters looked with alarm on the ideas of racial equality which Britain was not only disseminating, but putting into practical effect.

The truth was—and is—that racial policy is the predominant policy in South Africa. All things led back to that, all political actions were judged by it. To *all* white South Africans, the Commonwealth's value lay in how it affected racial relations. Later, there were to be some strange interpretations, oddly enough by the Afrikaners themselves.

Smuts could come to London and talk as learnedly and powerfully as he pleased about the Commonwealth, in his rôle as one of the world's elder statesmen. In so far as he spoke as the Prime Minister of South Africa, all that he said was conditioned and confined by the unique racial policy which held south of the Limpopo River.

What could one hope for from such a diversity of opinion, from such a meeting of leaders, all of whom were assailed by strong influences which, if not actually opposed to the Commonwealth, yet threatened to weaken its links beyond endurance? There was a prim note, at the end of it all, that "the representatives placed on record their appreciation of the value of the existing methods of consultation among Commonwealth countries which were peculiarly appropriate to the character of the British Commonwealth and preferable to rigid, centralized machinery."

Perhaps it is worth, at this point, examining what the common interests of the member countries were supposed to be, what in short it was their duty to preserve. All of them were dedicated to the idea of personal freedom on which democracy rested (though in South Africa it applied only to whites). All of them had adopted those democratic principles of law and government which Britain had created through the long centuries of her own turbulent history. In short, the independent nations of the Commonwealth were, just as much as Britain, committed to the preservation of democracy.

The Commonwealth and Empire had, also, formed a vital trading connection. The economic patter which had emerged from the historic fact of a central imperial power drawing raw materials from its colonies, and then providing them with goods and services, was buttressed by the system of Imperial Preference. And all of the Commonwealth and Colonial nations (except Canada), being members of the Sterling Area, had a common interest in the health of the pound. There was also a remarkable degree of co-operation over a wide field, in such matters as shipping, agriculture, migration, air communications, telecommunications and science.

One would have thought that, out of all these things, there could have emerged something coherent, an organization which in terms of power and influence was a reality. The self-congratulatory words of the Prime Ministers' 1946 communiqué—that the current methods of consultation were "preferable to rigid, centralized machinery"— gave the answer. A cynic might have found irony in the fact that the independent nations had staked their all on the Commonwealth during the years between 1939 and 1946, had stood alone for a fateful twelve months to save freedom, and yet rejected the idea of abandoning one tittle of sovereignty to strengthen it in peace-time.

To be fair, these young nations—Canada, Australia, New Zealand and South Africa—had their own massive problems to face, internal as well as external. They had not only to safeguard themselves in a challenging post-war world. They had also to continue with their own development towards powerful nationhood, to build and diversify their economies, to populate their own lands. How could they devote themselves to such daunting tasks and at the same time give themselves to the task of "powering" the Commonwealth?

Yet it still remained true that the Commonwealth, in that first year after the war, seemed to many people to be in grave danger of perishing from sheer inertia. The First British Empire had collapsed because Britain had refused her American colonists the right of self-government. Self-government having become the final goal of British colonial policy, it now seemed as if the British Commonwealth, in its turn, would collapse because those nations who had reached the goal would give up nothing of their own freedom to save it.

That atmosphere of complacency which was so marked at the Conference in London in 1946 persisted. What a powerful contrast it was to the tremendous upheaval going on in the Colonial Empire and in the East! But, there, they were not indulging in academic exchange of views. They were fighting for the reality of power.

CHAPTER VI

THE STRUGGLE IN INDIA

EVEN AS THE delegates of the Prime Ministers' Conference were homeward bound the greatest of Britain's imperial problems was rapidly developing into tragedy. In India, the clash between Hindu and Muslim reached a new depth of bitterness. Civil war, religious war with all its customary implacable hate, had long been darkly threatened by the leaders of Congress and of the Muslim League. Now it was no longer a form of political intimidation. It was all too possible. India's political leaders were reaping the whirlwind of their own past follies and rigid intolerance.

The Socialist Government of Britain, despite all rebuffs, clung to the idea that a united India was still possible. The greatest credit is due to Mr Attlee for his determination to hold on to the initiative in the face of every temptation to seek a quick way out. For in truth Britain's position in the sub-continent exposed her to hate and ridicule, and to the ancient charges of hypocrisy and lack of faith. Nothing could have been further from the hard truth. Britain's leaders wanted to hand over power with all speed, but they did not, to their eternal honour, intend to jettison their responsibilities.

In sad contrast, India's own leaders, able men though they were, showed a lack of judgement and responsibility, a tragic intolerance of each other's viewpoints, which has its repercussions to this day. They were not by any means solely—or even largely—to blame for the great abyss which had opened between the Hindu and Muslim peoples of India. They had inherited a situation brought about by the ambition and intransigence of former leaders, and also by the procrastination and lack of vision of former British Governments. But the charge remains that they made a pitifully small attempt to show some trust in each other and to co-operate with Mr Attlee.

The latest plan for India put forward by the Socialist Prime Minister was not only fair-minded and generous, but statesmanlike in its considered aim of preserving that unity which the British had introduced, whatever other errors of omission they had made. Briefly, the plan was to introduce an Indian Union with a central government drawn from British India and the Indian States, and provincial governments with a wide measure of authority. These provincial governments could form, if they so wished, into geographical groups with their own legislatures and executives.

It was an imaginative variation of the favourite British device of federation, and its great merit was that it gave India the chance of strong nationhood, whilst at the same time guarding minority groups. Above all, a new Muslim State of Pakistan would have emerged, and no plan stood the remotest chance of success without such an outcome.

Underlining their determination to bring full freedom to India without loss of time, the British Government sent out a man of rocklike integrity, a man of ideals who yet was a great man of action,

Lord Wavell. As Viceroy, Wavell was charged with bringing together the Indian leaders, so that an all-Indian interim cabinet could be formed and the new plan given a chance to prove itself. The British felt that time was the essence of the problem, that if a period was possible in which Nehru and Jinnah and their followers could work together for the common good of India, then the tragic alternative of partition for the sub-continent could be avoided.

Hope of such an outcome soon died. Hindu and Muslim bent their real efforts, not towards national unity, but to political manœuvre to outwit their opponents. Great riots, on a scale that even India had never known, were the bloody background to the political intriguing. Tens of thousands were slaughtered in religious massacres. Finally, both parties came together to form a cabinet, but they were like armed men waiting only for the signal of war. In that brooding atmosphere of communal hate and fear, the very word co-operation was obscene.

Lord Wavell, that much-revered poet and soldier, was the target of bitter abuse. Each side charged him with partiality. Each side tried to so influence events as to wrest advantage from their opponents, each tried to muscle the other out of office. The Constituent Assembly which was to have framed a constitution for a free India ended in a tragic farce, for the Muslim League members refused to co-operate and demanded postponement. The Congress Party proceeded with the futile passing of various resolutions, the Muslims denounced them and the Indian princes stood aside.

It was not so much deadlock as disaster. For it had been devoutly hoped that a united India, with an incomparable army and an efficient civil service, would preserve the peace in that vast area around the Indian Ocean, when the British withdrew. A vacuum of power in that explosive region would expose the world to perpetual tension. To many Britons, and particularly those who had served and loved India, there was an even more saddening prospect. That was that a great ideal was crumbling away, an ideal of a free and strong India taking her powerful place among the nations of the world.

It was only too clear to those who knew post-war Asia that time was running out. In China, the Communists under Mao Tse-tung were taking the initiative from the corrupt and cowardly hands of the Kuomintang. Not all the help and power of the United States could stabilize the position of Chiang Kai-shek, and the frightening prospect of the great country of China becoming communist began to face the statesmen of the West. Mao's 1945 manifesto, in which he promised the best of all worlds to as wide a range of his countrymen as could be encompassed, blew through war-weary and disillusioned China like a great wind. The young, the ambitious and the idealistic flocked to his cause, and so too did the long-sighted.

Whether the Russians gave Mao any measurable degree of support is doubtful. They had conveniently given the Chinese Communists the chance to occupy Manchuria and to take over vast stocks of surrendered Japanese arms. That was a powerful aid. But the Chinese leader and his colleagues planned and pursued their own triumphs. What had to be faced—and the American leaders were particularly reluctant to face it—was that the Chinese Communists had presented a doctrine to their countrymen, and growing numbers of them were more than eager to accept it.

Even at this early point of time the probability that the balance of power in Asia would be altered on a giant scale was apparent to those who suspected the international aims of communism. And chief among these discerning people was Winston Churchill himself. Early in 1946, at Fulton in the United States he delivered the famous warning of the imperialistic aims of Russian communism under Stalin. That speech evoked the strongest support and the bitterest criticism in roughly equal measure. The years have proved the exactness of Churchill's prophecies.

The urgent task of the democracies was to hold what was left of Europe. But Asia could not be left to chance whilst that was being done. An India plunged into civil war would be a desperate defeat not only for Britain, but for the Commonwealth and the whole of the free world. A stable and united India, whatever policies she adopted, would balance power in Southern Asia, for India was reared in democratic practice and her leaders were pledged to its continuance.

Britain could draw some comfort, at the least, from the continuing stability of Ceylon. Small though that island was, it was of the greatest strategic importance. And it was a heartening example of the painless emergence to self-government of a new democracy. The new parliament exercised complete control over Ceylon's affairs, save for defence and external affairs, and safeguards covering racial and religious discrimination. Ceylon was the first non-European territory of the British Empire to attain self-government. Mr Senanayake, the Sinhalese leader, was a man of great strength of character and comparable prestige. It was undoubtedly galling to an ancient people like the Sinhalese to hear patronizing references from British politicians and journalists to their having "served their apprenticeship" in government. The British themselves were to learn fast that to receive is harder than to give. But they could rightly find some cause for pride in the outcome of their Ceylon policy. And, perhaps even more, so could the Sinhalese leaders.

Southward, in Malaya, Britain had been forced to retrace her steps. The project for a Malayan Union was an admitted failure. Its most important positive outcome was that the Malays themselves, for the first time, created their own political alliance, the United Malay National Organization. That, in itself, was a considerable advance. It did emphasize that the easy-going Malays had awakened to the fact that they must begin to speak as a people if they hoped to hold their own in their own land.

The trend of thought, more in Britain than in Malaya, began to swing round to the idea of a Malayan Federation. And once again, as with India, the need for coherent action became all the more urgent because of that small but dangerous cloud on the horizon, the increasing pressure of the communist doctrine. It was deadlier than for India, because its evangelists were inside the borders of Malaya itself.

For some months the authorities in Malaya and in Singapore had seemed remarkably complacent about the continued lawlessness and labour unrest. In Britain, officialdom was even more dilatory in recognizing the growing danger to Malaya. All that was happening, it was inferred, was the natural sequel to a bitter war and occupation by a ruthless and bestial enemy. Considering what was happening in neighbouring Indonesia, across the Straits of Malacca, where the Dutch were fast losing control of their wealthy East Indian possessions, it was an extremely myopic view.

It was significant that the new federal proposals for Malaya were most strongly criticized by the left-wing Malay Nationalist Party, which rapidly made itself as powerful as the United Malay National Organization. But it was not in the limelight of national politics that the dangerous men were operating on an ever-increasing scale. It was in the background of the labour movement. Strikes which had more to do with subversion than the rights of labour, intimidation and violence for those who did not fall in line, these were the early weapons of the men who did not want democracy in Malaya.

At that time, of course, the Malayan Communist Party could still rest on the prestige it had gained through its war-time resistance to the Japanese. There was no gainsaying that its members had the right to pose as supreme patriots. In fact, the Secretary-General of the Malayan Communist Party, Ching Peng, even took part in the great Victory Parade in London in 1946. That was in the days of the shadowy dream world when the democratic countries—despite Churchill's sombre warning—thought that the shared tragedy of war had caused the communists to turn over a new leaf. Yet, as events were later to show Ching Peng and his lieutenants were even then planting cells in Malaya's trade unions, carefully hoarding their war-time arms, in case their plans for "peaceful" seizure of power went astray. Even today it is still apt to be assumed that the war of terror in Malaya began when guerrilla war in the jungle was launched. The facts are that it began with the labour troubles in Singapore and Malaya in 1946.

As this undercover revolution smouldered, Britain went forward with her plans for Sarawak, to the east. Mr Hall, the Secretary of State, blandly announced to the House of Commons that His Majesty's Government had "accepted" cession, and that Sarawak was to become a Colony. In Sarawak itself, no flags were hung out for the occasion. A mere two thousand dispirited Malays and Chinese gathered when the new Governor-General of the Malayan Union and Singapore, Mr Malcolm MacDonald, made a speech at the installation of the Acting-Governor of Sarawak. And the Datu Patinggi, the senior hereditary chief in Sarawak, cabled Mr Bertram Brooke (who was heir-presumptive, and opposed the Rajah's cession of the country to Britain) asking him to reopen the question.

There was no doubt that the majority of the people in Sarawak who knew what was happening—and that was most of them—resented the deal. They did not like the real power of government being withdrawn from their own land and transferred to a remote office in Whitehall, on the far side of the world. The advantages—and this is meant sincerely—that would undoubtedly flow from colonial rule made small appeal to them. Theirs was a happy and prosperous land; they were yeomen farmers, not coolies; they had a freedom almost unknown elsewhere in the East. How could you improve on that?

It still was true that it was a different world from that of 1939. The British Government clearly felt that it had a responsibility to safeguard Sarawak against a turbulent outside world. The very appoint-

The British return to Hong Kong in 1945. A Japanese envoy, followed by his interpreter, boards the flagship of Rear-Admiral Harcourt.

Released from the Japanese prison camp. (*Left to right*) Sir Percy McElwaine, Chief Justice, Straits Settlements; Sir Shenton Thomas, Governor, S.S., and High Commissioner, F.M.S.; Sir Harry Trusted, Chief Justice, F.M.S.; Sir Horace Seymour, Ambassador to China, who greeted the party at Chungking; Sir Mark Young, Governor, Hong Kong; Mr. C. R. Smith, Governor, North Borneo.

The Governor's arrival. Sir Charles Arden Clarke (*right*) arriving in Sarawak in 1946 as that territory's first Governor.

ment of Governor-General Malcolm MacDonald indicated the devout hope that a federation of Malaya, Singapore, Brunei, Sarawak
and North Borneo would ultimately develop. With that in mind,
one can understand, if not approve, the British desire to undertake a
rapid tying-up of loose ends as an opening move.

North Borneo shared, less painfully, in this same process. Just a
fortnight after the Sarawak "celebrations", on July 15, the British
North Borneo Company handed over government of the territory,
which it had exercised under Royal Charter since 1881, to the Colonial Office. This time, at Jesselton, Mr MacDonald met a rather more
heartening atmosphere. For North Borneo was, in the main, a wild
and largely undeveloped country, with many of its people not even
slightly affected by European civilization.

Nothing could more clearly have underlined the dramatic change
in the world for the great imperial power of Britain than these two
events—the departure, inside a fortnight, of the last of the chartered
companies and the last of the Sarawak rajahs. And in their place, as
the symbol of authority, Governor-General MacDonald, the son of
Britain's first Socialist Prime Minister.

As Arthur Creech Jones said: "In Britain the old imperialism has
come to an end." A few months after this "tidying up" in the Far
East he was appointed Secretary of State for the Colonies in succession to George Hall. And that in itself was as signal an opening to
a new colonial era as could be imagined. For it was Creech Jones
who was the arch-authority of the Socialist Government on colonial
affairs. He had been the main backroom thinker, and it was he who
was now expected to effect the Socialist transformation of the Colonies.
In a speech to the Anti-Slavery and Aborigines' Protection Society
he made forthright statements about "mistaken policies of the past"
having to be put right. "There are", he emphasized, "plural societies
with different standards, and common citizenship has to be evolved.
There is the practice, in places, of colour discrimination and colour
bars; there are also policies of segregation."

Creech Jones was a man with wide, if academic knowledge of
colonial affairs. He was also a man of real sincerity and the deepest
integrity. He meant what he said, and what he said about racial
relationships did indeed go right to the heart of the Commonwealth
ideal. But in the Colonies, the white population regarded him as
the evangelist of the coloured people. His coming to office filled
them with foreboding.

D

CHAPTER VII

THE MIDDLE EAST LINE

WHILST THESE GREAT events were moving in the Far East, Britain's old "Empire lifeline" through the Mediterranean and the Middle East was also under strain at key points. At a huge cost in men and material, after battle by land and sea and in the air, Britain had kept the lifeline open in the war years. Despite the dramatic advent of the atom bomb, it remained vital to her interests both in war and peace.

It was therefore all the more disturbing that troubles arose so quickly in Malta and in Cyprus. In Malta, which had borne so heroically the full savagery of enemy air attack, relations with the British deteriorated alarmingly within six months of the end of hostilities. The island's permanent problems of overpopulation, lack of resources and industries had naturally not been removed by the war. But the Maltese thought their gallant record entitled them to special consideration, to prosperity and responsible government for a start. Instead, they found unemployment, high prices and hard times. So did other peoples. But the Maltese had been tried to the uttermost limit; they had been raided nearly 4,000 times by German and Italian bombers, and over 27,000 buildings had been destroyed. Britain had given financial help during the war, and even before it was ended she had appointed Sir Wilfrid Woods to examine "the present and prospective financial position of the Malta Government in the light of the policy of H.M. Government that responsible government should be granted to Malta after the war". In short, how to equivocate freedom with chronic financial embarrassment. This indeed was to be the joint and evergreen problem of Malta and Britain for years to come. Sir Wilfrid calculated that Malta would need grants of over £40 million to get her finances on a level keel. He suggested that a succession of five-year plans was the way to tackle the problem.

The younger people of Malta were thinking in terms of emigration. There was talk abroad that British evacuation of the Suez Zone would mean that no British Navy would be needed at Malta. That in its turn meant that practically one out of every two families in the island would be heavily affected, for the dockyards were the backbone of the economy.

The British Socialist Government appointed a new civilian Governor, Mr F. C. R. Douglas, and there were high hopes that he would win the confidence of the Maltese. But he had hardly settled in when the Maltese Labour Party's nine Elected Members resigned from the Council of Government because of "their grave concern over Malta's economic and social problems" and an alleged lack of long-term planning. How resignation would help the problems to be solved or long-term planning to be set in motion was not explained. If the baffled and bewildered Mr Douglas could have seen into the future he might have found a grain of consolation in the fact that resigning to solve problems of state was to become almost a national political sport in Malta.

And whilst all this was going on, Sir Harold MacMichael had been busily studying the island for four months so that he could draw up a proposed new Constitution for Malta, to put before the Secretary of State for the Colonies. Sir Harold, of course, handled the preliminary approaches for the abortive Malayan Federation. It was a little ironic that the Malaya scheme collapsed even as Sir Harold was probing the Malta situation. The Malta politicians could be excused for finding this a little depressing.

If the situation in Malta was depressing, at the eastern end of Britain's Mediterranean chain, in Cyprus, it was even worse. The Greek Cypriots, who made up 80 per cent of the island's population (as against the 20 per cent of Turkish Cypriots), had never weakened in their passionate desire to be linked with Greece. British authorities were wont to claim that the nationalist leaders in Cyprus did not speak for the majority of Greek Cypriots, and it was customarily intimated that the ordinary people wished only to get on with their daily lives and to be spared politics. Whatever the truth of the official claim, the fact was that Greek Cypriot organizations, whatever other differences they had, rarely failed to speak with one voice in favour of union with Greece, *enosis* as it was called.

Such a union could not have failed to depress the living standards of the Cypriots; it would have been desperately resisted by the Turkish element, with the possibility of an open clash between Greece and Turkey developing; finally, the very fact that Greece herself had narrowly missed falling behind the Communist curtain hardly recommended her as the best of guardians of such a strategically important island as Cyprus. (There were significant reports that vital air and sea bases were to be developed there.) These facts never lost their force in the ensuing years. But neither did they make any more impact on the Greek-Cypriot leaders.

Nothing could have more emphatically demonstrated the obduracy of the *enosis* enthusiasts than the hostile reception which greeted British proposals for the future of Cyprus. These were announced in October of 1946 by Arthur Creech Jones. To the British Socialist Government they seemed not only generous, but the clearest possible indication that Socialism intended to liberate the Colonies from the evils of imperialism.

In truth the new proposals *were* fair and generous. Governor Sir Charles Woolley was to call together a Consultative Assembly, drawn from representative elements in the island, to consider the framing of a new Constitution, including the re-establishment of a central legislature. A ten-year development plan was also proposed, to place the Cyprus economy on a firm foundation. And as clear evidence that a liberal and conciliatory spirit was behind all, the strict laws which had been in force since the 1931 disturbances, such as the forbidding of meetings and processions without permit, were to be repealed. Deported persons were to be allowed to return, trade union leaders released from prison and—perhaps most significant of all—Cypriots were to be allowed free choice of an Archbishop, whose place had long been vacant.

The head and front of Greek nationalism in the island was centred in the person of the Archbishop. It was a certainty that whoever filled the vacant seat would be a resolute advocate of *enosis*. Britain, then, was taking an incalculable risk, but Creech Jones believed that no progress at all was possible without taking risks. As a final conciliatory gesture, Cyprus was to be given a politician as Governor, the former Minister of Civil Aviation, Lord Winster. This was in itself evidence that the British Government recognized that such territories as Cyprus, with a long history of culture and political experience behind them, needed to be guided rather than governed.

The response to these imaginative and far-reaching proposals was brief and blunt. All four political parties in Cyprus, the local Press, and the Ethnarchic Council retorted that the Greek Cypriots had one aim in mind—union with Greece. *The Times* correspondent in Cyprus sent a message to London which had a familiar ring. Impartial observers, he said, differed on whether the hostility represented the views of the majority of Cypriots. A cynic, even at that point of time, might have asked whether there was any such animal as an "impartial observer" in the island.

At this very time when the Cypriots were rejecting Britain's overtures, the Palestine problem itself was being brought startlingly home to the island. Illegal Jewish immigrants into Palestine, intercepted by British naval forces, were transferred to Cyprus, and by the end of October over 5,000 of them were imprisoned in five camps at Famagusta.

The Palestine tragedy was rapidly running on to its bitter and bloody climax. Jews and Arabs were now, even to the most hopeful eye, deadly and irreconcilable opponents. Britain held the ring in a contest in which there could be no winner and where the referee was likely to come out worst of all. Terrorism had become a daily condition of existence, murder and destruction were the weapons of both sides, but more ruthlessly so those of the Jews. Compromise had become a dirty word, and Jews and Arabs used the time that was running out so swiftly only to manœuvre for position in readiness for the final decision. The position was tragically similar to that in India.

The Anglo-American delegation which had been set up to investigate a solution for Palestine had finally produced a plan. The British Government lost no time in accepting it, but as it depended upon American co-operation there was a distinct air of unreality about it. The Americans were too deeply swayed by Jewish sentiment at home to be decisive and objective in this matter.

Briefly the plan proposed that Britain and the United States should press for the establishment of an international relief organization and should support an appeal to all countries to receive a proportion of the vast army of Jewish refugees who had been swept from their homelands by the storm of war. As for Palestine, the delegation suggested that federation was the solution with four separate areas—an Arab province, a Jewish province, the municipal district of Jerusalem and the Negeb which would remain under British control.

Behind this plan, which was almost a classic example of the British partiality for careful balance and compromise, there lurked the hope that a united Palestine would gradually emerge. But, against the background of bloody terror and bitter intransigence this cold and precise document was a pale and pedantic ghost. Practically at the same time that Britain agreed to the new plan, the King David

Hotel in Jerusalem, headquarters of the British military and the Government secretariat, was blown up. Nearly a hundred people were killed, many of them high government officials. The truth was that the Jewish terrorist organizations had two aims in view, to drive out the British and to crush Arab resistance. No compromise was possible with these fanatical men. The King David Hotel outrage was their answer to the would-be honest brokers of Britain and the U.S.A.

Palestine was but one, albeit the most important, of the Middle East problems. Since the collapse of the Ottoman Empire there had been no real unity in the Arab world. After Constantinople's writ became meaningless Britain had been the dominant power in the Middle East, and for long the trusted friend of the Arabs. This whole area, so vital to the safety of the route from Britain to the East, to Africa, to Australia and New Zealand, had become desperately more important because of the great oil discoveries. Yet now the carefully arranged façade was clearly tottering. A new wave of Arab nationalism was rising, provoked first by the humiliating domination of their territories by the Allies in the war, second by the grim determination of the Jews to found their own homeland. Out of it all there came a great alliance—the Arab League.

Behind the League was the sweeping ambition that the Arabs themselves would fulfil the ancient rôle of the Ottoman Empire, and unite the faithful. On paper the founder members gave an impression of potential power and influence. These members were Egypt, Iraq, Transjordan, the Yemen, Saudi Arabia, Syria and the Lebanon. But amongst them were deep-rooted jealousies and clashing ambitions. Disunity, which had so often betrayed the Arabs in the past, was eating at the foundations of the League almost as soon as it was formed. Yet, standing as they did over the cross-roads of the world, possessing the vast reserves of oil so vital to the industrial West, these Arab League nations were of towering importance.

Egypt, with the egregious and ambitious King Farouk at its head, had the best claim to leadership, but that did not mean that it was an accepted claim, not with the autocratic Ibn Saud of Saudi Arabia, and the Hashemite family of Iraq and Transjordan nursing equal ambitions. Yet Egypt was the only Arab state with real experience of international affairs. Her size, her comparatively advanced economy, and above all the presence of the Suez Canal in her territory further buttressed her aspirations.

Britain could not view the increasing influence of Farouk's Egypt with any comfort. She still had friends in the Middle East, but Egypt was not among them. An Egypt-dominated Arab League would be an anti-British League. When the headquarters and secretariat of the League were set up in Cairo, Britain had good reason to anticipate trouble. Yet she could not hope to continue to keep her troops in the Suez Canal Zone to guard her interests. The treaty negotiated with Egypt for the gradual withdrawal of all British forces from Suez drew a great fire of criticism both in Britain and in other Commonwealth countries. But with the Middle East states in such defiant mood, Britain had no alternative.

So that year of 1946 drew to an end with Britain, the Commonwealth and the Indian and Colonial Empire facing a dark and uncertain future. Everywhere the tide of nationalism—or, rather, of racialism—was rising. The communications of the Commonwealth and Empire were threatened, the East was in turmoil, the whole practice of colonialism, however benevolent, was under assault.

It was Britain's declared policy to advance her colonial charges to independence, in proper order. But now it looked as if the time left to her might be all too short for the job in hand.

CHAPTER VIII

CRISIS IN BRITAIN

As the winter turned into 1947 it brought to Britain some of the most savagely bitter weather in memory. Deep drifts blocked roads and railways, and added to the industrial chaos already caused by overloaded power stations and an acute coal shortage. A dazed and incredulous people at last became aware, almost overnight it seemed, that Britain faced disaster. The least knowledgeable of Britons knew that the country's former power and wealth had virtually been built on coal. Yet here they were so short of that black wealth that the country was running to a standstill. No other single happening could have brought home the change in fortunes with such bitter finality.

The Government produced an *Economic Survey* for 1947 as if to drive home the revelation, and the British people read that, in place of the Utopia which was the welfare state, they must bend all their energies to producing exports. The overseas buyer must have priority, not the housewife at home. The White Paper announced that "There is nothing temporary about our need for exports. Concentration upon exports must become a permanent part of our normal industrial life." It added, with a sort of melancholy satisfaction, that failure would mean continued food rationing, much less smoking and motoring and a great deal of unemployment. In short, a quarter of Britain's manufacturing capacity was to be reserved solely for the overseas customer.

Even this effort, as the Government admitted, was not nearly enough. The coal crisis into which they had blundered effectually prevented some of the major exporting industries from reaching a satisfactory output. It was plain that the Colonies, in particular, must curtail their development ambitions for some time ahead. They could produce the plans. Britain could not produce the tools.

The hard truth was that the British had been living beyond their means, and living on a fast-disappearing credit at that. Lack of trust between Government and industrialists, a relentless exploitation of their favourable bargaining position by the trade unions, an over-hasty attempt to nationalize and to create a comprehensive welfare state, a sheer refusal by the public as a whole to face the naked facts of economic life—all these things had helped to bring Britain to her knees. It added up to an adverse visible trade balance of £328 million, net incomes of £7,000 million chasing £6,000 million of goods, exports falling short of the required level by over 40 per cent.

The effect on the country's reputation abroad was disastrous. The founder of the greatest empire the world had ever seen, the centre of the whole Commonwealth from whom leadership, finance, aid were eagerly awaited, was struggling herself to avoid utter bankruptcy and impoverishment.

Eighteen months after the war had ended, recognition of Britain's great sacrifices was wearing more than a little thin. Instead, even the most faithful and loyal of her friends asked themselves how could Britain develop and control her still large Colonial Empire, how could she provide the money and the power to make a reality once more of her Commonwealth leadership?

As if Britain's domestic troubles were not enough, the India sub-continent had been racing on to what looked like final tragedy. There was utter and complete deadlock between Hindus and Muslims. A desperate last attempt to save the situation had failed towards the end of 1946 when Nehru, Jinnah and Lord Wavell travelled to London to try and reach a solution with the British Government. Civil war seemed inevitable.

Britain's stock had never seemed lower. The picture was one of a once-great nation stricken with some fatal palsy, ragged and weak, inept at home and nerveless abroad. And yet, at this nadir of her affairs, Britain began to show some of the old resolution, some of her former capacity for not only shouldering responsibility but discharging it. Clement Attlee, that Socialist Prime Minister who was so often under-estimated and even derided, showed the decision and courage that lay deep in his character.

In February of 1947, Mr Attlee made a public statement that Britain would withdraw from India in June of 1948. The decision was buttressed by a powerful and imaginative stroke. Lord Louis Mountbatten was prevailed upon to act as the last Viceroy and to guide through the transfer of power. Mountbatten's towering reputation in the East was allied to the real affection both he and his wife had for its peoples. In return, and without doubt, they finally commanded a like affection from those peoples. Instead of humiliating retreat, the choice of Mountbatten gave the British decision an air of magnanimity and goodwill. To top all, Lord Louis was a kinsman of the King of England and the Emperor of India. There was a grandeur about the act of abdication which contrasted oddly with the mild and self-effacing character of the man who made the final decision, Clement Attlee.

At the same time, the British Prime Minister had not only demonstrated Britain's sincerity, he had placed an onus upon the Hindu and Muslim leaders which they had so far succeeded in avoiding. There was every danger of the followers of Nehru and Jinnah now using the interval before independence to consolidate their respective positions, to practise obstructionism and intrigue at every step of the way. But in Mountbatten Britain had a man who was long accustomed not only to making quick and comprehensive decisions, but to seeing them thoroughly implemented.

Yet it was one thing to make an end of the India problem. It was quite another to end it in such a way that Britain could feel that she had discharged her duty. And it was yet another to accomplish the task whilst still retaining a Commonwealth link with the two independent states which were now to be created in the sub-continent.

In those tempestuous days before partition, the Hindu leaders' view of the Commonwealth was one of suspicion, even of dislike. On the other hand, the Muslim leaders, and particularly Mr Jinnah himself, had already concluded that the surest way of shaking themselves free of Hindu domination was to effect a continuing link with Britain. Membership of the Commonwealth was, they thought, the ideal way of accomplishing that.

Between them, these two men, Jinnah and Nehru, led 400 million people—people with brown skins, not white. The free and independent people of the British Commonwealth totalled some 75 million, all white, all officially accepting the British Crown. The accession to the Commonwealth of the multitudes of the Indian sub-continent would be a decisive triumph for the British ideal, just as their abstention from membership would be a saddening defeat. Whichever way the decision went, the Commonwealth had reached a watershed. Either it would go forward as a unique multi-racial organization, or it would contract into a partnership of peoples of European and mainly British stock.

What were they like, these two men Nehru and Jinnah who were due to play so formidable a part in the development of the Commonwealth? Both had been educated in England, both were men of considerable courage and resolution. Pandit Jawaharlal Nehru, son of a Kashmiri Brahmin, had been educated at Harrow and Cambridge, was a socialist and an internationalist. He was deeply loyal to Mahatma Gandhi, and still frequently deferred to the latter's opinions, not always with the happiest results. Yet these two men commanded the trust and faith of their people completely. The business man, the intellectual, the water-carrier alike held them to be the voices of Hindu India. Gandhi, who had once held the British in deep respect, had increasingly decided that India must find her soul. But Nehru had drawn from Britain more than perhaps he himself realized in the beginning, so much that in later years opponents were to deride him as a "brown Englishman".

Mohammed Ali Jinnah, trained in law like Nehru himself, had no spiritual father behind the scenes. Austere, dedicated and single-minded, he had not, as Nehru had, a united people behind him. Clashing rivalries between the mullahs and the younger intellectuals, between the landowners and the aspiring middle-class, between religious extremists and political moderates had worn Jinnah down, and only his sense of mission enabled him to go on leading his faction-ridden people. It could truly be said that the concept of Pakistan itself sprang largely from fear, fear of Hindu domination. Jinnah, then, was driven to be even more implacable than Nehru. And, as I emphasized earlier, he stood far more in need of outside allies.

On the very heels of Mr Attlee's announcement that the British were determined to quit India, Mr Jinnah underlined his implacable rejection of any form of compromise. He announced that "the Muslim League will not yield an inch in its demand for Pakistan". The Hindu leaders of Congress, though they had previously been sure of their superior strength and cohesion, were also at last bringing themselves to a reluctant recognition—that partition of India between Hindu and Muslim was now the only solution. Jinnah, ironically, had devoted the greater part of his political life to the conception of Hindu-Muslim co-operation. It was only when the Hindu-dominated Congress had arrogantly shown him, in 1937, that they believed they need make no concessions to Muslim pride, that he had so bitterly set himself to establish a Muslim nation.

Communal hatred mounted daily, with murder and terrorism running like a fire through India, most of all in the Punjab. Britain had left Congress and the Muslim League in no doubt that she was already holding them responsible for law and order. Indeed she could not now provide the forces to control matters. The prospect of freedom was at hand for India. And the prospect of responsibility was even nearer. Together, these two towering facts at last brought a sobering recognition of reality. "India's mad career of violence must end," said Mahatma Gandhi. The grim question was: Could it be halted in time?

It *did halt*, and nothing did more to halt it than Viscount Mountbatten's rapid assessment of the situation. His conclusion was that partition should be implemented with all speed. The British Government agreed, and on June 3 produced a plan providing for immediate partition. The threatened civil war was halted almost at once. The Punjab and Bengal were divided into Hindu and Muslim states. The North-West Frontier Province, Sylhat and Sind elected to join the new Dominion of Pakistan. The rest of British India became the Dominion of India, whilst the Indian princes were left to seek association with either of the new Dominions, or independence —though there never was a real hope of the latter for them. By August 15, the Indian Independence Act having been rushed through the British Parliament, partition had become a reality.

With startling speed, the Indian Empire had come to an end, not without vast human suffering. Yet if Attlee had lacked statesmanship and Mountbatten decision, if matters had been allowed still further to drift, nothing could have prevented a holocaust to defy imagination. Never since the East India Company went into India nearly 350 years before had the British shown greater political skill or better judgement. Generations of the British had served in India, bringing justice, stability and a mass of self-destructive prejudices. There had been glory and some shame in the association. But this could be said: Nothing so glorified the British as the manner of their going.

They had come to India as the Moghul Empire was declining. And when that Empire collapsed in a holocaust of war and pillage, it was British power which buttressed a disintegrating sub-continent. Whatever the sins of omission and commission over the colourful centuries, Britain left in the sub-continent the means of nationhood, a tradition of justice and of parliamentary democracy. More to the practical point, she had left the instruments by which those two supreme gifts could be safeguarded—a strong, able, dedicated civil service and highly-trained and experienced military forces. The division of these two instruments between the two new Dominions would clearly destroy a great deal of their potential, but both India and Pakistan would just as clearly inherit at least the foundations of potential strength and stability, without which independence is a self-destroying illusion.

The new Dominion of India was the more fortunate beneficiary, not simply because, as the larger nation, the larger part of the military strength accrued to her, nor even because her economic inheritance was far the larger. Most important of all, the seat of former imperial government, Delhi, fell to her, along with a trained secretariat and all the hoarded administrative experience of the years of British occupation. Pakistan had to start almost from scratch, to build up her own central civil service on the trained nucleus of men who came to her from the former Indian Civil Service.

In the years to come, Mr Nehru was to wound and disappoint many unrealistic people in the Western world who thought that membership of the Commonwealth would automatically bring India into the Western camp. Yet it was clear, from the very start, that he and the nation he led were the chief pillars of democracy in Asia, whatever policies he chose to adopt, and whatever criticisms were made of him.

The single towering fact was that India was dedicated to the ideal of democracy at the very time when Asia was breaking free from the centuries-long domination of Western imperialism, and when the new doctrine of communism was making a challenge for the leadership of all that great and proud continent. Over in China the hammer blows of a dynamic communism were at last revealing the decadence and the spiritual emptiness of Kuomintang, and an ocean of American dollars could do no more than delay the day of reckoning. And, at the same time, the writing was clearly on the wall for the Dutch in turbulent Indonesia, as it was indeed for the French in Indo-China. In neither area could the fierce upsurge of nationalist fervour be subdued, in neither area was the policy of the imperial power ever abreast of the ambitions of the people. When one looks back over the broad picture of South-East Asia in those chaotic days, the free world owed much to the courage and decision of the self-effacing Prime Minister of Britain, Clement Attlee. At one stroke he had given democracy a head start and he had brought the two segments of the Indian sub-continent into the Commonwealth as the first non-European dominions. How long they would stay there, or whether their entry would be beneficial or calamitous, lay in the uncertain future.

Elsewhere in the East, Britain's policies were having a mixed outcome. Certainly in Malaya there had been a retrieval of original error. The new proposal for a Federation of Malaya instead of a Union had proved more acceptable, and moreover it had been thrashed out thoroughly this time by the rulers of the Malay States, by the United Malay National Organization and by the British Government. Only the Chinese had protested. That was to mean much, later on. The old idea of a Dominion of South-East Asia, with Singapore, Brunei, Sarawak and North Borneo added to the Federation of Malaya, began to be projected again, particularly by the Europeans of Malaya. Yet all the time, that cloud which had been no bigger than a man's hand was growing, the cloud which authority publicly referred to as subversion, but whose real name was communism. The ambush of an armed convoy, the murder of a British rubber-planter, the murder of a Chinese miner—such constant incidents began to add up to something much more than post-war lawlessness.

Ceylon continued to be the bright and untarnished star. Led with monumental patience and a countryman's shrewdness by Prime

Minister D. S. Senanayake, Ceylon had been promised full and independent Dominion status, and the British Parliament passed the necessary legislation before the year was out.

Burma was the single failure, in so far as maintaining a link with the Commonwealth. There had never been a British élite so intimately identified with Burma as there had been with India. Lack of time, lack of continuing policy, misunderstanding of the temper of the diverse peoples—these were among the many factors which led to the break. Almost up to the last there had been hopes in Britain that U Aung San, leader of the Council of Ministers, would keep the link with Britain. But by June the Constituent Assembly made it clear beyond doubt that Burma intended to be an independent republic, outside the Commonwealth. U Aung San and six of his Cabinet Ministers were assassinated by Burmese opponents in a matter of weeks, but it made no difference. Burma, for good or ill, stayed out of the Commonwealth.

The year had begun with much foreboding, yet it had ended in the East on a note of hope, of real accomplishment. Considering the vast, wide chaos of the aftermath of war, the destruction of European prestige and Britain's own precarious position, the performance had fallen not far short of miraculous.

CHAPTER IX

THE ASSAULT ON AFRICA

"THE WILDERNESS AND the solitary place shall be glad: and the desert shall rejoice and blossom as the rose." Those familiar words from Isaiah might have been written to describe the British Labour Government's approach to Colonial development. The massive, planned attack on poverty, on illiteracy, on disease, the combined operation launched by a government determined to put an end to mere profit-taking, and to substitute the doing of the greatest good to the greatest number—that was the Socialist ideal. And it was not an ideal to be ashamed of. It appealed to the "one world" spirit which the end of the war had unloosed. To millions of British people, particularly those who had served in the war, it awakened,

at one and the same time, the spirit of selfless service and the awareness that Britain could again command a glorious future, this time
in a new and utterly unselfish way.

Early in 1947, this concept became reality. A White Paper (*A
Plan for the Mechanized Production of Groundnuts in East and
Central Africa*) was released by the British Government. It proposed
that—to meet a world shortage of fats for the next 10 to 20 years—
nearly three and a quarter million acres of land in Tanganyika,
Northern Rhodesia and Kenya should be put into cultivation. A
total of 107 mechanized units should be established to eventually
produce 800,000 tons of groundnuts a year. There was an epic poem
in this mundane proposal.

Mr John Strachey, the Minister of Food, lyrically compared the
proposed enterprise to a full-scale military operation. He added:
"The enemy this time is not another nation or another army but
the tsetse fly, the vast distances of Africa, the ignorance of the population and the backward standards. I envisage this as the first of a
large series of enterprises of this type, in which the national resources
are mobilized to make vast development schemes possible."

Mr Frank Samuel, the managing director of the United Africa
Company, whose plan originated the scheme, summed up the project even more dramatically. In an interview with a Tanganyika
newspaper he declared: "To a country thus far tilled by the primitive
methods of the hand-hoe, virtually unchanged from Biblical days,
we plan to bring in six years the whole range of Western agricultural
science—the bulldozer, the tractor, soil analysis, fertilizers, rotation
of crops, and mechanical harvesting."

Without doubt the whole vast project fired imagination in Britain
and raised new hopes in the Colonial territories. This was a revolution in imperial development of historic importance. It linked together Britain and her dependent territories in a joint bid for prosperity. It brought a vision of painless economic expansion, of new
educational horizons for countless backward Africans, of a whole
new world attained by mutual effort. A new railway and a new port
were envisaged for Tanganyika, townships would arise in the forbidding and desolate bush, thousands of Africans would enter into
a new and better way of life. And (as the White Paper rather
patronizingly observed) "the nature and scope of the project rule out
private enterprise . . . it would seem necessary to form a Public Corporation sponsored and financed by H.M. Government to operate

the project". The title later given to this body was the Overseas Food Corporation, and it was one which became something more than merely well-known.

There were a few criticisms from various quarters, particularly from East African agricultural circles. Dr. H. Martin-Leake, a former Principal of the Imperial College of Tropical Agriculture, wrote: "The urgency of the need has dictated the speed at which the project is to be put into operation and is responsible for the omission of certain preliminary investigations which would have determined some of the many doubtful aspects."[1] But almost the entire British Press gave the scheme an enthusiastic welcome. Nothing could have been better timed to lift the British people from the winter of discontent that they were even then passing through. A new horizon was what they undoubtedly needed, and a new horizon was precisely what the great groundnuts scheme gave them.

When the Government followed up their master-stroke with the announcement that a Colonial Development Corporation was also to be formed, with total borrowing powers of the order of £100 million, their reputation in the Colonial field soared to a peak. Arthur Creech Jones told the House of Commons that the object of the new Corporation would be "to establish or assist any enterprise in the Colonies which is designed to increase their general productive capacity". In short, it would supplement private enterprise and not displace it.

Creech Jones went on to paint an even broader and more inspiring picture. He said: "The United Kingdom Government are aware of the part which the Dominion Governments can play in the field of Colonial development ... the assistance of the Dominion Governments will, I am sure, be readily forthcoming as necessary with the large Colonial development plans, and there will undoubtedly be opportunity of Dominion investment in this field." The old dream of a united Commonwealth and Empire going forward in a united effort to develop its own vast resources was reawakened. Not even Lord Beaverbrook could ask for more.

The words of the White Paper on Groundnuts were being translated into deeds within a matter of weeks. Towns of tents arose in the wilderness around Kongwa in Tanganyika, jeeps bounced through the tsetse-ridden scrub, aircraft straight from London swept down onto the temporary airstrip. That desolate region seemed

[1] *The Crown Colonist*, April 1947.

Tungku Abdul Rahman became Malaya's first Prime Minister after uniting Indians, Malays and Chinese in a political front, and co-operating with Britain to defeat the communists.

Dr. Kwame Nkrumah, first Prime Minister of Ghana, defied the British in his early political career, and defeated the "old guard" of Gold Coast politicians in a struggle for ultimate power.

Flamboyant, vehement David Marshall, as Chief Minister of Singapore, tried to force the pace of constitutional progress in 1956—but failed. He said he had no intention of being a "shock absorber for colonialism".

Dr. Cheddi Jagan's attempt to defy Britain in British Guiana ended in failure. He was accused of attempting a communist *coup*. But later he came back to office as Minister of Trade.

to blaze with the burning enthusiasm of the groundnutters. The Africans, for whose ultimate benefit all this was being done, saw the first bulldozers arrive, saw them cut down the ancient bush with giant ease, or so it seemed.

As all this was happening, there came news of another great scheme proposed to the north, in Uganda. This visualized the building of a dam and hydro-electric power-station at Owen Falls, where the ancient, mighty Nile begins its long passage to the sea. Power, and cheap power, at that, for much of East Africa would be made available. This, in fact, was the realization of the dream of Winston Churchill when, travelling in Africa as a young man, he saw the dramatic possibilities of making the Nile leap through a turbine. Mr C. R. Westlake, who produced the scheme for the Uganda Government, said that the power available at Owen Falls equalled about 400,000 tons of coal a year.

Across the other side of the continent, on the Gulf of Guinea, another giant scheme was coming forward. This was the Volta River Project, in the Gold Coast. Its supporters claimed that the river could be dammed up in the interior, providing electricity and at the same time creating a 300-mile waterway to the sea, to bring down bauxite from the vast reserves near Mpraeso. All the schemes were big, but wasn't Africa big? It did not seem possible to think small about Africa.

Which was the Empire Party now? Who was following in Livingstone's footsteps and opening up the Dark Continent? Little wonder that Arthur Creech Jones, speaking in the annual debate on the Colonial Estimates in the House of Commons in July, ranged over the year's progress with pride. Twenty constitutions were being altered throughout the Colonial Empire; health services, education, trade unionism were all expanding rapidly; development was going forward on all fronts. But the Secretary of State was not dazzled by his own words. Cautiously, he concluded by warning that "however comprehensive our planning may be in regard to Colonial development, whatever enthusiasm and zeal we bring to the task, we cannot get far unless we have the co-operation and the understanding of the Colonial peoples themselves". These were wise words, and the years ahead were to prove them so.

Most of all, they were to prove true of Africa. The stir and the excitement over Africa's development—and 1947 was indeed Africa's year—obscured the rising discontent among those who were officially designed "the indigenous peoples"—the black men, the Africans themselves. In West Africa, all the ex-servicemen had returned, nearly 150,000 of them, and many were the willing followers of the rising, younger politicians, such as Dr Nnamdi Azikiwe of Nigeria. The Doctor, owner of a string of newspapers, led a delegation to London to press for self-government for Nigeria within 15 years. It was a fruitless quest, but he returned as a national hero.

In Kenya, the Africans, crowded in eroded reserves, coveted the farms of the white man. It was forgotten that the white settlers had produced fine and fruitful farms by hard work, and skilled cultivation. To the Africans, they were becoming the interlopers who had forced their way into Kenya and stolen the best land.

But there were few outside the white settler communities who realized the real dangers of the growing cleavage between white men and black. Certainly to Britain's Labour Government, at this point of time, the whole Colonial record, particularly in Africa, shone like a comforting light in the dark world. Even Ernest Bevin, the Foreign Secretary, brandished the flag of Empire. He told the Trades Union Congress in September: "I hope our Commonwealth, and certainly the Empire, will agree as to the possibility of a Customs Union for the Commonwealth." He had, somewhat characteristically, omitted to mention this breath-taking scheme to his Cabinet colleagues. But his words swept round the world, and more particularly round the Commonwealth and Empire. Australia was a little cautious, New Zealand was guardedly enthusiastic, Canada was cold. But Mr Bevin found himself with at least two powerful though embarrassing champions, Lord Beaverbrook and the Rt. Hon. L. S. Amery.

Sir Stafford Cripps, President of the Board of Trade, tactfully remarked that the Bevin plan "might have many advantages, but it is an accomplishment fraught with difficulties and it must take time to explore its possibilities". Sir Stafford could hardly have failed to recall that years before, when imperialism was a bad word, Mr Bevin himself had said of this very idea of an Empire Customs Union that "No more crazy idea has ever been submitted to intelligent people."

Yet it was true that close economic co-operation between the countries of the Commonwealth was not only vital to Britain's recovery, it was basic to the Government's deep-seated ambition to be the leader of world Socialism. A strong and co-operative Commonwealth would restore the power and influence of Britain and enable British Socialism to spread its ideals far and wide. However circumspectly Mr Attlee's Government might deal with Ernest Bevin's blunt statement, in order to avoid offending the more susceptible members of the Commonwealth, their real hopes were not so far different. As Harold Wilson, the Secretary for Overseas Trade, said at Geneva, "We shall find it necessary to have closer economic co-operation with other countries of the Commonwealth."

But Wilson, who had represented Britain at this same international Geneva Conference on Tariffs, had to report back to Parliament that some part of Imperial Preference had been bargained away. There had, he fairly claimed, been valuable concessions in return. But Britain and the Empire and Commonwealth were, as later events proved, being drawn into an American-conceived multilateral trading conception which made economic co-operation between Britain and the Dominions and Colonies increasingly harder of achievement. In short, the Geneva discussions, let alone the self-interest of the Dominion's had already dispelled Mr Bevin's pipe dream.

On the Colonial front, Arthur Creech Jones ended an exhilarating year with yet another revolutionary step, once again concerning Africa. During November, he called to London all the Governors of Africa to discuss the common problems of that continent—political and administrative, economic and social. Home to London in the fogs they came, from Nigeria, the Gold Coast, the Gambia, Sierra Leone, Kenya, Tanganyika, Uganda, Zanzibar, Northern Rhodesia and Nyasaland. These men who were the representatives of the King were the symbols of power in lands which totalled one and a half million square miles. They were the guardians of over fifty million people, brown, black and white; Christian, pagan, Hindu and Muslim. In size and in population, Britain's African territories represented about three-quarters of her Colonial Empire. Britain indeed was the greatest colonial power in Africa. This conference of Governors was of deep significance not only to all the British Colonial Empire, but to Africa as a whole.

Keeping in mind the steady political ferment in nearly all these African territories, and the rising ambitions for self-government, the conference which was to follow that of the Governors was of even greater significance. This conference, which Creech Jones announced would be held in the middle of the following year, was to consist of

Unofficial Members from the Legislative Councils of all the African territories. These Unofficial Members were the elected or nominated representatives of the people of the territories, those on whom the responsibility of self-government might finally be expected to fall—if Britain's careful plans worked out.

There were hopes in some quarters—and experienced quarters at that—that these two conferences might prove the beginning of a British African council or parliament. The hard facts of geography and of race were clearly against any such visionary concept. But it was the right way to think. Plainly, when one remembered the woes of Europe, the more cohesion there was in Africa the better. Not that it would be easy to attain, with African kingdoms and republics, multi-racial territories, European-dominated lands and five European colonial powers all pursuing different policies.

CHAPTER X

CLEARING UP THE CARIBBEAN

ONE MORE VIGOROUS effort was launched in 1947 by Arthur Creech Jones, to tidy up this vast, sprawling Empire collected by the British in 350 years of turbulent, thrusting expansion. In the late spring the Secretary of State for the Colonies sent a despatch to all the Governors of the West Indies proposing that a conference "to discuss closer association" should be held at Montego Bay in the September.

The collection of islands in the sunlit Caribbean and colonies on the American mainland which had come to be known as the West Indies recalled violent and colourful passages of British history. British Guiana, the Leeward Islands, the Windwards, their very names breathed of Columbus, of the Elizabethan adventurers and the struggle for the Spanish Main, of the buccaneers and the slavers. Now, for all their romantic past, these territories were in the main overcrowded and beset with economic problems, a source of grave and continuing concern to the Imperial Government in London.

It was only too clear that to try and base a federation on a mere three million people, scattered over a huge area of sea and land, was a doubtful proposition at the best. Yet what other future was there for them? As Creech Jones said to the delegates at Montego Bay: "I put it to you that it is essential to the progress of the West Indies that we should get along this road of federation as rapidly as we can."

What was known as "the island mentality" was one of the major obstacles in the way of federation. The vast distances, the lack of communication and the different history and traditions of the various territories all combined to produce an extreme degree of individuality and an almost equally extreme degree of suspicion, sometimes of outright hostility. It was true to say that there was an almost total lack of enthusiasm for closer union among the people themselves.

Jamaica, the largest and by far the most populous of the islands, was feared by all the others. Clearly it would play a major rôle in any federation, with its population of well over a million and its powerful political traditions. It was the politicians that were feared more than anything else—the bouncing, ebullient crowd-raisers, of whom the flamboyant and forceful Alexander Bustamante, leader both of the Jamaican Labour Party and of the unions, was the archetype. This extraordinary man was in constant conflict with authority and with those who sat in the seats of power. Creech Jones lunched with him, prior to the opening of the Closer Association Conference, and afterwards publicly praised "the vital public life of the Colony". A few weeks later, after a riotous election campaign, Bustamante was summoned on six charges, and it was alleged that he pulled a gun on a policeman. Creech Jones, who was by then on his way home, wrote a sorrowful little note of rebuke. "This is not the way for democracy to grow," he deplored. Still less was it the way to encourage the other West Indian colonies to plunge into partnership with Jamaica.

The two other most important islands of the Caribbean, Barbados and Trinidad, could view Jamaica with rather less apprehension than the scattered Windward and Leeward Islands, which found it difficult enough to achieve some sort of unity between their own constituent parts. But it was the mainland territories, British Guiana on the South American coast, and British Honduras on the Central American mainland, which showed the greatest caution. Not only were they fearful about being swamped by the islands, they nursed strong doubts as to whether their future lay with the Caribbean territories at all.

Both Honduras and Guiana had some cause for foreboding. The Secretary of State himself, earlier in the year, had indicated that the possibilities of both territories as settlement areas for the surplus population of the islands should be examined. British Guiana, as big as England and Wales together, had a population of 367,000; British Honduras, with an area of nearly 9,000 square miles, had a population of 60,000—no more than that of an English market town. Clearly both these lands stood in sad need of development, but though their leaders recognized that, they also believed that a flood of Jamaicans and Barbadians was not the answer.

Without the co-operation of the two mainland territories, particularly British Guiana, there would certainly be the utmost difficulty in establishing a federation on a reasonable economic basis. Even with them, it was difficult to see how the great dream of real nationhood could be realized. The great distances which struck at any sense of partnership, the differing stages of constitutional progress, the lack of a wide range of resources or of any advanced degree of industrialization—all of these were most daunting difficulties. Yet the idea of maintaining all the separate territories as individual entities was unthinkable. As Creech Jones pointed out to the delegates at Montego Bay: "It is clearly impossible in the modern world to hope for the present separate communities, small and isolated as most of them are, to achieve and maintain full self-government on their own."

At the end of it all, the delegates arrived at fourteen points of common understanding. This was a measure of agreement to astonish even the most ardent advocates of federation, and even more remarkable was the unanimous desire for a federation with Dominion status. A draft constitution for the federal machinery was agreed to. On closer examination, it was apparent that a coach and horses could have been driven through the fourteen points, so nebulous were most of them. The one thing clear was that practically all the delegates had a prior interest in preserving the position of their own territories, and very few of them had decreased their suspicions about their prospective partners.

Yet it remained true that federation in the West Indies became a politically practicable idea after Montego Bay. Whatever the reservations, public and private, most of the delegates had faced the cold truth that the Caribbean colonies could not dream in the sun any more. The decisive fact was the recommendation that a Standing Closer Association Committee should be set up, to plan federation. The delegates returned to their respective territories, to push forward their own local plans, to plunge into the maelstrom of island politics, to let the proposed Standing Committee get on with the details. After all, closer association had been talked about for years. As far back as 1938, a Royal Commission under Lord Moyne had declared federation to be the ultimate objective for the West Indies. But this time the delegates had set something in motion which, as it proved, was not to be halted.

Creech Jones had good reason for being satisfied with all that had been accomplished. He had good reason for being satisfied with his year. The tidying-up of the Colonies had gone well on the larger fronts.

Even in the far Pacific things were slowly moving forward. Throughout that wide ocean numerous groups of islands were scattered, and between them they presented a more baffling proposition than even the Caribbean. The native people of this area stemmed from the three major divisions of mankind: the Polynesians from the light-skinned Caucasian group; the Micronesians from the yellow-brown Mongoloid group; and the Melanesians, of negro stock. Culturally they ranged from Stone Age standards to a high degree of civilization. There were six controlling powers in the area —Britain, France, Australia, New Zealand, the United States and the Netherlands. It had been said, and with a good measure of truth, that practically every form of administration known to mankind was in operation somewhere in the Pacific.

In the main, the Pacific territories began their lasting association with the European powers in the great days of the navigator-explorers, Captain Cook, Tasman, Bligh and the rest. They were well situated for trade and for sea communications, and one after the other they were caught up in the repercussions of the general world struggle for military and economic power. The last war had brutally completed the process, for many of them were overrun by the Japanese in the early years of their non-stop triumph.

If the sad omissions of the past were to be rectified, if the tragic effects of the Japanese occupation were to be overcome, then action on a regional basis was essential, with co-operation among the controlling powers. During the dark days of the war in 1944, it was heartening to see such a proposal coming from a meeting at Canberra of Australia and New Zealand. These two Dominions had a close and direct interest in the Pacific, and the fierce struggles for supremacy in the Pacific during the war had sharpened their awareness of its importance to them. Moreover, they had charges of their own there. Australia was responsible for Papua and also held the mandate for New Guinea, whilst New Zealand was responsible for the Tokelau Islands off Samoa, and held the mandate for Western Samoa.

Britain naturally supported the two Dominions. Her colonies in the Pacific were the Fiji Islands (200 of them) and the Gilbert and Ellice Islands; there were also the British Solomons Protectorate, the tiny islands of Pitcairn and Nauru, and the native kingdom of Tonga, under British protection. The Phoenix Group was administered in conjunction with the Americans, and the New Hebrides in conjunction with France. Altogether, the Commonwealth interest in the Pacific was considerable and permanent.

Early in 1947, at Canberra, the six big powers in the Pacific agreed to set up a South Pacific Commission. In the main this commission was to be advisory, and it was to deal with economic and social matters. Working alongside the Commission would be two auxiliary bodies, the Research Council and the South Pacific Conference. This latter was seen as a sort of early development of a South Pacific parliament, and it was planned that leaders of the Pacific peoples themselves would meet at least every two years.

Ivor Thomas, Creech Jones' Under-Secretary of State, claimed that the Conference could be a valuable training in self-government. "We have thrown down a challenge to the capacity of the local inhabitants, first to discuss and then to manage their own affairs," he grandly proclaimed. Considering that the Commission's field of operations ranged over some thirteen million square miles, that their three million human charges spread over this huge expanse of ocean hardly knew of each other's existence, Ivor Thomas' remark had a kind of stupefying optimism. Yet within nine years the South Pacific Conference was to discuss with anxiety the rapid breaking-up of tribalism all over the area, the general acceptance of a European money economy, the urge for education and for industrialization. The delegates were to become conscious of the fact that there was no going back, that all their scattered communities were facing broadly similar problems—in short, that they had a great many things in common.

The West Indies, the South Pacific—the march of events in these two widely-separated areas emphasized that Britain, weakened though she was, still had far-spread responsibilities in a rapidly-changing world. And southwards yet to the last, remote land mass of the world another delicate situation was developing. Once more Britain was involved. Argentina recapitulated her claim to the Falkland Islands and to her "Argentine sector of the Antarctic". Britain rejected the claim completely, and Argentina and Chile retorted by proposing to call an international conference in Buenos Aires to decide legal claims to Antarctic lands.

From this time on the desolate and challenging Antarctic, with its deathly beauty and its debatable value, became a focus of international interest. Britain herself had been conducting research work in the Falkland Islands Dependencies (South Georgia, with the South Orkneys and South Sandwich, South Shetland, Graham Land and Coats Land) since 1943. The United States had despatched a large expedition to the Antarctic under the renowned Rear-Admiral Byrd, whilst Argentine and Chile also had expeditions there. It was hardly a coincidence that, at this juncture, the indefatigable Miles Clifford set out on the first-ever trip of the Antarctic Dependencies to be made by a Governor of the Falklands.

The Falkland Islands themselves, windswept and austere, had been of great importance in the old days before the Panama Canal was opened, when all vessels from the Atlantic to the Pacific had to double Cape Horn. For these rugged, windswept islands lay about 480 miles from the notorious Cape Horn. Their present importance lay in the fact that the largest whaling industry in the world flourished around their Dependencies. Their future value seemed to lie in their position as a gateway to the Antarctic itself.

The population of the Falklands consisted of about 3,000 people, mainly of Scots descent, whose principal occupation was sheep rearing. This they conducted with such success that the Colony was self-supporting, and had indeed built up comforting reserves. Certainly these hardy and healthy people could regard themselves as forming one of the most remote settled communities in the world, a vanguard on the frontier of the known world, for beyond them was only the empty ice world.

Britain had had links with the Falklands for 350 years, and had been in effective occupation for over a century. And she could claim to have led the way in exploration of the Antarctic itself. Cook and Weddell, William Smith and Captain Biscoe, Franklin, Scott and Shackleton, these were great names in its gradual discovery. But what was more to the present point was that Britain, Australia and

South Africa claimed about two-thirds of Antarctica between them. One could not altogether liken it to the 19th-century "scramble for Africa" but there were distinct points of resemblance. It was clear that a number of other nations besides Argentina would eventually contest the Commonwealth's position.

Drawing neat sectors on a map, claims by right of discovery, the sending out of small research expeditions is hardly the same thing as occupation by arms or by treaty, with all the buttressing of administration and development schemes. Down in the southern world of snow and ice a diverting situation developed in which bases were solemnly occupied and ships sailed with provocative flying of colours.

Yet there was a serious side to all this. The advent of nuclear power, the success of the Russians in developing their Arctic regions, the contraction of distance brought about by the rapid advance of aviation—all these factors made the future of Antarctica take on a real significance at last. No more did it seem the impenetrable and useless wilderness of ice which man could turn his back on. Who knew what decisive strategic value it might have in any future world conflict? Who really knew what wealth lay beneath the ice?

CHAPTER XI

WHITE AND BLACK IN AFRICA

THE REAL TESTING-GROUND for Britain's colonial policy, the testing-ground for the multi-racial concept which lay behind the whole Commonwealth ideal, was in Africa. For here were the territories in which the white man had put down his roots, here was where he held the power (or the prospect of power) though hopelessly outnumbered by people of a different colour. It was one thing to talk in Westminster of a Commonwealth of all races combining in partnership. It was most certainly another to be called on to implement such a partnership inside the borders of your own land, in your daily life.

It was already evident that the beginnings of African extremism, which were now too clear to be under-estimated, were calling forth a hardening in European opinion. In the Union of South Africa, where an election was imminent, Field-Marshal Smuts was losing in-

fluence. He was certainly not regarded by British Socialists as a
liberal, yet, as far as the political realities of South Africa permitted
him, he was. At least he was the symbol of tolerance, and his chief
lieutenant, Jan Hofmeyr, was both a realist and visionary. And
Smuts was a Commonwealth man, fervently believing that it was
a force of unique value to humanity.

His opponents, the Nationalists, were dedicated to the proposition
of white supremacy. In addition, they resented British influence in
South Africa, belittled the Commonwealth link and believed that
only a republic would ensure a realistic South African nationhood.
To them Smuts was at once a betrayer of Afrikaans ideals and of
white leadership.

On the other side of the Limpopo River, in Southern Rhodesia,
the shrewd and patient Sir Godfrey Huggins, Prime Minister for
14 years, also faced the prospect of an election. Most British Socialists
regarded him too as a reactionary, pledged to keep the white man
in power. A bitter irony lay in the fact that Sir Godfrey, like Smuts
in South Africa, was suspected by many in his own country of
"going Socialist", certainly of being too concerned with the welfare
of the Africans. It was this suspicion, plus his long tenure of office,
which led to forecasts that he would be swept from power at the
elections.

At this very point of time, the Gold Coast, that cherished model
of British colonies, exploded into violence. The combination of
rising prices and disillusioned ex-servicemen had created a potentially dangerous situation for some time past. But few Europeans in
authority had realized that, apart from these post-war problems,
African nationalism had been growing rapidly in strength. India,
Pakistan, Burma had gained freedom. The restless, dissatisfied African intelligentsia in the West African territories were fired with a
new hope. They were no longer to be satisfied with the prospect of
freedom in some vague and distant future.

The developing crisis in the Gold Coast brought forth a leader. In
truth, he played a major part in creating the crisis, crystallizing the
vague yet powerful ambitions of his more advanced countrymen,
translating their grievances into planned action. His name was
Kwame Nkrumah, and he had come back to the Gold Coast in
1947, after being educated in England and America, to take over the
secretaryship of a new political party, the United Gold Coast Convention. Leader of the party was Dr J. B. Danquah, an able and ex-

perienced politician of the older school. But it was the volatile and able orator Nkrumah who began to capture the minds and hearts of the people, who stirred in the younger folk, cutting across the old tribal animosities, a dawning idea of nationhood.

The flashpoint came on February 28. For some weeks past there had been an organized and surprisingly successful African boycott of European goods as a protest against rising prices. The Government finally announced that prices would be reduced and the Africans agreed to lift the boycott on February 28. On that same day a procession of ex-servicemen was due to march to present a petition for transmission to the Governor. There was an atmosphere of dangerous tension quite new to the peaceful Gold Coast. And when, with the opening of the shops, it was discovered that the price reductions were much smaller than hoped, it only needed one major incident to unloose disaster.

That incident, tragically, was provided when the ex-servicemen left their official route and arrived at a road leading to Government house. Barring the way was a small police detachment under a British police officer. The procession, swollen by the addition of excited civilians, now more nearly resembled a mob, and a mob which seemed bent on trouble. They were not to be turned back by words. Fearing an assault on Government House, the police opened fire. The first bullet brought an end of an era. The news was brought back to the capital, Accra, and at once the mob took over. Looting, arson and rioting swept through all the major towns for some days and a stunned country finally returned to a semblance of normality to find that 290 people had lost their lives, whilst 230 had received severe injuries.

The newly-arrived Governor, Sir Gerald Creasy, issued removal orders against Danquah, Nkrumah and four other leaders, whom he suspected of planning to stir up further violence; the Secretary of State immediately appointed a commission of inquiry to report on the troubles. But nothing could alter the fact that the old harmony between European and African in the Gold Coast was shattered. Indeed, the bitter hostility and frustration of the younger, educated Africans, their deep distrust of the Government came as a dismaying shock even to Europeans of long residence in the country, indeed more particularly to them. The riot had brought to the surface a dark and strong tide of Africanism, which drew its strength from a hatred of European domination.

The Report of the Watson Commission of Inquiry revealed this only too clearly. Bluntly it stated that "the most serious problem of the Administration in the Gold Coast is the suspicion which surrounds Government activity of any sort". It stated that there had been a failure on the part of the Government to recognize the decline of the Chiefs' influence, that there was political frustration among educated Africans and a rising resentment at the growing concentration of certain trades in the hands of foreigners. In short, the people of the Gold Coast believed that in government, in business, and in administration the way ahead for them was blocked, inside their own native land.

If all this were true, then there had been an unforgivable failure on the part of successive British governments and of the administration in the Gold Coast. Was it altogether, was it even largely true? To this day there has remained a bitter division of opinion. The critics of the Watson Report claimed that the strictures were grossly exaggerated, that the key to the situation was that inevitable problems of the post-war years in the Gold Coast had been cunningly manipulated by unscrupulous African politicians, particularly Dr Kwame Nkrumah.

One might fairly ask if the Watson Commission was equipped with sufficient experience of Africa to deliver such wholesale judgement after so comparatively brief an examination. The members of the Commission were Mr Andrew Aiken Watson, K.C., the Chairman, who was Recorder of Bury St Edmunds and Deputy Chairman of the East Sussex Quarter Sessions, Mr Andrew Dalgleish, a former Trade Union leader, and Dr K. A. H. Murray, the Rector of Lincoln College, Oxford.

Looking back, in the light of all that followed, it is clear that the Government of the Gold Coast had certainly under-estimated the rising strength of nationalist feeling and the sense of frustration. But it seems equally clear that the members of the Commission were not overburdened with a cautionary sense of their own possible fallibility. Their judgements were sweeping and their recommendations even more so.

It is of the greatest importance to assess the value of the Watson Report. For no other single document had so dramatic an impact on the Colonial Empire in the post-war years. Although the Burns Constitution had only been introduced two years before, the Commission advocating a reshaping of the Constitution and Government of the Gold Coast in ways that would give every African of ability an opportunity to help govern the country, so as not only to gain political experience but also to experience political power. The British Government had its own answers for some of the Commission's criticisms, but it accepted this key proposal. A committee of Gold Coast people under the chairmanship of an eminent African, Mr Justice Coussey, was set up to make definite proposals. The final outcome was that the Gold Coast took a gigantic step forward to independence, a far greater step than had been contemplated by the British in the first place.

But who can judge when the time to give freedom to a dependent country has arrived? Who can say, without reservations, when the pressure of nationalism is such that the controlling power must give way, even if it knows that the country concerned is ill-prepared to face a challenging world? Those questions underline the whole dilemma which faced successive Colonial Secretaries.

The Watson Report, and its consequences, led to a reappraisal, not so much of Britain's Colonial policy, but of its implementation. It influenced events far beyond the Gold Coast, in a way which could not have been foreseen by the British. Without question, it led to the speeding up of constitutional advance in other territories. For what Governor could now afford to ignore the lesson of the Gold Coast? And what nationalist leader would fail to learn the same lesson? That lesson was that a united people, under able leadership, could now force undreamt-of concessions from Britain, could short-cut the planned road to independence. If one studies the speeches of various Governors in those post-war years, and the lines of constitutional advance they contemplated, it is certain that few of them dreamed how quickly the pace would increase.

Has it been for better or for worse? It is hard to draw up a balance sheet. India and Burma had proved how dangerous procrastination could be. But India has also since proved that a country adequately equipped to face the modern world not only survives as a truly independent nation, but can make a powerful contribution to human affairs. In contrast, at the moment of writing this, Indonesian independence has meant the launching of an unstable and divided nation which is likely to prove a positive danger to the world.

Britain's policy is to prepare her wards for independence as and when they are ready for it. It is not only her policy, it is her duty. The foundation stones of democratic independence are an impartial judiciary, an experienced and incorruptible civil service, able and honest politicians, and an electorate with some understanding of and faith in the democratic process. These things are not conjured into existence by words or even by the most passionate patriotism. It is not enough to say that events have justified the action taken in the Gold Coast, that the gamble came off. We have yet to see whether the general speed-up of Colonial constitutional progress, which the explosion in the Gold Coast precipitated, will also be justified. Not all the present signs are favourable.

The faith of the Socialist Government in special commissions of inquiry seemed to dwindle after the Gold Coast upheaval. They were to burn their fingers once more—in British Guiana—before the lesson was thoroughly learnt. The theory that the impartial, independent commission of honest and able men can best resolve colonial deadlocks has much to recommend it. But the terms of such commissions should be most cautiously framed, the possible repercussions of their proposals must never be out of mind. It is difficult, indeed dangerous, once such a commission has produced its report, not to accept at least a proportion of its proposals.

The unfolding drama in the Gold Coast was watched with the closest attention throughout Africa. It would not be correct to say that it crushed any remaining hope of a liberal-minded government emerging in South Africa. *Apartheid* was already in the ascendant before Nkrumah launched his bid for power. But it did fortify the South African Nationalists in their belief that only their policy could save the white man in Africa. In the Union itself, the chaos in the Gold Coast could not but help the Nationalists' cause. This, they could claim, was precisely the sort of explosion they had prophesied for years. It was only what could be expected when "liberals" were allowed to put their weak and ineffectual ideas into practice.

It was in May that Field-Marshal Smuts finally lost power. Dr Daniel Malan, the former predikant of the Dutch Reformed Church, led his Nationalists to a victory at the polls. But this was not simply a victory for a political party, it was a victory for a tradition. It was not only Malan who had triumphed, but Oom Paul Kruger. Not only Smuts had been rolled in the dust, but Dingaan, once more. The Voortrekkers were back, bringing with them all the old bitter memories of English "oppression", and the deep-rooted conviction that they had been planted in South Africa by the hand of God to rule over the African.

Smuts, the only world statesman ever produced by South Africa, had been brought down by men of infinitely lesser stature. Saddening though that was, perhaps an even greater tragedy for Africa was the death, a few months after the election, of Jan Hofmeyr. This was the man, "the moral giant" as he was called, who was to have succeeded Smuts. Hofmeyr had brilliance and courage. "A policy based on fear must lead to disaster," he warned his countrymen. After he was gone, there was no other younger leader of his stature in the United Party, no one who was prepared to pose the realities of the racial situation, and to advocate a drastic reappraisal of the European outlook.

The defeat of Smuts, the rampant nationalism in West Africa, now seemed to make inevitable the defeat of Sir Godfrey Huggins in Southern Rhodesia. The men of moderation, of tolerance and compromise do not generally survive when fear and hatred dominate the minds of men. But Huggins was a political tactician of a calibre rarely seen in Africa. His Liberal Party opponents were convinced that after fifteen years of unbroken power the Rhodesians had had more than enough of Sir Godfrey and his band of rather mediocre lieutenants. But somehow the election came about when the true meaning of the victory of Dr Malan had begun to sink into the minds of British-stock Rhodesians. Somehow it got around in Southern Rhodesia that the leader of the Liberal Party, J. H. Smit, had nursed ideas about uniting the country with South Africa. It was enough to wreck his cause. Huggins overwhelmed his opponents, winning 24 of the 30 seats.

He immediately let it be known that a "United States of Africa"—the two Rhodesias and Nyasaland—was now possible. Roy Welensky, the leader of the Unofficial Members of the Legislative Council in Northern Rhodesia, had for some time past been convinced that the way to get union of the three countries was by federation, not by the amalgamation which Sir Godfrey still desired. Undoubtedly Welensky was right in believing that amalgamation was not to be thought of. Even federation, with a Socialist Government in power in Britain, presented formidable difficulties. Welensky set himself to convince his ally that federation was the only hope. It was his deep conviction that events were now moving so fast in Africa that no time must be lost in bringing the two Rhodesias together. He and Huggins must settle for what they could get.

Meanwhile, in the Gold Coast, Nkrumah was driving home the

advantage that the Watson Report had given to him. Wherever he spoke he drew huge crowds. He became the national hero, the man who had challenged the power of Britain and won. His policy was independence without waste of time, and without equivocation. The older politicians who had invited him back to the Gold Coast found that they had allied themselves with a tiger. The more discerning of them began to see that they, as well as the British, had no place in Nkrumah's scheme of things to come. The younger nationalists were solidly behind him, the young men with some degree of education who were tired of their own lack of opportunity. These young men were of the people, the first crop from a broader educational policy, and they gave Nkrumah something that was to prove decisive in the struggle for power—a direct and continuing link with the mass of the Gold Coast people. That was precisely what the older politicians like Dr Danquah lacked, for they were the professional men, the middle class, with one foot in that very European world which they now opposed. They were men of two worlds in a country struggling for independence, theirs was an unenviable position. The irony of the situation was that these discredited men were the ones who had had the benefit of British tutelage.

Just as the year 1947 had seemed the year of economic awakening for Africa, so did this following year seem that of political changes. But few people, in or out of Africa, realized just how significant the changes would prove to be. Nkrumah, Malan, Huggins and Welensky represented three different faiths in Africa, and only one of them could ultimately triumph.

CHAPTER XII

AFRICA COMES TO BRITAIN

HISTORY IS SOMETIMES made in the background, away from the main stream of events. The incident which seemed secondary to a greater occasion emerges, in the course of time, as decisive. Who thought, when the German leaders returned a handful of nondescript professional revolutionaries to Russia to further their own cause during the 1914-18 war, that they were unleashing a power destined to alter the whole course of human progress?

F

Yet history is often also made with the proper trimmings of drama and the true sense of great occasion. It seemed that a stage for great events was set when Africa came to Britain in the summer of 1948. For now that the Asian lands were independent, Africa represented the greater part of the Colonial Empire.

From the Legislative Assemblies of ten different territories came 61 delegates to confer, for the first time, on the common problems of Africa. London had never seen such an occasion, and neither had the delegates themselves. These Colonial leaders spoke for fifty million people, for the white settlers of the Kenya Highlands, for the black fishermen shouting their boats home on the roaring surf of the Gulf of Guinea, for the ambitious and bewildered Nyasaland boy footslogging his way down dusty tracks to work in the Rhodesian copper mines.

The nations of Europe had divided most of Africa between themselves, regardless of tribe or history. They had, they still pursued policies that reflected, not the aspirations or hopes of the African peoples, but the temperament and political and economic beliefs of the controlling nations themselves. On the face of it some of these policies were bound to fail. Naturally the British believed that their policy of guidance towards self-government was the right one. And what happened in Asia fortified them in their self-approval.

At least it could be said that this London Conference was a logical step towards co-ordinating Britain's policies in her various territories. The delegates represented Europeans and Indians, Arabs and Goans and, most of all, Africans, urban Africans and a great bewildering complexity of tribal people. They spoke for Christian, Hindu, Muslim, pagan. They spoke, in short, for what was being loosely called a huge melting pot of humanity. Only, in this particular melting pot, the ingredients refused to mix.

Did they really speak for all these people, those Colonial legislators? For the white mine manager of the Copperbelt equally with the pagan of Nigeria's Bauchi Plateau? Officially they did. Appointed or elected or ex-officio, they were the legitimate spokesmen of British Colonial Africa, emerging from the careful policies approved in Whitehall.

What was without question was that they came from a huge and torpid continent which was slowly struggling out of the lethargy of the centuries, a continent which had cradled human history in its northern reaches and had been lost in a long dark night of barbarism over much of its area south of the great deserts. Africa was variously described as an awakening giant, as the uncommitted continent in the world war of ideologies, as a largely untapped treasure trove for humanity.

For eleven days, at Lancaster House, the Colonial leaders discussed local government, information services, education and medicine, economic development and agriculture. They heard speeches by the Lord President of the Council, Mr Herbert Morrison, by the Secretary of State for the Colonies, by Field-Marshal Viscount Montgomery of Alamein, by the Secretary of State for Commonwealth Affairs, Mr Philip Noel-Baker. They were the guests at all sorts of dinners, lunches, and cocktail parties. There were visits to the Tower of London, to a housing estate, to Westminster Abbey, to the House of Commons. There was tea at the Scout Headquarters and a meeting with the Chief Scout, there was a trip on a launch round the London docks, there was a special service at Westminster Abbey. It could only have happened in Britain, this fascinating mixture of an annual political party congress and a conducted travel agency tour.

In fairness, the discussions did cover most of the major and basic problems common to all the territories, the obduracy of soil and climate, the wretched poverty, the daunting illiteracy and disease. Whether the delegates learned much from the rather platitudinous speeches and the stilted discussions is another matter. But without doubt they learnt a great deal simply by meeting one another, by the realization that they did face these many problems together.

Arthur Creech Jones, as Secretary of State for the Colonies, seemed to strike the authentic note when, beaming at the Secretary of State for Commonwealth Affairs, he said, "We can ... imagine Mr Philip Noel-Baker standing at the door of the Commonwealth Relations Office and beckoning all of you to hasten along and join those who have already assembled under the umbrella of his department."

Later in the Conference, and not so exuberantly, Creech Jones solemnly warned the delegates about a new menace in the Colonies —subversion. Legitimate agitation was one thing, he emphasized, communism was quite another. He also (for he was always an honest and courageous man) aimed a careful shaft at the rising black nationalism. The immigrant races in Africa were making a great contribution to its progress, and they had their rights.

Looking back, the significance of this Lancaster House Conference was that it was a watershed. The agenda, and the delegates in the main symbolized a passing era of Empire, an era of careful and ordered progress towards considered goals, with the emphasis on raising standards of education, health, housing and the like, and always in the background the solid, reassuring figure of the official, ready to encourage or to admonish.

It is a salutary exercise to examine, so many years after, the names of the delegates. Among the officials were such able and experienced men as Hugh Foot, Chief Secretary of Nigeria, and Robert Scott, Colonial Secretary of the Gold Coast, both of them later to be Governors; the European unofficial delegates included men still powerful in their territories such as E. A. Vasey of Kenya, and, above all, Roy Welensky of Northern Rhodesia.

Welensky, later to be a Prime Minister, was then a tough, repetitive and somewhat crude politician, an ex-white trade union leader with some of the shortcomings of that type. But he was also a man of considerable natural ability, with an uncommon imagination and great power of leadership. He alone during the eleven-day Conference disturbed the placid flow of talk by cumbersomely dragging in a reference to the desirability of linking the Rhodesias and Nyasaland.

Among the African leaders were the great chiefs like the Gold Coast's Nana Sir Tsibu Darku IX, the Omanhene of Asin Atandesu, Sierra Leone's Paramount Chief Bai Koble of Marampa, and Nigeria's Oba Aderemi, Oni of Ife. There were the Emir of Katsina, Usuman Nagago and Sulemanu, Emir of Abuja. And, prominent among the middle-class Africans, was that able politician from the Gold Coast, Dr J. B. Danquah. All these were the men who had become practised in democratic government, under the careful guidance of the British. To them, or men of their calibre, in the natural order of things, full power would ultimately descend. That was how it looked in those hopeful days of 1948.

There were other men in Africa who aspired to leadership, but their names were not among the list of delegates. Few people outside of Africa had heard of them. Such men as Kwame Nkrumah, Dr Nnamdi Azikiwe, Harry Nkumbula, Tom Mboya and Julius Nyerere. These were the missing men. Their names were to ring out over Africa when many of those present at the Lancaster House Conference were forgotten or powerless men.

Three years before this colourful, much-publicized conference at Lancaster House, there had been another conference, at Manchester of all unlikely places. It was attended by a handful of men, most of them of no seeming consequence, living in seedy lodgings, eating and arguing in cheap cafés. Yet most African leaders of the present time would unhesitatingly place this conference far above the Lancaster House affair in importance. It was the Fifth Pan-African Congress. Pan-Africanism, prior to this meeting, was mainly an intellectual exercise for American negro leaders or an emotional appeal to West Indian subconsciousness. The Manchester Congress marked the emergence of the movement in the continent where it really belonged, Africa. Dr W. E. B. Dubois, the American Negro intellectual who organized the first four African Congresses, was in the chair, but the congress was dominated for the first time by Africans from Africa—trade union leaders, business men and aspiring politicians. The two organizing secretaries were Kwame Nkrumah himself and George Padmore, the former West Indian radical who was to become Nkrumah's Adviser on African Affairs. Among the delegates was another outstanding African, later to be still more widely known. His name was Jomo Kenyatta, and his native land was Kenya.

It is important to look back to this Manchester Congress and to compare it with the Lancaster House Conference. Not simply because, in the best dramatic tradition, the rejected, unrecognized nondescripts swayed the African masses in the years to come. But because the different themes of these two significant gatherings give the clue to the continuing clash in Africa, to the seeming incompatibility of white and black viewpoints. As I have already pointed out, the Lancaster House Conference symbolized the policy of "careful and ordered progress to considered goals" with the emphasis on raising standards of life, and political progress being handled just as cautiously. Manchester, on the other hand, represented the passionate desire of a people, who felt themselves the despised and rejected, to stand up like men, after four centuries of oppression. In grey and grimy Manchester, which had seen its own violent rebellion against oppression, that gathering of coloured people from many lands of sunlit seas and deep rain forests pledged themselves to liberate Africa from colonialism. In George Padmore's words, Pan-Africanism stood for "Racial co-existence on the basis of absolute equality." That, of course, meant that power would inevitably lie in the hands of African majorities throughout Africa.

A working Pan-African organization is far more easily talked about than achieved. The wide range of cultures, of traditions, of peoples in Africa weakens the prospect of a common front. But what is important is the spontaneous sentiment behind the Pan-African idea—that Africans must rule Africa, must not be the under-privileged and the disenfranchised in their own lands. It is that which binds together the new generation of African leaders, and Britain cannot afford to forget it. Otherwise the Secretary of State will stand for ever waiting, in the lyrical words of Mr Creech Jones, "at the door of the Commonwealth Relations Office beckoning all of (these leaders) to hasten along and join those who have already assembled under the umbrella of his department".

A solid proof of this emerged immediately after the Lancaster House Conference. For attendance at it proved to be political suicide for the eminent Dr Danquah from the Gold Coast. Kwame Nkrumah's followers branded Danquah as guilty of collaboration with the imperial enemy. Even though he had previously been de-tained along with Nkrumah by the Gold Coast Governor, and had apparently qualified as a national martyr, his appearance at the con-ference was regarded as treachery to the nationalist cause.

In his book *The New Ghana*[1] J. G. Amamoo recalls that *The Accra Evening News* warned Dr Danquah in particular not to accept the invitation to the conference. "But Dr Danquah chose to go, and with other members of the delegation he left port for London ... he at once forfeited public confidence, and long before he re-turned the ground was very much prepared for a change." The Doctor, of course, had no opportunity of voicing Gold Coast political aspirations, even if he had thought it prudent to do so. The agenda saw to that. But his crime lay in his going at all. He never recovered from the slur of being a "moderate". That was as fatal for an African politician as being a "liberal" was for a white politician in South Africa.

The Lancaster House delegates were not the only distinguished visitors to London in those stirring autumn days of 1948. The Com-monwealth Prime Ministers (or their deputies) came together for their second post-war meeting. What made it an historic occasion was the attendance, for the first time, of Asian leaders, Mr Nehru from India, Mr Liaquat Ali Khan from Pakistan and Mr D. S. Senanayake from Ceylon (which had now attained full nationhood with the passing of the Ceylon Independence Bill).

[1] Pan Books Ltd.

It has always been fatally easy to glow with pride at the very sight of coloured Prime Ministers conferring with white Prime Ministers in London, and to talk of a "brotherhood of nations". Vague slogans about common aims and mutual understanding is no substitute for practical policies. The 1948 meetings set a standard in woolly communiqués which was unfortunately all too easy to follow in subsequent years, and which led one of the Prime Ministers to describe the proceedings as "mothers' meetings". Yet 1948 was the year in which it could be truly said that the "Fourth British Empire", the greater Commonwealth, emerged. For two major points were discussed, each of which had a significant bearing on the development of that Commonwealth.

First of all, there was the recognition that members of the Commonwealth should take an initiative in their own regional affairs. This arose from Britain's participation in Western Union, the joint defence organization of Western Europe. Though there were previous fears that Britain might have taken the first steps towards becoming involved in a European federation, it was agreed by the Prime Ministers that, so far, this association with Europe was "in accordance with the interests of the other members of the Commonwealth". But it was also agreed that Britain should keep her Commonwealth partners in close touch "with the progress of this co-operation with Western Europe".

There were critics who deplored this development as loosening Commonwealth ties. But a stronger body of opinion believed that it would enable the Commonwealth to play a larger part in the world when the precedent was followed—as it very shortly was—by other Commonwealth members. And in any case (so ran the argument) it was better to face the realities of the situation, and to recognize that members would take regional action on their own account, with or without Commonwealth agreement. At least the other members would be kept informed, so that the prospect of a co-operative approach in any world crisis would be always possible.

The second matter discussed by the Prime Ministers which had a signal importance was the question of Eire's relationships with the Commonwealth. Premier Costello and his government in Eire, satisfied with nothing less than the purity of utter independence, had determined to sever the last link with the Crown by repealing the External Relations Act. However, Mr Costello also described Eire as "a sovereign democratic state associated with members of the

British Commonwealth". In short, Eire wished to go on reaping the benefits of Commonwealth membership without being a member. This was to make nonsense of the Commonwealth association. In the event, the Prime Ministers could make nothing of Eire's position, try though they did. It had been hoped that a compromise might be reached by recognizing Eire citizens as British subjects under the terms of a new Act. But even here Eire would not agree.

It was not so much the position of Eire as this particular Act which was really significant. For, acting on the recommendation of a committee set up by the Commonwealth Prime Ministers in 1946, a British Nationality Act had been drawn up in consultation with the Dominions and passed through Parliament in July of 1948. For the first time it set up a status of dual citizenship. Any citizen of the United Kingdom or the Colonies, of Canada, Australia, New Zealand, South Africa, Newfoundland, India, Pakistan, Southern Rhodesia and Ceylon was henceforward also entitled to the status of British subject. So all Commonwealth countries recognized each other's citizens as British subjects (though, if they chose, they could call themselves "Commonwealth Citizen" instead). This might have been thought a simple legal matter. In fact, it was a decisive change, and at a later date enabled India to remain a member of the Commonwealth when the signs were that she must sever the link. It broadened the whole concept of the Commonwealth at a time when it appeared extremely likely to come to a standstill.

Often it has been claimed, and rightly, that one of the major benefits stemming from these Prime Ministers' meetings was not simply the general discussions but those which took place privately between two or three of the Prime Ministers on problems affecting them alone. Sir Godfrey Huggins had one discussion in London that autumn that was quite certainly of the most extraordinary significance. It was not with another Prime Minister, but with Roy Welensky of Northern Rhodesia. These two talked over their plans to bring the two Rhodesias and Nyasaland into closer union.

Welensky was desperate for action. He had talked over the proposal with Creech Jones and found that the British Government had no sympathy at all with the idea of amalgamation. "My party would never agree to handing over the control of four million Africans in Northern Rhodesia and Nyasaland," the Colonial Secretary had said, with the utmost firmness. But he had added that if some solution could be found which would meet the legitimate wishes of Welensky and

Huggins and at the same time protect the interests of the Africans, the British Government would be prepared to consider it.

Welensky went to see Oliver Stanley, the previous Conservative Secretary of State for the Colonies. Stanley told him that, even if the Conservatives were returned to power, there would still be no prospect of amalgamation. But he intimated that "some sort of federation" might be the solution. Federation, of course, was what Welensky had been urging on Sir Godfrey Huggins. Now, he thought, his viewpoint had been confirmed to the hilt. He left Oliver Stanley and went straight over to meet Sir Godfrey at his hotel. Without preamble, Welensky told the Southern Rhodesia Premier that it was no good going on with the idea of amalgamation. "I've seen Creech Jones and Oliver Stanley as well," he said. "The only thing we have a chance with is federation."

It was not an easy thing for Sir Godfrey to abandon the amalgamation policy, which had long been a major plank in his political platform. But he recognized that time was running out, that unity of approach could not be much longer delayed. He promised Welensky that he would put the federation alternative to his Government colleagues in Southern Rhodesia. "I'll call a conference," he added. "We can hold it at Victoria Falls."

The agreement made between those two men in that London hotel was to change the course of Central African history, and to launch an experiment which bore heavily on the future of Africa, and indeed on the whole Commonwealth.

CHAPTER XIII

TURMOIL IN THE EAST

AFRICA HAD FACED Britain with perplexities and anxieties during 1948, yet they did not even begin to assume the terrifying significance of those in the East. Only in Ceylon, small and vulnerable, was there still a picture of comparative peace and stability.

The partition of the Indian sub-continent, the independence of India and Pakistan, had removed the very heart of British defence strategy in the East. India under British rule had been, for long past, the powerful guarantor of stability in South-East Asia. From India the command of the Indian Ocean was maintained and in the Second World War she had not only been the giant commissariat of the Allied forces in the East but had provided almost two million servicemen. Now, that magnificent body the Indian Army had been divided between the two new Dominions. Worse still, as the year wore on, it became tragically clear that the gulf of suspicion between India and Pakistan was widening. In Kashmir there had been open fighting. Both Dominions were equally obdurate in claiming that the state belonged to them.

Pakistan itself was torn with internal troubles. Already hopelessly undermanned in the civil service, and economically unbalanced, the country was even more perilously threatened by political and religious intrigue. At this very time when the new state desperately needed him, Mohammed Ali Jinnah, the architect of the country's independence and the first Governor-General, died all too soon. The long fight for a free Pakistan had proved too much for Jinnah, the only man capable of rallying the new nation. Indeed in his own person he was the symbol of Pakistan's fight for nationhood.

The parlous situation in which the country was plunged so soon after the early days of rejoicing lost her the great opportunity of grasping the leadership of the Muslim world. Had she been able to do so, much of the later dangerous chaos in the Middle East might have been avoided, and the Commonwealth's position would have been strengthened.

Ten centuries before, the ancestors of the Muslim people of India, spreading out from the Middle and Near East under the banners of Islam, had debouched into India and conquered. Now history had given them a chance to look back whence they came, to the lands which their Turkish ancestors had once ruled. It was too soon and they were unready. Pakistan had enough to do to ensure her own survival.

Egypt had grasped her opportunity and was now making the running in the Middle East. The Palestine tragedy was approaching its climax. The United Nations, into whose faltering hands Britain had passed over the mandate, had set up a special commission which recommended partition of the Holy Land, safeguards for the Holy Places and a transition period under U.N. auspices. But the Arabs did not believe in partition at all, let alone a transition period in which it could be effected.

Britain was still the nominal authority in Palestine, pending the transfer of power to the two new governments. But, poised as she was between the deadly enemies, the target of both and the unhappy instrument of a United Nations organization which had been unable or unwilling to set up its own police force, she finally decided to break clear. It was announced in London that Britain would relinquish the Palestine mandate by May 15 of 1948 and withdraw her troops by August 1 at the latest.

The sorry truth was that Palestine had become untenable for any single controlling power. On the Christmas Day of 1947 more than 100 people were killed or injured, in a land holy to both Jews and Arabs. In 26 days from December 1, the total of dead and injured amounted to more than one thousand. Inside Palestine, the terrorists on both sides strove to outmatch each other in slaughter. Outside it, the surrounding Arab states crept in closer for the kill.

On May 15, the day when Britain relinquished authority, the Jews proclaimed that the new Israel was born. Born of suffering, Israel was at once faced with the threat of extermination. The Arab countries invaded. Egypt struck well into Palestine and captured Gaza. But the Jews held fast, savagely determined to survive. When a cease-fire arranged by the U.N. gave breathing space, it had already become clear that the Arabs, far from crushing Israel, had been mauled and humiliated.

This fierce and overriding desire to eliminate the Jewish state was the only point of unity in the Arab world. The uneasy peace over that great and historic region of the Middle East which had been maintained in the main by Britain for thirty years was now gone, and with it the greater part of British influence. It was a sad reflection that British prestige, which had been so high with the Arabs, had been all but swept away by the tide of nationalism. The attempt to mediate between Jew and Arab had only gained her hatred and contempt. Transjordan and Iraq were Britain's only reliable friends in the area, and their friendship was tempered with caution.

The swirl of events in the Middle East in 1948 was of deep concern, not only to Britain but to the Empire and Commonwealth. It was becoming steadily clearer that a satisfactory agreement with Egypt over the future of the Suez Canal would be difficult to obtain. Furthermore, Egypt's aims to secure an overlordship of the Sudan, which she was supposed to be ruling in conjunction with Britain, was no longer in doubt. King Farouk's ambitions were in inverse ratio to his personal abilities and character, but there were other men in Egypt, of stronger metal, young and frustrated military officers, who also dreamt of glory and expansion. It did not need an extraordinary perception to see that Britain's vital military bases in Egypt, which she had occupied for sixty-five years, could not be considered secure. The time had come to consider alternatives.

Cyprus, in the Eastern Mediterranean, appeared the best prospect for a military base if and when the Canal Zone was no longer available. But even here there was unrest and uncertainty. The *enosis* movement for union with Greece had rapidly gathered strength in 1948. Early in the year, the left-wing Greek Cypriots on the island had campaigned for immediate self-government as a first step towards *enosis*. Just as resolutely, the Turkish Cypriots, who formed one-fifth of the population, categorically rejected the proposal. The right-wing Greek Cypriots prudently abstained from the campaign, but not because they were less in favour of *enosis*. Indeed, in October they called a meeting of 18,000 people to demand "Union and only union with Greece". It was the biggest political meeting in the history of Cyprus, but only for four weeks, for the left-wingers countered with a meeting attended by 30,000 people.

Once more Britain was faced with a situation in which reason was drowned by emotion. It did not matter to the Greek Cypriots that Greece herself had only just averted internal collapse and civil war and was still in a parlous state; it did not matter that *enosis* would mean economic disaster for Cyprus, and very possibly war with Turkey. All that counted was the call of blood and religion, and that came down to unity with Greece. Overriding even these things was the probability that Britain, in a brief enough space of time, would be out of her main Middle East bases. Cyprus would be the last foothold. For her own sake, for the sake of the Commonwealth and the non-communist world, she would surely have to stay there in strength.

Whilst all this was happening in the Middle East, what was happening in the Far East, that other link of the former "Empire lifeline"? India, for all her quarrel with Pakistan over Kashmir, and the heartrending problem of the refugees, had made a remarkably good start. Nearly all the Indian rulers had come to terms with the new Indian Government. Over 500 separate states had been welded into sixteen manageable units. Hyderabad, where the Muslim Nizam wanted independence, was the outstanding exception. The manner of its incorporation into India—police moved in on the excuse of mounting terrorism—was a blot on the record, though it could fairly be said that the Nizam's ambition was both unrealistic and positively dangerous to the new nation.

But India, like Pakistan, saw the man who had been the very soul of the nation struck down. Gandhi, the great advocate of free Asia, was shot down by a young Hindu fanatic, after he had undergone one of his famous fasts in an attempt to bring Hindu and Muslim nearer together. The tragedy of the eleven million Hindus, Sikhs and Muslims, uprooted and seeking new homelands, had moved him to this last effort. His murder showed only too well how deep were the communal hatreds sown through the years, and how far from fulfilment was the hope of Clement Attlee at the time of partition, "that the two new Dominions we now propose to set up may in the course of time come together again to form one great member-state of the British Commonwealth of Nations".

If ever a stable and strong power was needed in that turbulent area of South-East Asia it was then, in that year of 1948. The Chinese Communists had swept on from victory to victory. The forces of Chiang Kai-shek had been decisively defeated in the north of China, and the Kuomintang had been finally discredited. It was now only a matter of time, and a short time at that, when a Chinese Communist State would emerge. How would that new power react to world events? How would the Chinese adapt communism to their own purpose? It was already clear that South-East Asia, broken free of colonialism, was looking for a political panacea, and one which would guarantee a better way of life for all. Communism was prepared to guarantee that. At the cost of individual freedom—but what was freedom to the humble millions of Asia whose only recognized enemies were hunger and disease?

While the battle for China still continued, communists were scheming, thrusting, consolidating throughout the East. From the southern border of China down that long line of former European colonies that led to the Australasian approaches there was struggle and intrigue. This, as President Sukarno of Indonesia later said, "was the main artery of imperialism". It had also been the Japanese road to triumph. Along that road was now advancing something more dominating than imperialism, far more deadly than the military power of the Japanese. Communism believed in conquering the minds of men, not simply their bodies.

At the northward end of the old "imperialist artery" in French Indo-China, France was finding that her power was being steadily eroded. For nearly two years guerrilla warfare had been waged, and all the time the Communist leader Ho Chi Minh, trained in Moscow and a thorn in the side of the French for eighteen years, was consolidating his new republic of Vietnam (comprised of the former three French possessions of Tongking, Annam and Cochin-China). It was a masterly performance, for during that period of consolidation neither Russia nor China could be of much help.

Burma, which had left the Commonwealth and declared itself a republic, had also been faced with a communist revolt—which petered out—in 1948. But that was only a part of Burma's woes. There were a series of rebellions all over the country, and only the great influence of Prime Minister U Nu, a man of deep religious faith, was holding the country together. At this point of time, a link with the Commonwealth would have served Burma well. Without doubt it would have helped to bring about internal peace, and even more certainly it would have disposed of Burmese fears of eventual Chinese encroachment. But the link was broken, and there had never seemed any possibility of repairing it.

Britain, in any event, was faced with trouble enough of her own in Malaya. In the February of 1948, the new Federation of Malaya had come into being. Nobody pretended that it satisfied everybody, but at least it had been devised in close consultation with the rulers and political leaders of Malaya. Within six months of its inception the Federation was plunged into a reign of terror. The long postwar story of sedition and sporadic violence, of labour unrest and general lawlessness, reached its climax. In June, there was a sudden and shocking explosion of violence. Rubber estates were attacked and planters murdered; British and non-communist Chinese were murdered. Behind it all was an implacable aim to establish a Communist Republic of Malaya.

The leader of the revolt was Ching Peng, able and determined. His lieutenants, like himself, were fighters hardened in the guerrilla war against the Japanese, masters of jungle warfare. It was during the Japanese occupation that the plot to establish a communist state had first been laid. Hundreds of young men had been transformed from patriots to ardent communists during those hazardous years. Dumps of food and ammunition had been built up for the day when the Japanese had been beaten and Malaya was ripe for the taking. The trade unions had been deeply penetrated, the dossiers had been drawn up, the whole apparatus of totalitarianism was there in embryo.

One of the root causes of the tragedy was undoubtedly the over-complacent attitude of the British Government to events in Malaya. Repeated warnings of the approaching dangers had not been dis-counted, but they had been played down. Even when the revolt came, most Europeans in Malaya itself believed that it could not last long. Many of them suffered from their own brand of complacency, which was that nobody but themselves understood Malaya. The fanaticism, the ruthlessness, the sheer cold-blooded efficiency of the communist revolutionaries in Asia had still to be revealed to White-hall and the Raffles Hotel.

The neighbouring islands of the Dutch East Indies were in an even worse state than Malaya. The uneasy agreement made in 1946 between the Dutch and the Indonesian nationalist leaders, which was supposed to lead to a Netherlands-Indonesian Union, had only served to emphasize the wide and bitter gulf between the two parties. It was only to be expected that the Dutch would fight to retain their power. Their East Indian possessions were linked firmly with the Netherlands economically, almost indeed part of them. The Dutch had settled there, intermarried, become part of the East Indies. They had poured endless money and effort into the territories, which en-joyed great prosperity before the Japanese invasion. But it was all insubstantial in face of the unswerving resolution of the Indonesians to rule themselves.

By 1948, fighting was constant, and in the December of that year the United Nations stepped in, for the second time, to demand a cease-fire. What added to the tragic chaos was that the civil war was not only between the Dutch and the Indonesians, but between the rival Indonesian factions, the democrats and the communists. Politi-cal parties and sub-parties sprang up like tropical flowers after the rains. It was this seeming picture of irresponsible demagogy which fortified the Dutch in their determination to stay put, to resist ex-travagant demands, and to see themselves as the only possible stabilizing influence. It was an understandable error, but a fatal one. For behind the proliferation of politics, behind the turmoil, there was a deep and widespread desire for freedom, dangerous and pain-ful though it might prove to be.

Not only the British were alarmed at this rapid onrush of events in South-East Asia, and the unpredictable consequences of those events. The Australians and the New Zealanders were even more directly concerned, after the nightmare of the Japanese war. Colonialism was dissolving fast, and with it the old peace and prosperity. What could take its place? The Australians knew they must learn to live with South-East Asia. They were realizing that they were practically part of it, and no longer merely a proud and grateful outpost of Britain. But how could they live with fanatical, anti-European nationalists or, worse, even more fanatical communists?

It was now that the towering significance of India, and more particularly of Mr Nehru, became apparent. The Indonesians looked to him to find them a way out of the impasse, and he suggested that a conference be held in Delhi early in the New Year. Such was the recognition of his potential influence that the Dutch as well as the Indonesians acknowledged the value of his intervention. Nehru indeed was already becoming an almost god-like figure in South-East Asia. The immense prestige that had come to him when he led India to freedom, and so signalled the beginning of the end of colonialism, was buttressed by his own personal qualities of leadership and imagination, and above all by his burning idealism.

Nehru's strength lay in his being an ardent Asian. A British public school and university education had served only to strengthen that deep instinct. Not even the communists could label him a tool of imperialists. Not even his fanatical opponents in India who derided him as a "brown Englishman" could convince the masses that he was so. His neutralist foreign policy, his willingness to borrow economic ideas from the communists as well as the democrats, clearly illustrated his utter independence. He was in nobody's pocket, and though cynics accused him of using the Cold War (like Tito) to get the best of both worlds, his independent policy carried great weight, more particularly among the uncommitted countries.

Nehru's maddening tendency to lecture other world leaders, his bland assumption that the weight of experience behind the diplomacy of the older countries was only a catalogue of human folly best forgotten, his obduracy over Kashmir, all these things goaded his critics. The Western world, particularly the United States, thought that his contacts with Russia showed blind folly at the best, and at the worst, plain treachery. They would not bring themselves to recognize, then, that he was the first and greatest of the Asian leaders, finding his way to a policy for India, which in itself would be a policy for Asia, and for the countries released from colonialism.

He was a democrat, despite his critics, a passionate believer in the rights of the individual man. His very independence of mind, his choice of policies that frequently ran counter to those of the Western democracies, the fact that he could sometimes even cast the whole weight of his influence against them, paradoxically served only to emphasize his democratic faith. If freedom of the mind was the essence of democracy then Nehru was demonstrably more democratic than its avowed champions in the West.

Whatever criticism was, and is, advanced against his neutralist policy, he emerged as the most important man to the democratic nations in all Asia. And if the Commonwealth was to be anything more than a mutual benefit society of people of British stock, then he was quite certainly the most important man in the Commonwealth also, as it began to emerge in its new form in 1948.

The measure of his stature was that he was able to make so great an impact on the world scene at the very time when he was endeavouring to establish India herself on firm foundations. Let there be no under-estimating the magnitude of that task. In India were the best part of 350 million people, only about one in ten of whom was literate. Undernourished, beset by disease and the sheer brute hardship of existence, these were the people whom Nehru determined should rise and rise quickly to a better way of life. As if there were not enough daunting problems, India was the country of caste, which stood in the way of progress. And, most terrifying of all, the population was increasing at a rate of some six million a year.

There was a grim irony in the fact that Nehru, the leader of so poverty-stricken and backward a country, should have established himself as the keeper of the world's conscience, more than ready to rebuke and admonish those very powers on whose assistance he must depend if his economic plans were to succeed. But it was true beyond doubt that neither Britain nor the Commonwealth, nor indeed the democratic world as a whole, could afford to see Nehru fail. The alternative to Nehru was already in evidence beyond the Himalayas, in China. Mao's task there was infinitely easier than Nehru's. For it could be accomplished by a pitiless suppression of human liberty.

CHAPTER XIV

"A GOAL OF DISINTEGRATION"?

OTHER PEOPLE'S EMPIRES might crumble about them, as had all other empires in human history, but the British had long felt that they alone had perfected a policy of evolution which preserved the work of the imperial centuries. That comforting sense of superior perspicacity had not been gravely shaken even by the onrush of events in the East. But it began to waver in 1949. Not only were there growing doubts about the wisdom of British Colonial policy. It was even more possible to wonder whether the expanding Commonwealth which was the anticipated fruit of that policy was not turning sour.

There was a significant correspondence in *The Times* at the beginning of 1949 which uncovered such doubts—and they were felt by many people well-versed in Colonial affairs. Mrs Elspeth Huxley, the distinguished writer on Africa, alleged that "we have set up a goal of disintegration, countenanced the separatist, and have been slow to open the highest of opportunities within the imperial service to Colonials". She claimed that "with our persistent emphasis on the political goal of self-government, we have set a contrary aim to the Roman ideal of empire".

It was easy to point out that the Roman Empire had not survived, but that did not dispose of the danger that the British Empire would not survive either. There were clear signs that other countries still doubted the ability of a weakened and impoverished Britain to discharge her Colonial responsibilities. Superior advice from the United Nations on how to advance backward peoples coincided with vociferous "claims" on various British possessions. It was true that the claims had generally been made often enough in the past, but now they were being pressed with increasing vigour. Taking the pessimistic view, the situation did bear points of apparent resemblance to historic instances of dissolving empires. As for the Commonwealth, the world saw in it neither the material potential of the United States nor the mental dynamic of the U.S.S.R.

These depressing judgements sprang inevitably from the sight of Britain herself struggling through crisis after crisis. The efforts to establish nationalization and to concurrently implement a huge social welfare programme could not have been more ill-timed. The war had drained away so much of Britain's wealth, the changing economy of the world had faced her with so many new trading challenges, that her full efforts were needed for the single task of survival, without the complications of a precipitous social revolution. The self-imposed burdens under which Britain staggered were so clearly too much for her that the value of sterling itself began to be increasingly challenged.

The desperate need was for more dollars. The Colonial Empire, already a net earner of $200 million a year, was one of the main hopes for the bridging of the dangerous gap. Not only could the Colonial territories obviate the spending of dollars by producing more, they could *earn* still more dollars by the same token. The Colonies, in short, were basic to the British Government's plans for recovery. Yet political ambitions in those very territories were outrunning economic planning. That was the dilemma of the British Government. It had come home to Britain's Socialist leaders that the Empire had not simply been a happy hunting ground for hard-faced capitalists, but that it had evolved from hard facts basic to Britain's survival as a great trading nation. Those facts—that Britain needed bases, markets and sources of raw materials—still remained. The genuine idealism of Socialist thought did not remove them.

There was an irony in the accusation of a Select Committee on Estimates that there was no evidence of a coherent strategy of economic planning behind the extensive developments being undertaken under the Colonial Development and Welfare Act. This, to a Government of Planners! The Colonial Office acidly retorted that there was a distinction between Soviet planning and the "outline planning" of Britain, which deliberately left a degree of freedom of decision to individual Colonies.

But, even if there was no central economic plan for the Colonies, worked out in and directed from Whitehall, the British Government had produced definite plans for such a development of Colonial resources as would materially contribute towards the overcoming of Britain's external insolvency. The Four-Year Economic Plan submitted to the Organization for European Co-operation laid down definite Colonial production targets, to be fulfilled by 1952-53. Groundnuts were to increase from 335,000 tons to 880,000 tons; rubber from 435,000 tons to 830,000 tons; copper from 202,000 tons to 356,000 tons. And many more equally ambitious increases were planned. Later on in the year, Harold Wilson, President of the Board of Trade, told a Royal Empire Society meeting that "It is in the future development of the Colonies that so many of us pin our hopes of a great contribution towards a long-term balance between the Sterling Area and the rest of the world." He pointed out that 10-year development plans for seventeen territories had already been approved, providing for a total expenditure of £180,000,000. "Against the background of world economics the development of these territories, Colonial and self-governing, may in 10 or 15 years prove to be the most important event of the present century," concluded Mr Wilson. "Given time, it may revolutionize the world economic position and balance of trade."

Time, that was the essence of the whole matter. In the face of rising political ambitions inside the Colonies, and international interference outside them (not to mention communist intrigue) would there be time for the fruition of development plans? Where was the guarantee that Colonies, when they became independent, would meekly participate in British plans for the consolidation of the Sterling Area? In their Four-Year Plan, Britain's Socialist Government assured the Colonies that "the purposes of Colonial development are complementary with those of European recovery". They would have been hard put to it to find a single nationalist leader in the Colonies to subscribe to any such theory. On the contrary, almost all those leaders bitterly resented being tied to the economies of European countries. They preached that their inferior position in the world was due to their being forced into the rôle of producers of raw materials. They believed that future prosperity lay in industrialization (had not Europe itself proved that?).

The truth was that the Colonies were going through so rapid a stage of transition that the Socialists were forced into a period of reappraisal. During the annual debate on Colonial affairs in the House of Commons in 1949, Arthur Creech Jones stated that "the broad purpose of British Colonial policy is to co-operate with Colonial peoples in the effort to bring stability, good order and prosperity to the world by building up in the Colonial territories responsibility and the conditions of good living. This purpose (he added) can be achieved only in so far as it evokes the response, understanding and confidence of the Colonial peoples themselves."

That was not so much a statement of policy as a recognition of facts. What was much more significant was Creech Jones' declaration on political development. "I do not think it can go on speedily until the social services have been expanded," he said, "nor until a sound economic basis has been built in the territories to sustain the social services."

The idealistic picture of a Socialist Galahad riding to the rescue of the oppressed and enslaved Colonial Empire, which had been presented in so much Socialist writing before and during the war, was fading fast. It was not only that Socialism needed the Empire and Commonwealth as much as, if not more than, Capitalism. The truth was that no political doctrine could ignore the plain fact that Britain's prospects of future prosperity and influence rested on the continuing existence of that intricate system of world-wide trade and development which her money and her enterprise had supported for centuries past. The Sterling Area (which meant in the main the Commonwealth without Canada) was responsible for 40 per cent of the total external trade of the world. Its operations had not only given Britain her unique place in the world; they had also brought into the main stream of world trade all sorts of remote and backward territories which otherwise would have remained isolated. This system, clearly, was of extreme benefit not only to Britain, but to all the other members. But to the new generation of nationalist leaders arising in the Colonies it was a system of exploitation built up through the years by which the imperialist oppressors had waxed fat at the expense of backward peoples. Indeed, earlier generations of Socialists had told them so.

It was at this point of time when the Socialist Government of Britain became painfully aware of the clash between the economic and political plans for the Colonies that their favoured instrument of development, the Government corporation, began to come under fire. The East African Groundnut Project of the Overseas Food Corporation was running into difficulties that were as daunting as they were unexpected. And whilst that Corporation was being heavily criticized for a lavish outpouring of money, its companion, the Colonial Development Corporation, was being assailed for a quite contrary reason, that it was over-cautious in laying out capital. Only a little over £3 million had been invested in the first year of operations, and Colonial leaders were complaining that the C.D.C. seemed only willing to tackle the sort of projects which private enterprise was quite ready to undertake.

The spectacle of the Socialists facing up to the realities of imperial responsibility could hardly fail to arouse an attitude of complacent "we told you so" in the breasts of the Conservative Opposition. But the Government deserved credit for facing up to the circumstances before them. And in truth there was not so very much difference in the Conservatives' declared approach. If the Socialists had to cut their political suit according to the economic cloth available, it was equally true that the Conservatives were—even out of office—brought to recognize that their earlier conception of the speed of political advancement was out of touch with the times. It is not unjust to reflect that the settlement Britain had effected in her Asian territories, tragic though some of its consequences had been, and unsatisfactory though it was in part, might not have been achieved under a Conservative government.

The Conservative Charter for the Commonwealth and Empire, which was published in the summer of 1949, laboured to emphasize the difference in the party's approach from that of the Socialists. It advocated improved machinery of consultation in the Commonwealth and more frequent meetings of the Prime Ministers; it looked forward to a Commonwealth Defence Council and a Combined Staff; it reapproved the Conservative belief in Imperial Preference, and asked for a joint economic and migration policy.

On the Colonial side, the Charter supported self-government within the Commonwealth for the Colonies as soon as they were ready for it; it advocated as rapid a programme of development as possible, with the private investor playing his part as well as the government; bulk purchase schemes for Colonial commodities were condemned, though the need for guaranteed markets and agreed prices was recognized.

With slight alterations, this summary of the Conservative policy could have been presented by the Socialists. In the annual debate on Colonial affairs in the House of Commons, Alan Lennox-Boyd, speaking for the Conservatives, did say that his party intended that "priority would be given to the development of the material wealth of the Colonies, because neither an improvement in social conditions nor any real political advance was possible without firm economic foundations". But he was attacking the Socialism of yesteryear. What he was advocating the Socialist leaders were already implementing.

Oliver Stanley, the former Secretary of State, not only agreed with the cautious approach of the Colonial Development Corporation but appeared to go against his own party's Charter when he said, "I have always realized that there might, in certain cases, be a need for bulk buying in the Colonies." And he concluded his speech to the House with a moving appeal for a common approach. "I believe that about the most important matter for the United Kingdom over the next ten or twenty years will be the development of its relationships with the Colonial Empire," he declared. "About the most important element in its success or failure will be the maintenance of some unity of purpose between the various parties."

In three years, the Conservatives and the Socialists had indeed moved remarkably close to each other in their approach to Commonwealth and Colonial affairs. There were extremists in both parties who laboured away at the ancient differences, but by 1949 the majority on each side recognized that they had a common duty to preserve the Commonwealth and to discharge Britain's duties towards the Colonies. There were too many danger points for responsible politicians to play too hard at the party game in this field. There were too many self-announced and self-appointed heirs to the various parts of the British Empire in the expected event of its dissolution.

In Central America, Guatemala was pressing her claim to British Honduras more vociferously than ever. The Argentine authorities refused to recognize the validity of documents issued in the Falklands and reiterated their claim to sovereignty over the Islands. Chile, which had already established two garrisons in the Falklands Antarctic Dependencies, sent out an expedition to establish a third naval, military and air base in the British Zone.

Meanwhile, the position in Cyprus was steadily worsening. Lord Winster, as Governor, had brought out from Britain plans for a Consultative Council to open the way again for constitutional advance. The Greek-Cypriot leaders turned it down, whereupon Winster resigned and the island for a time was without a Governor. When the new Governor, Sir Andrew Wright, arrived, both right wingers and communists in Cyprus let him know that if he did not bring with him a declaration recognizing the Cypriots' claim to be united with Greece then he might as well go home at once. When he attended the annual Agricultural Exhibition he was bombarded with leaflets, and the police had to break up demonstrators howling for "Union with Greece".

To complete the sorry picture in the Mediterranean, General

Franco was demanding that Gibraltar be returned to Spain, whilst Malta's Deputy Prime Minister, Mr Mintoff, resigned because he violently disagreed with Britain's approach to the George Cross Island's economic difficulties. Unemployment was steadily increasing and a mood of bitterness towards Britain grew with it.

But most disturbing and dangerous of all was the mounting threat of communist terrorism in Malaya. Even more depressing than the communist successes was the apparent continuing official complacency. For when Mr Rees-Williams, Under-Secretary of State for the Colonies, said that Britain would need another two years to wipe out the terrorists, he was acidly reminded by the High Commissioner, Sir Henry Gurney, that "We cannot contemplate, and do not contemplate, the present state of affairs continuing for two years, or for any time of that sort." The General Officer Commanding, Major-General C. H. Bouchier, bluntly observed that Rees-Williams' estimate "must surely have been intended to cover the period required to gaol, deport or hang the last militant communist". By September, the Government of Malaya was talking about the last phase of the campaign and announcing that communist terrorism was to be brought to a final ending. As events turned out, the only criticism that could have been made against Rees-Williams was not that he was pessimistic, but rather that he was indulging in wildly excessive optimism.

Hong Kong was naturally perturbed by the Malayan crisis, and even more by the approach of the victorious Chinese Communists to the borders of the New Territories. At least, the official leadership in the Colony was. The "old hands" of the commercial section believed that they could do business with the Chinese whatever happened. But the building up of the defences went forward rapidly. Lieutenant-General F. W. Festing, G.O.C.-in-Chief, announced at a press conference that "the gun density, when completed, will be equal to that of London at the height of the blitz". More and more troops arrived, and General Festing pointed out that though Hong Kong was a highly vulnerable target, it was a comparatively easy place to defend. And this time it was different from the Jap assault of 1941. Now, Britain commanded both sea and air.

In reality, not even the oldest "old hand" knew what the Chinese communists would do. By October, the British had an estimated garrison of 30,000 troops in readiness. On October 16 the communists arrived on the Hong Kong border. Quietly they took up positions at

Shumchun and other border posts. They provoked no incidents with the British posts. Quickly and efficiently they began to establish their authority on the Chinese side of the border. So far, so good. But who knew what was in Mao's mind?

All these tensions throughout the Colonial Empire, the uncertainty over the outcome of Britain's policies, had an inevitable and disturbing effect on the very men on whom the Colonies most urgently depended, the members of the Colonial Service. A growing cynicism, a steady lowering of morale, shockingly foreign to the traditions of the Service, could no longer be obscured. It was becoming apparent in most grades, throughout most age groups.

The replacement of members of the Service by indigenous people had proceeded gradually. The process had long been recognized not merely as inevitable but as wholly desirable. But it had been planned as a cautious and co-ordinated operation, and Colonial officials had looked ahead to many more years of service. Now, the clamorous pressure of Colonial politicians left no doubt that the cherished plans for a gradual hand-over of authority would be rudely revised. Local politicians, all over the Colonies, were making a special target of the Colonial officials, particularly the administrators. Arthur Creech Jones, speaking at the annual Colonial Service dinner of the Corona Club in London, said: "We are a bit anxious about the future of the Service, because insufficient numbers of men are offering themselves for the administrative and technical services. I trust that the members of the Club will publicize the aims and opportunities of the Service and discredit the idea that it no longer offers a satisfying career." At this time, there were nearly fourteen hundred vacancies in the Colonial Service, and the prospects of filling more than a small percentage of them quickly enough were remote.

Apart from the general shortage of staff, another factor was increasing the strain on the Colonial official. This was the multiplication of duties, the flood of paper work bound up with all the new plans emanating from Whitehall for social, economic and political advance. More and more the average official became divorced from the people he served. Longer and longer periods were spent at the desk, to the detriment of work "in the field". The days when the district commissioner was "the father of his people" were already passing into history. The dangers of this, at a time of great transition when it was vital to hold the confidence of the Colonial peoples, were only too clear.

Dr W. E. H. Stanner, an Australian anthropologist who had visited ten British Colonies, said that the thing which had impressed him above all else was "something that was fast disappearing"— the close contact between the European official on the one hand and the native people on the other. He added these warning words: "Already the minds of some Colonial peoples are without real comprehension of what our administrations are hoping and working for. Some are filled with a confusion of half-truths, the other half being supplied sometimes by those who themselves have little understanding of, and sometimes not even the wish to understand, the dignity and mission of British Colonial policy. Those who fully understand our purposes are a minority."

These sombre words were only too true. It was easy to claim that India was off to a heartening beginning as an independent nation because of the stength of her indigenous civil service. But that civil service had been organized over a far longer period than was the case in practically all the Colonies. Embittered Colonial officers, at the very time when British M.P.'s were deploring the obstacles put in the way of the Colonial intelligentsia, could fairly point to the widespread evidence in Africa that Western civilization had made only the slightest impact. The notorious "Ritual Murder" in the Gold Coast was still fresh in the memory. In the June of 1949, a Basuto chieftainess and one of her followers were executed for ritual murder. In Nigeria, in October, a Yoruba chief and his witch doctor were hanged for a similar crime. Whatever was said in the debates of the British Parliament or those of the United Nations, to the average Colonial official the task before him of introducing Western civilization to the backward did not appear to have changed in its essentials from pre-war days.

The Colonial Service, from the very austerity of its traditions, did have its weaknesses. Certainly, the stupid "Precedence list" which existed in the average Colony led to a ridiculous form of social snobbery. And as all too few local people were high on the list, the snobbery took on a racial aspect. The wives and daughters of officialdom were much to blame. The outlook of British suburbia, lunatic in the circumstances, was apt to take the place of the friendly dignity which was sorely needed. The local people were all too often led to complain that they felt "second class citizens".

But, against this admittedly dangerous fault, reflect on the virtues of the British Colonial Service. There was, above all else, the genuine

sense of mission, the deep sense of disinterested service, the determination to lay at least the foundations of justice, fair dealing and
ordinary humanity, and to raise the Colonial people above the clod-
like existence which was the grey and comfortless lot of the majority.
To retain these qualities amongst primitive and bloody-minded
people, often in climates trying in the extreme, in territories where
innumerable diseases flourished and the land was poor and arid,
where life was customarily short and bestial, demanded men of considerable calibre. There were the failures, the weak ones, the office
seekers, but by and large the Colonial official *was* a man of calibre.
The very circumstances of his work lent themselves to autocracy and,
sometimes, rigidity. But even those were a profitable exchange for
inhumanity, illiteracy, and murderous despotism. And, in the very
nature of things, only discipline and autocracy could have produced
progress in lands called upon to bridge fifteen centuries in three
generations.

Without a Colonial Service dedicated to its mission and assured
that it could in large measure fulfil that mission, all the plans so
carefully worked out in Whitehall were useless before they were
launched. That was the real heart of the matter.

CHAPTER XV

THE REPUBLICAN REVOLUTION

IN THE COMMONWEALTH itself, that greater entity of self-governing
nations to which all the Colonies were supposed to be aspiring, a
great and revolutionary change was in prospect. The member
nations were faced not only with a deepening economic crisis, but
with the declared intention of India to become a republic. This at
once raised constitutional issues which struck at the very concept of
the Commonwealth. For all the members owed a common allegiance
to the Crown. How could India remain a member—and Mr Nehru
and his government sincerely wished to do so—when she intended
to end her allegiance?

Clearly, only a broader and looser conception of Commonwealth
membership would allow a republican India to remain a member.

Supporters of the old imperial tradition vehemently claimed that such an accommodation for India would so weaken the links of the Commonwealth as to make them meaningless. But others claimed that the departure of India would herald gradual decay. It was not an argument which ended quickly. Indeed it persists to this day. But when the Prime Ministers of the Commonwealth ended their deliberations in the April of 1949, they had taken a step of fateful significance.

The communiqué which was issued placed this declaration on record: "The Governments of the United Kingdom, Canada, Australia, New Zealand, South Africa, India, Pakistan, and Ceylon, whose countries are united as Members of the British Commonwealth of Nations and owe a common allegiance to the Crown, which is also the symbol of their free association, have considered the impending constitutional changes in India.

"The Government of India have informed the other Governments of the Commonwealth of the intention of the Indian people that under the new constitution which is about to be adopted India shall become a sovereign independent republic. The Government of India have, however, declared and affirmed India's desire to continue her full membership of the Commonwealth of Nations and her acceptance of the King as the symbol of the free association of its independent member nations and as such as the Head of the Commonwealth."

That was the key to the problem, the acceptance of the King by India as Head of the Commonwealth. It was no longer necessary to owe allegiance. All this, of course, had stemmed from the previous year's decision on Commonwealth Citizenship, which had made clear that such status did not depend on allegiance to the Crown. If citizenship of the Commonwealth did not entail allegiance, then the membership of a nation need not.

Australia and New Zealand, in particular, were not really happy about the compromise, and Prime Minister Robert Menzies was to attack the loosening of Commonwealth links at a later date. But Britain tactfully smoothed down feelings (she nursed the hope that Eire might return to the family circle) and South Africa was certainly not wedded to the concept of allegiance to the British Crown. The Nationalists had their own ambitions about republicanism, and it was with genuine feeling that Dr Malan was able to say to the Union Parliament on his return that "the main reason, in my opinion, why the Commonwealth can remain together, in spite of the changes and developments which have taken place, is that the Commonwealth has shown an ability to adapt itself to changing conditions in a changing world. It respects freedom, not only freedom for all the members jointly but freedom for every member as distinct from the Commonwealth." Dr Malan was clearly looking ahead. One could almost see him drafting his own republican constitution. It was not often he was to find himself approving of Pandit Nehru, but this was certainly one of the occasions.

Nehru himself reported back to the Indian Parliament that it had been made perfectly clear "that the King had no functions at all. He has a certain status. The Commonwealth itself, as such, is not a body, if I may say so. It has no organization through which to function and the King also can have no functions." Such an explanation may have aggravated the more devoutly loyal of the King's subjects, who believed that India was simply making a convenience of the Commonwealth and would finally kill the ideal behind it. They did not appreciate that the Commonwealth, to the mass of Indians, still meant British imperialism and was correspondingly suspect. Only the fact that Nehru supported the maintenance of the connection made it palatable to the mass of his fellow countrymen.

Two factors of supreme significance stemmed from India's adherence to the Commonwealth. Firstly, it deeply influenced nationalist leaders throughout the Colonial Empire, and inclined some who cherished the idea of following Burma's example to think again. It had not been widely appreciated in Britain how immense was Nehru's reputation among dependent peoples, and how eagerly his decisions were noted by them.

Secondly, the continuing membership of India decided at least the shorter-term future of the Commonwealth. It was to be an expanding association, ready to go to extreme lengths to accommodate all those peoples who had come to nationhood under British guidance. The concept of a Commonwealth based on allegiance to the Crown and deep loyalty to Britain had been by-passed.

Was the decision taken at the 1949 meeting of the Commonwealth Prime Ministers the right one? Even as this is written, the question remains unanswered. It was in the nature of a gamble. For who could say what the Commonwealth link would mean to the next generation of Indian leaders, those not educated in Britain and familiar with her ways? To them, the link might be no more than a sentimental embarrassment, best severed. But it remained true that the 1949 decision was in keeping with the fundamental ideal of the Commonwealth as a brotherhood of nations, as apart from an alliance of people of the same stock.

But if India was in, Eire was out. Britain's hope that the unpredictable Irish would change their minds was sadly off the mark. Yet Eire, by some sleight-of-hand not apparent to the bewildered eyes of the outside world, still seemed to reap most of the benefits of the Commonwealth association after having decisively rejected it. Only the English and the Irish themselves, having lived in exasperated recognition of each other's oddities for centuries past, could understand how it came about. And even they could not have put it into words.

The towering gain from this 1949 meeting of the Prime Ministers was that India, at the very time when the whole fate of Asia hung in the balance following the Communist triumph in China, was still in the Commonwealth. Mr Nehru might exasperate Western leaders with what they believed to be a wholly unrealistic concept of peaceful co-existence. He himself might declare that he was ready to draw inspiration from both democracy and communism, that he sided with neither world; but it was beyond dispute that he was running a democracy in the heart of the very continent where its survival was of decisive importance to the future of the world.

Constitutional issues were not the only grave problems facing the Commonwealth. Its economic position, repeatedly threatened by crisis since the end of the war, had deteriorated with alarming speed. Gold and dollar reserves had been melting away, and prices for the commodities produced by the Sterling Area had dropped steeply. These depressing facts were known to the Prime Ministers, but they left it to the Finance Ministers of the Commonwealth, who arrived in London in July, to try and stop the rot.

It was all too clear during the course of the discussions that the divergences of outlook were so wide that co-ordinated action on a scale that would be really effective was well-nigh impossible. The smokescreen of complacent platitudes did not disguise the truth that exhortation was being substituted for action. In the last resort all depended on each country "playing the game" in the true spirit of British cricket. After all, Britain had introduced it as a national game to all the Commonwealth countries except Canada.

The Finance Ministers recognized the causes of the Common-

wealth's near-bankruptcy clearly enough. They talked gravely of
the strength of sterling being essential to the world as a whole; they
agreed to recommend to their governments measures to stop the drain
on gold and dollars; they made vague and pious references to the
desirability of a multilateral world trading system; they indicated
that everybody must earn more dollars and spend less, and that the
resources of the Commonwealth must be developed.

All this was very discerning, and without doubt the Finance
Ministers pressed on their respective governments the desirability of
"playing the game". But the root of the whole matter lay in the fact
that each country was trying to do too much, too quickly, and with
only a hasty glance over their shoulders at what their colleagues
were doing. Was it to be expected that India would keep a straight
bat and mutilate her huge plans to raise her people's wretched living
standards? That Australia, still haunted by the spectre of isolation
from her allies in the last war, would halt her plans for industrialization? That Pakistan would hold back on that desperate effort to
widen the base of her economy on which her survival depended?
And could the Colonies be fairly asked to increase the output of
their dollar-earning products, whilst their conditions of existence remained far below those of the more advanced countries of the Commonwealth? What Solomon would decide the level of sacrifices to
be made?

It was already clear that—whatever the Westminster Statute intimated about the sovereign right of countries to order their own
affairs—the Sterling Area would never cure its recurrent ills unless
the members were prepared to give up some portion of that
sovereignty on the economic side. Even in 1949 it was painfully clear
that an exhaustive survey and analysis of resources was needed, followed by an agreed order of development priorities. The short-term
measures were simply desperate tourniquets to stem the continual
blood-letting of hard currency.

There was much complacent talk in Westminster of the remarkable value of Commonwealth consultative machinery, whereby
Governments of the various member countries kept each other constantly informed of their plans of action. Valuable it was, but it was
all the less effective for the want of an honest co-ordination of policies
at the highest level. And indeed, even these methods of consultation
were soon to be revealed as falling short of what was indisputably
desirable.

For at long last, the British Government had to face up to the painful truth that their estimate of the value of the pound was far from coinciding with that of the outside world. A long and despairing game of bluff ended in the devaluation of the pound by approximately one-third. It was a staggeringly large depreciation, and it was carried through without reference to the other members of the Commonwealth. Sir Stafford Cripps could claim that to divulge this step would have been to invite a disastrous flood of speculation which might have brought the whole Sterling Area crashing into complete bankruptcy. Understandably, it aroused angry criticism from other members of the Sterling Area, whose fortunes were, in the main, just as closely tied to the pound sterling as were those of Britain. In brief, a major decision of economic life-or-death importance was not revealed in advance. The claim that there was complete mutual trust did not stand up to this major test.

The economic foundations of the Commonwealth, as 1949 drew to a close, were under the most severe strain. So many aspects of policy clashed one with the other that the compromise inevitably reached was of the weakest nature. The Colonies and the Commonwealth were being called upon for further production at the very time when the money for equipment was being curtailed. Britain's own capacity to expand production to bridge the dollar gap was bedevilled by the constant drawing upon the sterling balances (those debts contracted with Commonwealth countries during the war by Britain in the common fight for survival). In the year ending in June of 1949 India and Pakistan alone drew almost £150 million. That meant that Britain sent out exports to that amount for no return at all in the way of raw materials. In the Colonies, development plans were being slowed down in a period when it was only too obvious that they needed speeding up to keep abreast of political aspirations. Devaluation meant that the Sterling Area would have to increase the quantity of goods she sold in dollar markets by fifty per cent, when it had already proved difficult enough to hold sales at the original figure, with commodity prices falling.

Political and economic policies tended to cancel each other out. For example one might talk of restricting Indian withdrawals of sterling balances. But how could that be equated with the desperate need to stabilize a great democracy in Asia when communism was beginning its bid for the soul of that continent? And if India's special case was recognized, how could Pakistan, her proud and suspicious neighbour, be denied? Even the hard and clear mind of Sir Stafford Cripps, the British Chancellor of the Exchequer, could not clarify the confusion of events and policies. He himself had spoken, before devaluation, of the "series of expedients which led to a series of crises as each expedient became exhausted".

Stalwart evangelists of the Commonwealth ideal might speak of the invisible bonds as strong as steel which would enable the association to survive. To the cynics, it seemed that the best hope lay in the recognition by all the member countries that they would sink or swim together, that if they did not hang together they would hang separately. At this point of time there was not very much evidence even of that.

CHAPTER XVI

A LIGHT IN THE EAST

IN THE LATTER months of 1949 it had become steadily clearer that Mr Attlee would not wait much longer before he staged a general election in Britain. His party had been in office for well over four years and had effected a social revolution. But now they appeared to have run out of ideas. The burden of office had proved heavy and exhausting; the Socialists had laboured to implement a far-reaching programme in Britain in a period when the nation lived under a perpetual threat of bankruptcy, and when the international scene had darkened steadily. Mr Attlee might talk of "a renewal of the mandate". What he and his followers really needed was a breathing space to reflect on the value or otherwise of all they had done, and—this above all—to devote calm consideration to their next instalment of policies, always supposing that the electorate gave them a further term of power.

Nowhere had the Socialists been more sternly tested than in the sphere of the Commonwealth and the Colonial Empire. They had come through the test with some credit. They had, more often than not, been prepared to reassess their policies in the light of experience. There had been some resounding failures, but equally there had been heartening successes.

H

It is only necessary to study the Parliamentary debates on Colonial affairs to see how rarely the Opposition found it necessary to turn their heavier guns on the Government. Indeed, it was the Colonial leaders themselves who made the greatest play with the differences (often imagined) between the policies of the two parties. In the months immediately before the British election, it was illuminating to study the utterances of Colonial politicians and the editorial views of newspapers. Clearly, in multi-racial territories (Northern Rhodesia and Kenya were the classic examples) the Europeans prayed for the advent of a Conservative Government, whilst the Africans were no less fervently hoping for a return to power of Mr Attlee. In "black" Africa—in such territories as Uganda, the Gold Coast, Nigeria— there was still a heavy preference for a Socialist Government—but with distinct reservations. (The Socialists were no longer the saviours of the oppressed, but rather the lesser—though quite definitely so— of two evils.) Quite another viewpoint was revealed in a "fortress colony" such as Malta. There, a powerful hope existed in some quarters that the Conservatives would spend more on defence. Whether this would be because they were the purer patriots or the more belligerent of the two parties was not made clear.

In the Eastern territories of the Commonwealth, the British Government could make some claim that they had at least anticipated events instead of being overtaken by them. For this the major credit goes to Mr Attlee. It was recognized inside the Socialist Party that no aspect of policy touching on Asian affairs escaped the Prime Minister. The major decisions were his, and he brooked no interference, no misinterpretations. It might have appeared that Mountbatten's strong and determined approach contributed most to the resolving of the India problem. Mountbatten played his considerable part, but behind him stood the slight, almost apologetic figure of Attlee, even more resolute, even more dedicated to the task in hand. This was the real master, and the magnitude of his accomplishment has yet to be realized.

At the very beginning of 1950, some two months before the election, an event of great significance put the seal on Attlee's efforts. This was the meeting of the Commonwealth Foreign Ministers in Ceylon, at Colombo.

As far back as 1948, when the Prime Ministers had met in London and spent much of their time discussing the international situation, it had been resolved that there should be meetings to discuss foreign affairs at a ministerial level. The Colombo meeting, held at the invitation of Prime Minister D. S. Senanayake of Ceylon, was the first such conference. From it there emerged a recognition that self-government was not enough, that the political stability of South-East Asia depended "mainly on the improvement of its economic conditions". The Foreign Ministers agreed to recommend to their governments "the establishment of a Consultative Committee of the Commonwealth Governments interested in the area, the first meeting of which should take place in Australia".

This recommendation had two highly significant aspects: it was the beginning of a joint democratic attack on the poverty of Asia; it signified a positive and joint use of the Commonwealth's potential by the member countries. It has been claimed that the Colombo Plan (which was the fruit of this 1950 meeting) was in the first place an Australian idea. That would have made it all the more significant —that a Dominion should take an initiative instead of Britain. But to this day British Socialist circles claim that the Colombo Plan was the monument of the late Ernest Bevin, the Foreign Secretary of the day. Burma, it is said, needed British aid, but Bevin foresaw that if he gave it the Commonwealth countries—India, Pakistan and Ceylon —could hardly be denied the same assistance. This would at once expose the pro-Commonwealth Prime Ministers of those three countries to the charge of abetting the return of imperialism. The way round the problem, said Bevin, would be to make it an all-Commonwealth operation of mutual aid.

The concept of the Colombo Plan came not a day too soon. China had been given full political recognition at once by Russia. By February of 1950 the 30-Year Pact between Russia and China had been signed. A third of the world's population were now united in the same ideology, and it was certain that these two giant countries would lose no time in imposing their doctrine, one way or another, on the rest of Asia. Indeed, there is good evidence that the conference of the World Federation of Trade Unions held at Peking in November of 1949 was in reality an inaugural meeting of an organization to direct communist movements throughout South-East Asia.

The Western Powers, by painful experience, knew that Soviet methods combined intimidation and blandishment, and that the instrument nearest to hand, political or economic, was never neglected by Moscow. There was every reason to assume that China would adopt the same approach, and in the case of South-East Asia a demonstration of communist superiority in solving economic problems was the obvious policy.

Australia, so keenly aware now of her involvement with South-East Asia, was desperately anxious to press ahead with positive action. There was a meeting in May at Sydney of the new Commonwealth Consultative Committee, and it was decided to recommend to all the Governments concerned that a six-year development plan for the whole of South and South-East Asia be prepared. The Governments of India, Pakistan, Ceylon and the Colonial territories within the area were invited "to provide information on the state of their economies and to prepare six-year programmes of development". Invitations to join in the scheme were sent to the non-Commonwealth territories in the area—Burma, Thailand, Indonesia and the three Indo-China Associate States. This was the beginning of the famous Colombo Plan.

The Australians would have liked speedier action, but the foundations of the Colombo Plan laid at Sydney represented a considerable achievement. Even at this early stage it was obvious that the whole imaginative concept could only have been manipulated through the Commonwealth. And the Socialist Government of Great Britain could claim that it would have been altogether impossible if India, Pakistan and Ceylon had not already been given independence.

But even before the Sydney meeting—in March—Mr Attlee had gone to the electorate. The result was one which could give no real satisfaction to either Socialists or Conservatives, and even less to Britain's friends and allies. For the Government retained power, but with so small a majority that they could not begin to govern effectively.

When Mr Attlee formed his new Government at the beginning of March, it was certain that he could not hope to force through contentious issues. Moreover, opinion abroad was disturbed at the sight of an ineffectual Britain at the very time when she needed a strong and able government. Yet some period must elapse before the people could be asked to resolve the stalemate. In the meantime, the Government could at least depend on the support of the Opposition for the broad principles of their foreign and imperial policies.

One of the casualties in the election had been Arthur Creech Jones, the Secretary of State for the Colonies. His departure was possibly more sincerely regretted by many of the people of the Colonies, whose affairs he had been handling, than by a number of his colleagues. Creech Jones had not carried the weight inside the Cabinet that was so essential for a Colonial Secretary in a period of delicate transition. It was not because of any lack of ability. Creech Jones was thorough and informed. He was more than merely sincere, he was devoted to the betterment of the Colonial people. Perhaps above all else, he had the strength of character to change some of his most cherished ideas when they failed in the face of reality.

His successor was much more powerful in the Socialist Party, and much less fitted to handle the affairs of the Colonies. James Griffiths was a man of great sincerity with a long record of devoted service to the Socialist Party. He was warm-hearted, emotional and—as an ex-miner—passionately interested in the advancement of people whom the world had served ill. But he knew very little of Colonial affairs, and this was no time to begin an apprenticeship. It was not a happy appointment, and amongst the Europeans in the Colonies it was regarded with anger as simply a reward for services to the Socialist Party, with no reference to the good of the Colonies. But there are good grounds for believing that at least one major event which bene-fited the Europeans, the introduction of the Federation of Rhodesia and Nyasaland, might very well never have come to pass if Creech Jones had remained in office.

Despite the crippling of their power, the Socialists were able to go ahead and play their part in the development of the Colombo Plan. In September, yet a third meeting of the Commonwealth Consultative Committee took place in London. Answers from the non-Commonwealth countries invited to participate in the scheme had not been received in time, but from the London meeting a compre-hensive plan covering the Commonwealth countries finally emerged. An assessment of the total resources of capital and technical assistance needed in South-East Asian territories of the Commonwealth was made, and it was thus possible to indicate how much help would be needed from the more advanced members. By November, the Report of the Consultative Committee was published, having been approved by all the Governments concerned.

It would be misleading to regard the Colombo Plan as some sort of economic "united front" or even as heralding a co-ordinated development campaign. In essence it was a collection of individual plans, with no real central command. Yet it did provide a panoramic view of South-East Asia's economic needs; it released a sorely-needed flow of outside capital into the area and brought into being machinery for technical assistance. It gave the countries concerned at least the chance to plan ahead to the best advantage.

The Colombo Plan was in fact the Western liberal approach to the appalling problems of Asian poverty. It would clearly stand or fall by its performance in comparison with that of communism. From the very first, it could at least claim to be the sort of aid which did not offend the self-respect of the beneficiaries. And that was important in Asia. In any case, it was the first concerted effort to solve a gigantic human problem, and on that score alone the Commonwealth could justifiably be proud of its handiwork.

But whether economic aid alone was going to be enough was debatable. The communist shadow was lengthening across South-East Asia. The position in Malaya was deteriorating. What officialdom still complacently referred to as "banditry" was near enough to civil war. Malcolm MacDonald, the Commissioner-General for South-East Asia, was at least realistic enough to describe the situation as "very serious indeed". And so it was. In May, the new Secretary of State for the Colonies and the Secretary of State for War, John Strachey, visited Malaya to investigate the situation, and on their heels came the Chief of the Imperial General Staff, Field-Marshal Sir William Slim.

There was no denying that the morale of the terrorists was rising as markedly as that of the general public in Malaya was falling. At the root of the guerrilla successes was the succour they received from the Chinese squatter population, the flotsam of war. That succour was not altogether the result of intimidation; it also stemmed from Chinese fears that the British were not going to be tough enough for the situation. Until these people were confident enough to stand up to the terrorists themselves, little improvement in the general situation could be expected.

One imaginative move was the appointment of Sir Harold Briggs to the civil post of Director of Operations, in which he was expected to plan co-ordination between the police and the military. One of his first moves was to build up the number of Asian police inspectors, and to increase the number of Chinese in the regular and special constabulary. Priority was also given by the Government of Malaya to the resettlement of the Chinese squatters, who now totalled about 300,000. The old delusion that the crisis could be resolved in a short term of time had now disappeared and Sir Harold himself continually stressed that the task ahead could not be hurried.

Meanwhile, in neighbouring Sarawak there was still a brooding discontent. The cession of the state to the British Crown was the subject of litigation by which the heir-presumptive to the Raj of Sarawak, Captain Bertram Brooke, and his son Anthony Brooke sought a judicial declaration that the act of cession was illegal. In Sarawak itself an anti-cession movement emerged and rapidly assumed a nationalist character, in which no less than sixteen associations were allied. Their common aim was the restoration of Sarawak as an independent state under British protection and Brooke rule.

Members of one of these associations, the Malay Youth Movement, disastrously overstepped the mark when they helped to form a secret and illegal organization called "The Thirteen Essential Ingredients". The simple objective of the organization was to murder the Governor and other leading officials. Tragically, they did succeed in killing the new Governor, Mr Duncan Stewart, in a stabbing attack, only three weeks after his arrival. Four Malays were hanged and another seven of the conspirators were sentenced to long terms of imprisonment, but the anti-cession movement still remained as strong as ever.

Although there was little doubt that the Communist Government in China were giving aid and encouragement to the rebels in Malaya, they were remarkably quiet about Hong Kong. James Griffiths was able to refer to the Colony in the House of Commons as "an oasis of prosperity and peace in the Far East". He could say that with justice. Trade had reached a new record, and new manufacturing industries were springing up regularly. The huge influx of refugees from China (the population had quadrupled since the Japanese occupation and was now two million) was at once an embarrassment and a tribute to Hong Kong's stability. Considering the tragedy that befell the Colony in the last war, morale was astonishingly high. There was no panic, no run on the banks, no dark forebodings. On the contrary, the great entrepôt of the East was well-armed and in good heart. The leaders of the great and long-established commercial enterprises saw no reason why bigger and better business should not eventually come their way. If anyone was drawing comparisons between the British Empire in this dark period of time and the decline of the old Roman Empire, Hong Kong provided no fitting text. For here the legions were not streaming home, nor was the *pax Britannica* crumbling away.

In Burma, too, hope was rising. The saintly U Nu was beginning to establish some semblance of national confidence in his government, though it was in large measure due to the utter inability of the many communist factions to achieve a united front in opposition to him. But in two other countries the communist thrust had brought war.

Vietnam was split in two and torn by fighting, but it was Korea that most troubled an anxiously-watching world. There the civil war threatened to burst into world conflict. Who was responsible for originating it is still not certain. But it is clear that the first overt action was an attack by Communist North Korea against the South. There was no evidence that China was in any way implicated at this point, and indeed for some months the Chinese leaders behaved as if the conflict was no concern of theirs. Not so the Americans. President Truman decided that, whilst the U.S. Army might not consider South Korea worth defending, it presented a point of principle that he could not ignore. This was aggression, in his view, and appeasement of the aggressors would be as certain a way to world war as it had proved to be in 1938.

The Americans took the case to the United Nations, invoking the machinery of collective security. They secured the support of the Security Council and, what was more, the active support of sixteen U.N. nations in resisting the aggressors. The American determination was to confine the war to Korea by all possible means. But when the North Koreans had been driven back across their own frontier in defeat, the U.N. forces, which were very largely American, followed with the intention of seizing this opportunity to unify the country. At that point, China intervened. Large forces crossed into Korea to buttress the shattered forces of the North, and overnight it seemed that the world would be plunged into catastrophe. Bitter and protracted fighting followed, and a situation which had seemed within reach of solution became a menacing, constant threat to all mankind.

So soon after its inception, the Chinese Communist State was giving early evidence of its determination to protect what it conceived to be its own. So soon, its tentacles were spreading out over South-East Asia. It could well be that the Chinese Communists believed that the U.N. advance into North Korea was but the prelude to an American campaign in China designed to reinstate Chiang Kai-shek. Or it may have been an evidence of their determination never to be put on the defensive, as were the Russian Communists after the First World War, but rather to attack in advance if necessary, and all the time to expand and to buttress their power.

The United Nations' advance over the 38th Parallel had its violent reaction inside China. A regime of terror began which ended, two years later, with a total of two million executions. To the communists, the threat outside their borders must be answered by the liquidation of all suspected "counter-revolutionaries". Moreover, social and economic reform must be pursued with all possible speed. Above all, this meant land reform, China being so largely an agricultural country. The peasants and the poor farmers were to be the main beneficiaries of the new order of things, the landowners were to be the guilty. This process of violent and ruthless reform added its quota to the long list of the executed.

But this grimmer aspect of the Chinese revolution was not the whole. Without doubt, the communists had inspired a new and dynamic national spirit, a feeling of incipient greatness. The young and eager were on their side. Corruption and nepotism were swept away. The curse of continued inflation over many years, which was at the root of many of China's ills, was attacked with great resolution. By iron regimentation the resources of the nation, human and material, were bent to the purpose of establishing a sound foundation for the economy. There were great errors of omission and commission, but there was almost incredible progress. A great wind was sweeping through China, purifying and fortifying.

What was the alternative offered by the democratic world to this tremendous revolution? As it evolved in South-East Asia in particular it was a mixture of socialism and capitalism not very different from that being applied in Britain. It stood fast, in the last resort, on respect for the individual, not on soulless regimentation. But what was its performance, contrasted with that of communism, in raising the living standards of grossly-underprivileged millions? Matched with the regimentation of communism, with its inevitable concomitant of a massive bureaucracy, was a combination of state planning and individual enterprise.

This much could not be denied. If it was accepted that the world was divided into communists and democrats, then in South-East Asia the bastions of the democratic world were the nations of the Commonwealth. If Britain had never achieved anything else in the world that single fact was the measure of her unique contribution to human history.

CHAPTER XVII

AFRICANISM AND PARTNERSHIP

IN AFRICA, so far behind the Asian territories in cultural heritage, there seemed to be no checking the speed of events. It was not only the example of Asia which fired the younger African nationalist leaders, but the determination to prevent the Europeans so consolidating their position that they could not be challenged. In the Gold Coast the tide ran for Nkrumah after an early and shattering setback; and in the two Rhodesias the European leaders, Sir Godfrey Huggins and Roy Welensky, pushed forward with their plans for federation. The return of a weakened Socialist Government in Britain had been a disappointment, but they believed that Government would not long survive, that it would be replaced by a Conservative Government which would be markedly more sympathetic to their aims.

The younger African nationalist leaders, on the other hand, were equally determined to advance their cause whatever party was in power in Britain. The old dream of a Socialist Government which would yield to their most extravagant demands had faded. But the humanitarian outlook of that Government provided an alternative approach. Colonial politicians were well aware that there had never been any great danger in political extremism under the rule of a liberal, democratic power like Britain, and there was less than ever now. Not only was there not the slightest prospect of liquidation, there was the positive advantage of being able to claim a martyr's crown. The British authorities had a long and uncomfortable experience of this strategy, particularly in India, and they were no nearer a solution. (They could always reflect that Pontius Pilate had known the same dilemma.) However conscious they were of the dangers of creating national martyrs, there was always a point at which action must be taken to preserve law and order, when arrests must be made and men clapped in gaol. Then followed the inevitable shocked questions in Parliament, the commission of inquiry, the broadening of the constitution. This had been the pattern during the first spell of Socialist rule and it had not taken long for astute politicians in the Colonies to appreciate that handsome results could be obtained with comparatively little risk.

European settler leaders were very conscious that they had not the same power of manœuvre. They could hardly claim to be the natural leaders in a multi-racial country and at the same time try to force the Colonial Office's hand by a show of irresponsibility. Nor could they afford the discouragement of outside investment. Sir Godfrey Huggins and Roy Welensky were most keenly aware of this. It was their policy to convince the British Government that they could safely be entrusted with the future of the Africans. The beginning of the year 1950 had filled them with grave doubts about the wisdom of being so patient. Creech Jones had not altered in his dislike of the federation proposal and Sir Godfrey went so far as to tell an audience in Gatooma that Southern Rhodesia might well have to drop the idea and go forward for Dominion status on its own.

As it happened, the defeat of Creech Jones in the British election saved the day for Huggins, and a decisive advantage was gained by the Rhodesian leaders whilst the second Labour Government was still in office. James Griffiths, at the Colonial Office, proved to be less rigid in his approach to the Rhodesian problem than Creech Jones. Or was it less astute and experienced in African affairs? In any case, he did not oppose a proposal by Sir Godfrey Huggins that a Conference of Officials (of the Colonial and Commonwealth Relations Offices, and of Southern and Northern Rhodesia and Nyasaland) should be called to examine what grounds existed which supported the case for closer association between the two Rhodesias and Nyasaland. Creech Jones afterwards said that the approval of such a conference gave the principle of federation a degree of recognition from the British Government which opened the way to victory for Huggins and Welensky. Behind this opinion was the natural chagrin of the politician who has lost control of great events through no fault of his own. Yet Creech Jones honestly thought that the federation of the three Central African territories would be disastrous for the Africans of the area, and that it would be used to buttress the power of the white men. Griffiths, however, felt that if a federation could be established, assuring justice to the African, then no time should be lost. Otherwise, he feared that matters might get out of hand, with the British Government unable to control the situation.

It is possible now to see beyond all doubt that the holding of the Officials' Conference *did* open the way to the Federation of Rhodesia and Nyasaland. The British Government cautiously announced that the Conference would be merely exploratory, that its findings would commit none of the governments concerned. Yet if the Conference found small enough difference between the racial policy of Southern Rhodesia and those of the two Colonial Office territories, then the chief argument against federation would be destroyed. Huggins and Welensky were publicly cautious and non-committal; privately, they were satisfied that a deadlock which had lasted 26 years was within sight of being broken.

In West Africa, over in the Gold Coast, Kwame Nkrumah was keeping abreast of the Rhodesians in the race for power. His Christmas Day Message to his followers reminded them that their motto was "We prefer self-government with danger to servitude in tranquillity." Having jeered at the chiefs ("They will run away and leave their sandals," he said) he announced a "Positive Action" campaign against the Government on January 8 of 1950. This started promisingly enough for Nkrumah with widespread strikes and a serious dislocation of trade and transport. But energetic action by the Government, the condemnation of the campaign by the chiefs, and—this most of all—a bewilderment and indecision apparent in the mass of the people turned the tide. The Nkrumah mystique failed for the first time, and for some weeks the power of his party seemed to be broken.

Nkrumah and several of his lieutenants were arrested on charges of sedition and initiating an illegal strike. There was no demonstration on their arrest. Nkrumah was sentenced to three years' imprisonment, his companions to lesser terms. At this point, the remarkable advantages of political martyrdom became apparent. Nkrumah, through the efforts of his able colleague Kobina Gbedemah—who came out of gaol practically at the moment his leader went in—was built up as the self-sacrificing patriot leader.

In municipal elections at Accra, Kumasi and Cape Coast Nkrumah's Convention People's Party gained overwhelming victories. As swiftly as Nkrumah's star rose the fortunes of his opponents, the United Gold Coast Convention, plunged. The undisputed ability of many of its leaders, their undoubted experience in the art of government could not save them against men who had mastered the more mundane art of electioneering and who had the gift of capturing the ear of the mass of the people.

The first general election in Gold Coast history was due in February of 1951. But six months before that it was sure that Nkrumah, even behind prison bars, would be the victor. Now the consequences of the Watson Commission were clear. For the Coussey Commission which had followed that had recommended universal adult franchise and a constitution which brought complete self-government within easy grasp. On the face of it, the rapid course of events was bringing to power a man whose influence rested largely on a semi-literate urban electorate, brought into being by the advances planned by Britain herself, and whose climb to leadership had been marked by violence and intransigence. It was the very antithesis of what the Colonial Office had envisaged over the years of careful and detailed planning.

There was some comfort in the fact that the new Governor of the Gold Coast, Sir Charles Arden-Clarke, had proved to be one of those strong and capable men, yet able to temper his strength with imagination, that Britain seems often able to call on in moments of crisis. After the "Positive Action" disorders he pointedly repudiated any need for a commission of inquiry. "I know of nothing that cannot be dealt with justly and effectively by the Courts of the Gold Coast and established disciplinary procedure," he said.

Neighbouring Nigeria, four times the size of the Gold Coast and Britain's largest colony, had her troubles, not so immediately challenging but no less tragic. Towards the end of 1949, a go-slow strike at the Enugu Colliery ended in a violent clash between African miners and police. Twenty people were killed and for a critical few days there was the dark prospect of a country-wide upheaval. At the subsequent inquiry a Government political intelligence officer declared that there were terrorist parties organizing in Nigeria, and that plans to seize explosives and ammunition had been uncovered.

Like the Gold Coast, Nigeria had a resourceful and determined Governor in Sir John Macpherson, whose aim was never to let himself be overtaken by events, and to keep one jump ahead of general political aspiration. Also like the Gold Coast, the country had its astute and purposeful politicians, chief among them Dr Nnamdi Azikiwe. But Nigeria was split by jealous tribal factions and by religious animosities. Were it not for these things, it would assuredly have taken the same road as the Gold Coast.

In an address in London to the Royal Empire and Royal African Societies during this period, Mr J. H. Huizinga, a Dutchman, said that after only two generations European civilization seemed to be preparing to abdicate its mission in Africa. "How," he asked, "can the spectacle of West Africa's sudden leap towards self-government fail to arouse powerful and legitimate jealousies in the breasts of all those other African groups who may well feel that on grounds of merit they have as good a right to emancipation?" He went on to warn that "the refusal to admit that what is sauce for the West African goose must be sauce for the East African gander can hardly fail to be resented as an injustice and, worse than an injustice, a refusal to practise what is preached".

Mr Huizinga's prophecy was already in process of fulfilment. In Kenya, north of Lake Baringo, three hundred African tribesmen, mainly of the Suk tribe, attacked a district officer and his police escort. The D.O. and two European police officers were speared to death, and twenty of the attackers were killed in return. Such conflicts and such tragedies were part of the occupational risk for Colonial officials. But this was different. For the party had been sent to rearrest an African who had been convicted for being an adherent of the proscribed and fanatical religious sect, the Dini ya Msamba, the "Cult of the Good Spirits".

This sect had been in trouble before, but what raised alarm in Kenya was that it seemed to underline the warnings given by experienced men that the gulf between African and European had never been wider, that there were strange happenings tied up with an "Africa for the Africans" movement which scorned and rejected the white man's creeds and looked back to the old, dark Africa.

In the same month as the tragedy at Lake Baringo, the Comet jet airliner made its first landing at Nairobi. It had flown 2,200 miles from London to Cairo in 5 hours 8 minutes and a like distance from Cairo to Nairobi in approximately the same time. From London to Nairobi in a little over ten hours' flying time! But it was still ten centuries from London to Lake Baringo. That was the real African tragedy.

In Tanganyika, there was trouble of a different order, but it was no less harmful to European prestige. The great Groundnut Scheme had finally run into heavy trouble, though the Minister of Food, Mr Strachey, desperately tried to paint an optimistic picture of progress. The truth was that a gamble had failed. Drought and the reluctant soil had been major factors in the ignominious failure, but bad planning, faulty administration, a lack of preliminary research had damned the project from the start.

The name of Kongwa, which had been the centre of the main effort, rang through Britain. The Committee of Public Accounts said that they were "left with the impression that the basic fault in the scheme was the failure to realize the impracticability of the original plans in the conditions which existed immediately after the war". A salvage operation was launched, and there was some adroit face-saving in the announcement that the plan would go forward as a broad project of Colonial development rather than one purely to produce food.

There was no avoiding the real truth that a most worthy conception, ill-devised and distorted by political manœuvring as it was, had died. In Britain, the very idea of Colonial development lay under a cloud. In Africa, Britain's ability to tackle such development was doubted as it had never been before.

Northward, in Uganda, distrust and suspicion between European and African was replacing the old, pleasant tranquillity. In the April of 1949 there had been the planned rebellion against the Kabaka and the Buganda Government which had stemmed from a number of causes, but which without doubt had gathered its strength from the feeling among the mass of Africans that they were the exploited "have nots". That rebellion had been crushed and its ringleaders punished, but the distrust of the white man only gathered strength. The Governor, Sir John Hall, warned the people to be less credulous of self-appointed leaders. He asked, "Why do you disbelieve those who have done you so much good, and readily believe the lies, the obvious lies, of evil and self-seeking men just because they are of your own race?" It was the age-old plaint of the imperial proconsul and as ever it fell on unheeding ears.

Throughout East Africa, amongst the literate young Africans, this rising distrust of the British grew more marked. The deepest suspicions were entertained of the East African Assembly, which was increasingly seen as simply the instrument which would bring about an East African Federation dominated by the white men. Every move concerning the proposed Federation of the Rhodesias and Nyasaland was noted. What seemed inevitable in Central Africa, thought African nationalists, could well happen in East Africa.

It was natural that every step taken by South Africa's Nationalist Government would be equally closely watched. Dr Malan had given Africans no cause for comfort, and when he announced his intention to ask the British Government for the transfer of the High Commission territories to the Union, African opinion was deeply disturbed. It was inconceivable that any British Government should hand over these three British-protected territories—Basutoland, Bechuanaland and Swaziland—without the consent of their peoples, and the less so to a South African government pursuing a policy of rigid race separation and white supremacy. Yet it remained true that the economic case for separation was sound; for all three territories the Union was the principal market and the principal avenue for employment. Britain would gladly have transferred them to a South Africa pursuing the same policy as herself.

The significance of the High Commission Territories was not only that they brought into the open a fundamental clash of policy between two members of the Commonwealth but that they symbolized the African dilemma. Here were black men's countries dependent on the white man's economy and at the same time determined to resist his supremacy. On the other hand, Dr Malan needed these territories under his control if his *apartheid* policy was ever to be practical. This, indeed, was his opening move in a campaign based on recognition of the fact that he had not the land left inside his own borders to implement his plans. African and European rejected and desired each other at the same time, as they did all over the continent. In the welter of conflicting policies practised in Africa was there any hope of an answer to that paradox?

Africa as a whole now presented a picture of disheartening confusion and apparent lack of purpose. It was difficult to discern the threads of a coherent British policy which would lead to the democratic front that was Britain's real monument in Asia. But there *were* the threads of such a policy, and as various factors—in particular, geography—had prevented communism making any great impact, there was at least a little time left in which to draw those threads together.

The clash between the interests of the white and black races had obscured another force at work in Africa. The influence of Islam, spreading down the Nile valley, across the great desert regions, was more powerful than the Europeans of southern Africa assumed. Apart from the Egyptians, the Muslim peoples of North Africa, of the Sudan and of Africa "South of the Sahara" were technically backward, suspicious of European influence and frequently torn by sectarian feuds. But basically they had a common cultural and religious heritage which gave them a purpose and a homogeneity that the Christian and pagan Africans, split by tribalism, lacked. It is only necessary to reflect on the cohesive strength of the Muslim population in Nigeria, the Sudan and French West Africa to see the undoubted truth of this, and to realize that Islam could certainly not be written off as too corrupt and decadent to affect the flow of events.

Studying the map of Africa, one can see how these Islamic states of the north, "black Africa" in the centre and "white Africa" in the south form rough divisions, the fingers, as it were, of each reaching out to the borders of the others. Add to this confusing division the bewildering number of policies being applied by the Colonial powers, and it seems quite hopeless to prophesy how Africa will emerge. Yet it was and is true that if peace and a measure of prosperity will keep Africa as a continent in the camp of the free world, then British policy gives the best chance of succeeding in that aim.

Even as far back as 1950, that policy had two main aims: self-government and co-operation between European and African. Those aims gave room for widely different interpretations—certainly many Socialists did not think co-operation meant white settlers—but they *did* offer the best hope for the emergence of a peaceful and prosperous Africa.

CHAPTER XVIII

"SOF'LY, SOF'LY KETCH MONKEY"

IF EVENTS IN British Africa seemed to be proceeding with the maximum of pandemonium and publicity, it was extraordinary to see how completely opposite was the scene in the Caribbean. There, too, the talk was still of federation. But a dense fog seemed to have settled down. There is a West Indian saying, "Sof'ly, sof'ly ketch monkey". It fitted the federal negotiations admirably. Officialdom seemed to be going about the matter so silently that those outside the sacred inner circle had no idea of what was afoot.

At the beginning of 1950, the publication of the report of the Standing Closer Association Committee was still awaited. Towards the end of the previous October, the Committee had completed its year-long examination of the proposal for a Federation of the West Indies. Its conclusions had been placed before a special conference of the Caribbean Governors held in Barbados. Their Excellencies had in fact two special reports to study, dealing with the questions

I

of a customs union and the unification of civil services. They had a great deal to talk about, but the unfortunate thing was that no hint of their discussions escaped from the Conference chamber. If ever a project appeared likely to die of sheer inanition it was the West Indian federal project at this point of time.

The West Indian press and public had been primly informed that the Governors were only exchanging opinions and not shaping policy, so that there was no need for publicity. The Standing Committee itself, during its twelve months of labour, had held all meetings in secret, and had decided, at the end of it all, that the report should go to the Colonial Office and to the various legislative assemblies of the Caribbean before the public were allowed to know the details. It was over four months after the Governors' conference that the report was finally issued. How ironic it is to reflect that from that time on one of the chief criticisms made by outside observers was that the general public in the Caribbean territories seemed to be apathetic about federation.

However, the report of the Standing Closer Association Committee did firmly recommend a British Caribbean Federation as "the shortest path towards a real political independence for the British peoples of the region, within the framework of the British Commonwealth—what is meant, in fact, by 'Dominion Status'". The Federation, said the Committee, would have a central Legislature having exclusive power to deal with 21 subjects, including defence, external affairs, exchange control and the raising of external loans. Another 38 subjects—such as banking, criminal law, currency, development of industries, immigration, sea and air communication—would be covered by both Federal and Territorial Legislatures, Federal Law prevailing in case of inconsistency. There would be 23 senators and 50 members of the Federal House of Assembly.

This was the suggested allocation of seats for the House of Assembly: Barbados, 4; British Guiana, 6; British Honduras, 2; Jamaica, 16; Antigua, 2; St Kitts-Nevis, 2; Montserrat, 1; Trinidad, 9; Grenada, 2; St Vincent, 2; St Lucia, 2; Dominica, 2.

The basic weakness of the proposed Federation was implicit in these figures. For they demonstrated the potentially overwhelming power of Jamaica and Trinidad. And they included two Colonies which were far from being convinced that the Federation was a good thing—British Honduras and British Guiana. The *Daily Chronicle* in British Guiana voiced an opinion broadly held in the

Colony when it said that "West Indians do not appreciate British Guiana's problems as a continental country and its destiny as part of the great South American continent." The newspaper somewhat complacently added that "the Mother Country has a responsibility to us individually which she will not fail to discharge".

The truth was that neither of the Colonies wished to be dominated by politicians from Jamaica and Trinidad. Most of all they disliked the idea of Mr Bustamante (who had just won the general election in Jamaica) being the leading man in the proposed Federation. Yet Mr Bustamante was nearly as lukewarm as they were. He declared that a large interest-free loan was needed if the Federation was ever to be born. "If I can find out where the money is to come from I may be interested in Federation at the earliest possible moment," he remarked.

The British Government was most firmly in favour of Federation, and so was the Opposition. In a House of Lords debate, both sides praised the Report of the Standing Closer Association Committee. Lord Hall said that the Government were only waiting to hear what the various legislatures in the West Indies had to say about the Report. But he hastened to add that Britain's support for the project did not mean that she was trying to avoid any of her financial or economic responsibilities towards the territories. That, of course, was to reassure suspicious West Indian politicians who harboured the notion that Britain only wanted the Federation to save the drain on her own pocket.

In spite of the hostilities and suspicions, there was a firm enough foundation for an eventual Federation in the West Indies. But that was most certainly not the case in another area, where federation seemed highly desirable. In East Africa, the old dream of a united Kenya, Uganda and Tanganyika was still cherished. Men who had served a lifetime in East Africa as Colonial officials still believed that they would have failed in their purpose if they did not see the three territories brought together. But few suspected how dark and deep the African hostility towards the European was now running, in all three territories, but in Kenya and Uganda far more than in Tanganyika. Few Europeans appreciated how strong was the influence of the despised new generation of African politicians, not only among the urbanized and detribalized Africans, but among the rural population.

As 1950 drew to its close, and whilst this African resistance was rising (soon to erupt in a terrible form) the desire for a federation was intensifying among the Europeans. The promise of progress soon being made towards the same goal in Central Africa sharpened ambitions in Nairobi, where Sir Godfrey Huggins, the Prime Minister of Southern Rhodesia, was greatly admired, not so much for his statesmanship as for his alleged astuteness in outwitting the Colonial Office.

Sir Godfrey was indeed astute, so much so that he was able to resist the blandishments of the Kenya Europeans. When he was invited to attend private talks between the representatives of Kenya, Uganda and Tanganyika, he cheerfully promised any help or advice he could give, but made it extremely clear that Southern Rhodesia could not be concerned with East African affairs at the present stage. Sir Godfrey had no intention of jeopardizing in any way the forthcoming London conference on closer association between the two Rhodesias and Nyasaland.

The Secretary of State for the Colonies, James Griffiths, made a statement in the House of Commons on December 13 which was clearly designed to remove what he himself called the "growing uncertainty" in East Africa. Without doubt, that uncertainty had been sadly intensified by his own Minister of State, John Dugdale, who came to cross-purposes with European settlers in Tanganyika during a tour of East Africa. Dugdale left an impression behind him that the Socialist Government had no sympathy with the point of view of the Europeans in East Africa and had no intention of drawing on their knowledge and experience. There were faults on both sides, but it made all the more difficult the Secretary of State's efforts to reassure people in East Africa that he believed in a partnership of all the races.

Griffiths emphasized in his House of Commons speech that though British Colonial policy still aimed at eventual self-government and inclusion in the Commonwealth of all three East African territories, they would develop separately for the time being. Self-government, he emphasized, would include "proper provision for all the main communities which have made their home in East Africa", but the Africans must be brought forward to the stage where they could "take their full part ... in the political and economic life of the territories". He made it clear beyond all doubt that until that happy day, the British Government would continue to exercise ultimate control in all three territories.

This was by no means what the more forceful of the Europeans had in mind. They were not mollified by the thought that the East African High Commission and the Central Assembly provided a useful bond between the territories. But the British Government's policy was not only the right one; it was the only conceivable one under the circumstances. The only doubtful thing about it was that it rested on the assumption that time would create a new harmony among the racial groups. Once let the Africans, the Europeans and the Indians know that Britain was holding the ring until they joined up with each other and all would be well—so ran the argument. But what if, instead of harmony, deeper animosities developed? What if the different races merely used the breathing space created by Britain to outmanœuvre each other? That very thing had happened in Palestine and in India.

Down in Southern Rhodesia, Sir Godfrey Huggins was being extremely circumspect in all his public utterances as the year neared its end. His Africans were to become "liberal democrats", he announced to a meeting of Rotarians. "Liberal democracy is not the creed of slaves or the dispossessed," he added. "It is the working faith of men who have acquired a stake in society, men who are sure of themselves and their own worth." He and his colleagues, he emphasized, were anxious to build up Southern Rhodesia on the basis of a partnership between the various races, not to use colour as a test of man's ability and culture. "There is nothing altruistic in this," he disarmingly declared. "Any other plan in this dangerous world would lead to the removal of our European descendants. We can only develop and hold this country as partners."

Whether it was dangerous or not, South Africa was now steadily implementing a racial policy that was the complete reverse of partnership. The new Minister of Native Affairs, Dr Verwoerd, was not only a rigid believer in *apartheid*, but a man of grim resolution and great administrative capacity. But not even Verwoerd could really resolve the inherent contradictions of the policy. At the very time that he was explaining his plans to the Native Representative Council, South African industries were being slowed down by a manpower shortage. Yet the use of non-European labour was still supposed to be severely restricted. In practice, it was not so, and all sorts of devices were resorted to. Over 75 per cent of the chemical industry's labour was estimated to be non-European, and quite certainly many Africans were doing semi-skilled jobs in manufacturing industries which were supposed to be reserved for Europeans.

The European unions, as well as the Government, opposed African advancement. They stood fast on the wholly hypocritical claim that equal pay must be given for equal work or—they piously claimed —the whole sacred principle of trade unionism would be betrayed. As the mass of Africans were hopelessly under-educated and rarely able to serve an apprenticeship, they clearly could not equal the European workers. Strangely enough, this contemptible device— which was used later in the Northern Rhodesian Copperbelt—succeeded in deceiving the British trade union leaders for quite some time.

Dr Verwoerd held out a rosy and quite impracticable vision to the Native Representative Council. *Apartheid*, he explained, would mean industries, towns and "even cities" arising in the native reserves. They would be largely created and controlled by the natives themselves. But he gave little indication as to how this black Utopia would be brought about, and as it would clearly wreck the national economy if it ever came into existence, there was little enough point in his going into detail. The African leaders pointed out that this policy of segregation had been conceived by the white man, without any consultation with the African. Unilateral policies, they warned, would have increasingly little chance in Africa, however well they were conceived. Not unexpectedly, the discussions quickly reached a deadlock.

Far more immediately menacing was the revelation that the Nationalist Government shortly intended to remove the Cape Coloured voters from the common roll, where they had been for 98 years. As the Cape Coloured people were in the main staunchly anti-Nationalist, their removal from the roll would strengthen the Government's future electoral prospects. But over and above that, this announcement showed the determination of Dr Malan and his followers to curb the non-Europeans and to buttress white supremacy. It was little wonder that more and more Europeans, apprehensive of the future, were crossing the Limpopo River into the Rhodesias. But even this was welcomed by the more extreme Nationalists. The newspaper *Die Transvaler* could see no tragedy in "10,000 people or so" moving north each year. "It is an investment for the preservation of 'whitehood' for which both the Union and the Rhodesias will be grateful for in the long run," it announced.

Over in the Gold Coast, Kwame Nkrumah's followers were launching their campaign for the February general election. Africa had never known such days. The Convention People's Party had clearly mastered all the tactics of electioneering, and they seemed to have the necessary finance. Their canvassers were everywhere, their propaganda vans, carrying the red, white and green "liberation" flag, were to be seen in the remotest parts of the land. "Home Rule for the Gold Coast" was the slogan of the day. Nkrumah was still in gaol, and every day he stayed there increased his propaganda value for his lieutenants.

It was a spectacle that thoroughly alarmed two British Members of Parliament, David Gammans and Geoffrey Cooper, who were studying labour conditions in the Gold Coast. In an article in the *Daily Telegraph* they claimed that they found an alarming lack of experience, of knowledge or of any other of the qualifications necessary to people granted the vote. They pointed out that 90 per cent of the electorate could neither read nor write, and that few of the people seemed to know what the election was about. All this was possibly true, but the hard fact was that the election was the culmination of the train of events set in motion by the ill-advised Watson Commission of 1948. What had been sown then was about to be reaped.

CHAPTER XIX

A CHANCE FOR GREATNESS

In January of 1951, under the menacing shadow of the Korean War, the Commonwealth Prime Ministers met in London for what promised to be the most significant of all their meetings. The world had never, since 1945, been nearer to global war. The Commonwealth, with its wide and intimate connections throughout the world, its vested interest in peace in every major region, seemed the one organization that could give a practical lead to the rest of the world. Indeed the main purpose of the meeting was "to review the international situation and to consider what further positive action Commonwealth governments could take to secure and preserve world peace".

The Prime Ministers ranged over the world in their discussions. The terms of a peace settlement for Japan—still hanging fire five years after the war—were considered. So, too, was the situation in the Middle East and that in Europe. Economic problems arising from the shortage of raw materials were examined in detail. The result of all these labours was depressingly small. The two practical gains were that a meeting of Defence Ministers—but not those of the Asian members—was arranged for June, a later meeting of Supply and Production Ministers for September. The communiqués issued after these two meetings rivalled those of the Prime Ministers in platitudinous vapidity. But at least the consultative machinery on economic questions was strengthened, which was a faltering step in the right direction.

The truth is that a chance for greatness was fumbled. It was fumbled because the very idea of sacrificing one jot of national sovereignty was regarded by almost all the Commonwealth nations as sacrilege. This extraordinary attitude, taken by nations heavily leaning on the charity of the United States, intimidated and inhibited by the thought of communist power, and living under the shadow of nuclear war, had its touch of sad irony. The Australians at least were desperately anxious for the Commonwealth to take on bone and sinew. Robert Menzies, the Australian Prime Minister, had already spoken of the need for closer consultation and particularly for a Commonwealth Committee on Foreign Affairs. His Minister in London, forceful and outspoken Eric Harrison, had boldly spoken out in public for a Commonwealth Charter and a Council of Commonwealth Affairs, so that defence, foreign affairs, economic development and trade policies could be co-ordinated.

Harrison stressed that his views were his own and did not represent those of the Australian Government, but there is little doubt that he was flying a kite for Mr Menzies. The Australian Prime Minister certainly urged his views on the other Prime Ministers, but he got little enough support, and most of that came from Huggins of Southern Rhodesia, who was particularly perturbed at the weakening of the Commonwealth's economic links. Strangely, Menzies did not get the support he anticipated from Holland of New Zealand. The experience left a lasting sense of impotence with Australian leaders, but it is to their credit that they never allowed themselves to be disheartened. Yet it is clear that the increasing tendency of Australians to look to the United States for increased help both in defence and in economic development was given a decisive impetus by the rebuff they received in London in 1951.

At some stages of the Prime Ministers' stay in London it looked as if the unresolved differences between themselves loomed more importantly than anything else. Most delicate and dangerous of these differences was the standing quarrel over Kashmir between India and Pakistan. The forces of both countries still stood ready for conflict in that lovely state. Those who had hoped that Commonwealth influences would move either a little closer to compromise were sadly disappointed. The best that could be said was that their Commonwealth membership kept both countries in a sort of peaceful contact and diminished the chances of actual war.

India had, too, a bitter grievance with South Africa, over the racial policies of that country and their humiliating impact on Indians in the Union. India's third problem concerned the discrimination against yet more of her people overseas, the Tamils in Ceylon, though so far this situation had not developed dangerously.

Dr Malan of South Africa had his own particular difference with Britain herself. Her policies in relation to coloured races generally, and most certainly in Africa, he considered to be not merely foolish but positively disastrous. After the meeting of the Prime Ministers (where he was represented by Dr T. E. Donges), in this same year of 1951, he gave an interview to the Nationalist newspaper *Die Burger* in which, astonishingly, he disclaimed any share in the responsibility for the consequences of British policy in recognizing India, Pakistan and Ceylon as members of the Commonwealth. He accused Britain of acting on her own in this matter, but this was manifestly inaccurate. He himself—or any other of the Prime Ministers—had every opportunity of making his views known well before the Asian members came into the Commonwealth, and indeed he had indisputably been a party to the unanimous decision to allow India to stay in the Commonwealth as a republic.

The truth was that two matters dominated Dr Malan's mind, the inviolability of the *apartheid* doctrine and the desire of him and his followers to make South Africa a republic. These obsessions had the sometimes perplexing effect of making South Africa's Prime Minister appear to condemn and to praise the Commonwealth at the same time. In this same interview he intimated—clearly with the Gold Coast in mind—that the policy of converting British Colonies into free independent nations of the Commonwealth "means nothing less than the undermining of the foundations of the Commonwealth and its gradual liquidation". Yet, only a few weeks before,

Dr Malan declared at a Cape Town banquet in honour of Mr Patrick Gordon Walker, the Secretary of State for Commonwealth Relations, that South Africans could only express satisfaction with the development of Commonwealth relations and the stage they had now reached. "The outstanding feature of that development", he added, "has always been freedom, conceded and recognized in accordance with the growth of their own nationhood in Colonies which formerly were mere component parts of a single empire, until the stage has been reached of that complete equality in status and independence now possessed by all members of the Commonwealth."

But the Doctor was not alone in assessing the value of the Commonwealth very largely in relation to his own country's problems. The real wonder is that the participants at the 1951 talks were able to so far rise above their own national viewpoints as at least to dimly see that they gained something positive from the Commonwealth link.

It is salutary to look at the Prime Ministers individually, and to see them not as godlike figures descending on London but political leaders whose power rested on the approval of their people. Mr Attlee himself, on whom fell the major burden of keeping the Commonwealth together, was not only responsible for the political and economic development of over forty colonies, but knew only too well that he had not at his disposal the military and economic strength which had buttressed the Commonwealth and Empire before the war. Moreover, his own government was hanging on to power by the barest majority, knowing that another election must soon come which might well see them tumbled from office.

Robert Menzies of Australia, that powerful and able advocate of the Commonwealth, was none the less well aware of this country's dependence on American strength, and later in the year he brought Australia into the much-criticized A.N.Z.U.S. pact with the United States and New Zealand. At the same time as he advocated closer Commonwealth co-operation he was thus driven into a defence pact from which Britain was excluded, and was at the same time impelled to pursue a wide and speedy policy of industrialization. This was, understandably, aimed at making Australia more self-sufficient and at the same time making her more populous, but its accomplishment could not but affect trade with Britain.

New Zealand's Prime Minister, the solid, worthy but unimaginative Sidney Holland, had just come into office and ended fourteen years of Labour rule. Overwhelmingly loyal though he was to the British connection, he was committed to justifying his election promise of "making the pound go further". Just before he came to the London meeting, his trade mission returned from Britain with the complaint that negotiations for bulk purchase contracts had been unsatisfactory. The British, on the other hand, made wounding comments on the tendency of the New Zealanders to strike a hard bargain. From this time on, British trading arrangements with both New Zealand and Australia were to suffer repeated and generally painful adjustments.

The man who sat in perhaps the most uneasy seat of all was Liaquat Ali Khan of Pakistan. This brave and able man had taken on a task to daunt most men merely in succeeding the revered founder of Pakistan, Mr Jinnah. On top of that he was uncertain of his army's loyalty, plagued by the intrigues of the mullahs and threatened all the time by the very instability of the Pakistan economy. The final complication was the jealousy between the western and eastern wings of the State. And as far as the mass of his countrymen were concerned, if the Commonwealth could not get Kashmir back for them then it was pointless for Pakistan to be in it.

The month after Liaquat Ali Khan's visit to London there was a gathering in Karachi which well illustrated the difficulties he had in curbing religious reaction. This was the grandly-titled World Muslim Conference, which advocated welding Islam into a bloc to stand between communism and democracy. There was more than a hint of communist promptings in the references at Karachi to "the machinations of the Western imperialist Powers".

Mr D. S. Senanayake knew well that Ceylon needed the Commonwealth link desperately. But this Asian squire who was the "father of his people" also knew that behind the façade of staid and responsible advance in Ceylon there was a rampant nationalism and a religious intolerance. The pressure of the younger Sinhalese intelligentsia who wanted the Europeans out with all speed was only matched by the machinations of politically-minded Buddhist priests who not only wanted the Europeans out, but all trace of European influence destroyed.

Not even Pandit Nehru, unchallengeable though his position was in India, could act in London without looking over his shoulder to Delhi. Many of his followers believed the Commonwealth link was useful to India only because Nehru said so, and that the time was to come when he had to fight hard to justify the link. Above all else, what Mr Nehru wanted from the Commonwealth was its influence in the cause of world peace. All the members, of course, desired peace as fervently as did Mr Nehru, but they were not prepared to seek it in neutralism, and they sometimes found his exhortations irksome.

The Canadians, who had become increasingly aware that they had a Pacific as well as an Atlantic coast, were anxious to have the goodwill of the Asian members of the Commonwealth, and particularly that of India. But they also provided the link between the Commonwealth and the United States, and Mr Nehru (who stood extremely high in Mr St Laurent's estimation) was increasingly leaning to the opinion that United States' policies were as menacing as those of Russia to the cause of peace. Mr St Laurent's Government had allied itself so closely to the U.S. that a steadily-growing number of his countrymen were apprehensive at the prospect of losing all real power of decision. But this criticism was partially answered when, in the delicate stages of the Korean War, Ottawa was in closer touch with London than with Washington.

Sir Godfrey Huggins of Southern Rhodesia, long experienced in these Commonwealth meetings, was at once the most practical in his approach and the most resilient. The central ambition of his life was to found a British Dominion in Central Africa, and he was willing to be all things to all men to ensure that ambition. This most seasoned and shrewd of politicians had not handled his ebullient Rhodesians for so many years without knowing how far a policy could be pushed. He did not want any of the Asian members of the Commonwealth influencing the British Government too much about African affairs, but neither did he want too much obvious support from the other members. In short, Sir Godfrey wished to avoid his much-desired Dominion in Central Africa becoming a matter of contention inside the Commonwealth, at this delicate stage of his campaign.

Looking back on this 1951 meeting of the Prime Ministers two things stand out clearly: as the whole concept of government which Britain had herself perfected and passed on to all the other members of the Commonwealth was that of parliamentary democracy, in which each government depended on the changing will of an electorate, effective unity between the members depended on the strength of individual governments in their own countries, and on the degree of tacit understanding they had with their political opponents on Commonwealth policy. Britain, Canada, Australia and New Zealand could probably reach agreements which would be continued after a change of government. That hardly was the case with the other members.

And secondly, there was evident from this time on a racial stress inside the Commonwealth which was apt to influence all relationships. Britain, above all, worked constantly to discount this stress, and to implant the notion that the racial differences were actually a source of strength, as in the Commonwealth they could be brought into the open instead of simmering dangerously under the surface.

One matter in which the Commonwealth Prime Ministers could take great and legitimate pride was the evolution of the Colombo Plan. The Commonwealth Consultative Committee had surveyed the whole vast area of South and South-East Asia, where 570 million people (a quarter of the world's population) lived, and had finally produced a plan for development spread over six years, at an estimated cost of £1,868 millions. This plan, which appeared just before the meeting of the Prime Ministers, was prefaced by the solemn warning that on its success depended "the political stability not only of the region of South and South-East Asia but of the world".

More than two-thirds of the estimated cost of the plan was for India, and Britain immediately announced that her own contribution, including the repayment of sterling balances, might well amount to well over £300 million, or one-sixth of the whole. The technical co-operation scheme was to be assisted over a three-year period by a sum of £2,800,000 and by the provision of trained men. But as Lord Milverton, one of Britain's greatest Colonial administrators and a former Governor of Nigeria, pointed out in the journal *New Commonwealth*,[1] the development of South-East Asia still depended on "the restoration of Japan's industrial capacity, peace in India and in Pakistan, and settlement in Indonesia". Even more, the eventual support of the United States, the only country in the world with a large amount of capital to invest, was quite essential.

The Commonwealth was without question the one association through which such a concept as the Colombo Plan could be organized in South-East and South Asia. The Commonwealth countries concerned had the administrative framework to hand, they had the foundations of stability, they had the habit of co-operation, and they

[1] November 1950.

were either independent or on the road to independence. Moreover, they had in the single person of Mr Nehru the greatest asset of all. His blessing on the Plan ensured its respectability in Asian eyes. And to cap it all, the Plan had been devised to emphasize self-help and to remove the suspicions attached to foreign aid.

Even at a cautious assessment the value of the Commonwealth in the East was strikingly clear. That was all the more emphasized by the comparative failure of the United States policy in the region. A fortune in money had been poured out, only for everything to end in the loss of China and the running wound of the Korean War, plus the embarrassing acquisition of as discredited a handful of allies as could be found in all Asia—Chiang Kai-shek himself, Dr Syngman Rhee in South Korea and Pibul Songgram in Siam.

The chief hopes of the Americans were pinned on Japan, the bestial and discredited foe of only six years before, to whom sovereignty was restored by the Treaty of San Francisco in September of 1951. During the seven years of the American occupation the Japanese had humbly and dutifully submitted to "democratization". But as soon as the Treaty was signed, the discredited politicians filtered back, the commercial cartels re-emerged, the militarists gathered strength. To the Americans the Japanese were to be the bulwark against communism. But at the best they were uncertain and ambiguous allies, and to the rest of Asia they were still suspect, if not despised.

It was, remarkably enough, not the Japanese but Pandit Nehru who was unreliable, unrealistic and untrustworthy in American eyes. To the State Department he was not the man on whom all liberal hopes depended, but the blind egoist who was leading non-communist Asia into a trap. The Americans were fortified in their estimation of the situation when Tibet was annexed by Communist China towards the end of 1951. Under the British, for nearly forty years, Tibet's autonomy had been carefully preserved. The independent Himalayan states such as Tibet, Afghanistan, Nepal had long been designed as buffers to protect the northern frontier. Now, the Chinese action forced a reluctant India to return to this old "imperialistic" policy. But it did not seriously change Mr Nehru's pacifist outlook. Indeed, Indians argued that Tibet actually proved Mr Nehru's view that aggressive American policies in Asia provoked equally aggressive retorts from the Chinese.

What became increasingly clear was that the Commonwealth had a powerful influence in both camps, in that led by Mr Nehru which believed that communism could be peacefully contained, and in that dominated by the Americans, who believed that only armed strength could resist it. Through the Commonwealth links, each camp was at least in touch with the other, which was a more powerful gain to the democratic world than seemed apparent in these early, confusing years of the renaissance of Asia.

CHAPTER XX

EXPERIMENT IN AFRICA

CLEMENT ATTLEE, IN a short six years, had ended an era in Asia by bringing independence to India, Pakistan, Burma and Ceylon. He seemed now to be beginning the same process in Africa. The decision to implement the major proposals of the Coussey Report in the Gold Coast meant that the Colony would be brought to the verge of self-government following the elections in February of 1951.

Is it exaggeration to compare what was happening in the small West African territory of the Gold Coast, with its area of merely 90 thousand square miles and population of under four million, with the great sweep of events in the East? It heralded the end of an era of massive European domination quite as surely. In that famous interview with *Die Burger*, Dr Malan had said: "Whatever happens in West Africa must almost inevitably affect all the other Native territories. And if those other territories are now equally successfully going to demand what the Negroes of West Africa have obtained, it will mean nothing less than the expulsion of the white man from virtually all that lies between us and the Sahara. The white man's civilizing work and leadership, which has only recently begun and which for generations to come will remain indispensable, is then at an end."

Making full allowance for the Doctor's obvious wish to harden opinion among Europeans (particularly in South Africa) in favour of his own "white supremacy" policies, it remains true that the advance of the Gold Coast was to fire African ambitions all over the continent. In later years, the African politicians of multi-racial territories in East and Central Africa were increasingly unwilling to settle for anything less than what the Gold Coast had been granted.

On the surface, the long-awaited election in the Gold Coast seemed to bear out Dr Malan's gloomy prophecy of "an idealism which must end in tragedy because it refused to recognize the facts". The spectacle of illiterate people having to be carefully schooled in what they were doing, voting for a blue fish or a brown elephant symbol because only thus could the parties be identified for them, was most certainly startling when compared to the sophisticated electorates of Europe. But without doubt, many of those who most heavily criticized the election would have thought it an imaginative exercise in the democratic function had the Gold Coasters rejected Nkrumah. But, as had seemed inevitable for some time past, Nkrumah and his supporters triumphed, though the victory was not nearly so decisive as they had hoped. The final result showed that out of 84 Elected Members of the new Legislative Assembly, 48 were either members of Nkrumah's Convention People's Party or ready to support it.

Nkrumah and several of his lieutenants were still in prison, but this was by no means as embarrassing a situation for Britain as some of her more malicious critics imagined. The Governor, Sir Charles Arden-Clarke, took a handsome share of Nkrumah's popularity by releasing the C.P.P. leader and his comrades as an "act of grace". There were no strings attached to the action, and Nkrumah was invited to Christiansburg Castle and invited to form a government. He could hardly reject such magnanimity. Nor did he want to. Like Cecil Rhodes, he needed time. Dr Nkrumah was well aware that after the accession to power comes a real time of proving, and that what talent he had in the ranks of his party was quite unproven in the hard art of government.

The scene when the Doctor was released from James Fort seemed so in keeping with the whole bewildering sweep of events as to be virtually symbolic. For a huge crowd of Africans bore their leader to a local arena and there slaughtered a sheep to propitiate and thank the gods of their fathers. Then the hymn "Lead, Kindly Light" closed the proceedings. The hero of the hour, with his acute sense of occasion, said little. No words, indeed, could have improved on the classical perfection of Nkrumah's personal drama as it had unfolded in the past twelve colourful months. The "liberator" had come into his own.

At the opening of the first session of the new Legislative Assembly the Governor brought down the emotional temperature by stressing that new Members would now begin to carry the heavy burden of responsibility for the welfare of the people. "This is the test," warned Sir Charles, "and here the world will expect to see the quality of the people's representatives displayed." He went on to point out that "the future of territories outside these boundaries will be influenced by the evidence which this House gives of its capacity to discharge its duties in a manner which commands respect".

Whatever his more impatient followers thought, Kwame Nkrumah knew that the Governor's words were most carefully chosen. Nkrumah needed not only time but yet more decisive support from his own people. He let it be known that though his party still believed in "self-government now" it would give the new Constitution a trial, though opposition to it previously had been the very thing which put Nkrumah and his lieutenants behind bars. He had good reason to consider that enough was enough.

Dr Malan was not alone in criticizing the British policy in the Gold Coast. Sir Godfrey Huggins improved the occasion with a little homily on the "shocks from the Colonial Office in the past few years". He went on to say: "I think the speed at which they have gone is absolutely disastrous. Not only are they hurting Africans in the territories they look after, but they are creating a threat to Southern Rhodesia. I have reason to believe that they have seen the red light now, but whether it is too late I cannot say. The political pace has been so fast with these primitive people that it would be extremely difficult for them to put the brake on now, and if they cannot there will be absolute chaos."

Sir Godfrey was certainly not seconding Dr Malan's views. Indeed at this very time he was launching a scheme to induce more Britons to emigrate to Southern Rhodesia to offset the influx of South Africans. Such speeches as this were made with the intention of underlining what the Rhodesians considered the folly and injustice of allowing illiterate West Africans to leap forward to self-government whilst holding back the advanced Europeans of Central Africa. And the prospects of those Europeans hung on the outcome of the London talks on closer union in Central Africa.

To this day there are recriminations about the direction taken in the London talks, allegations that the officials concerned overstepped their brief in making outright recommendations. For the Report on Closer Association bluntly said that such association between the two

K

Rhodesias and Nyasaland was not only desirable but that the need for it was urgent. A Federation in Central Africa was recommended and even the actual Constitution was outlined. It was true that the safeguarding of African interests was kept well in the picture with the proposals that there should be a Minister for African Interests and an African Affairs Board, plus nine Members in the Legislature to represent Africans, four of them of that race. But there was no denying that the Report was an outcome which was hard to equivocate with the earlier announcement that the Conference would be purely exploratory.

The Secretary of State for the Colonies, James Griffiths, now realized the ambiguous position into which he had fallen. He temporized with a declaration in the House of Commons that "None of the Governments—including the British—are committed at this stage." But it was clearly difficult for the British Government to draw back now that the Conference they themselves had approved had produced (albeit unasked) a positive scheme for Federation. The reaction of African leaders inside and outside of Central Africa is the best indication as to whether the Report committed no one. Almost to a man they condemned it. Kwame Nkrumah himself declared that Central Africa would now inevitably become "a second South Africa".

In truth, it would be difficult to recall any report that more directly and decisively bore on the central principle of the whole Commonwealth. In its text, directed though it was at a Central African problem, it underlined the racial stresses of the Commonwealth and in its proposals attempted to solve them. The Socialist Government of Britain clearly realized this, and they can hardly be criticized for postponing comment on the Closer Association Report, let alone action. Finally, James Griffiths announced that he and the Secretary of State for Commonwealth Relations, Patrick Gordon Walker, would visit Central Africa to hold a conference with the territorial governments.

That conference finally took place at Victoria Falls, and was quite definitely a failure. The African delegates from Northern Rhodesia and Nyasaland were utterly opposed to federation and Griffiths himself was only too aware that without any hint of African support he could never—even if he so wished—get the project backed by his own government. The end result was bitterness on all sides and a decision by the Secretary of State for the Colonies that it was best to put off further talks for nine months.

In the event, what James Griffiths decided was of no account. As the talks drew to an end, Mr Attlee announced in London that he intended to stage another general election in October. His government's position had steadily grown more untenable. His heavily-burdened ministers were weary and his opponents, smelling power in the air after their long sojourn in the arid wilderness of opposition, had had enough of compromise and were ready to try their fortune at the polls again.

Britain had stood for some months past in desperate need of a strong and vigorous government, and above all one which commanded a large enough majority for decisive leadership. The Korean War, the stresses in Africa, the continuing anxieties in the Far East—all these menacing developments were made so much the worse by the existence of a British Government which could not govern.

It was at this very time of uncertainty and indecision that two of Britain's friends were murdered and the long-threatened eruption in the Middle East came. In the March the Persian Prime Minister Razmara, who had resolutely opposed the nationalization of his country's great oil industry, was assassinated. Hussein Ali, his successor, quickly put through the Persian Parliament the legislation blocked by Razmara and the stage was set for an outburst of nationalism which from the very beginning threatened disaster to Persia and severe hurt to Britain. Moussadek, who succeeded Hussein Ali as Prime Minister, cast himself for the key rôle. He seized all the properties of the Anglo-Iranian Oil Company, including the huge refinery at Abadan.

This wild and ill-considered action by the tragi-comic Moussadek proved calamitous to both Britain and Persia and in the end to the Persian Prime Minister himself. The Persians soon discovered what should have been apparent to them all along, and that was that they lacked technical experts and tankers, and had destroyed confidence in their own reputation. But there were deeper lessons, and for the West particularly, in this episode. Firstly, it demonstrated what had been too often laughed down—the furious, if blind, strength of nationalism in the Middle East. Secondly, it exposed the dangerously heavy dependence of the British on the oil regions of that area. Thirdly, it revealed that the great oil companies had, in the main, failed to realize that their position of strength had been gradually eroded, that "partner" and not "benefactor" was their only safe rôle in the turbulent world of "Arabism". Above all else, Abadan exposed the frightening gap between American and British policies—no, even worse, the lack of a coherent policy on either side.

The second disaster for Britain was the murder in Jerusalem in July of her trusted and resolute ally, King Abdullah of Jordan. He had long dreamt of a new Arab kingdom of Jordan, Syria and Iraq. If ever that had materialized it would have stabilized the whole of the Middle East and banished the spectre of communist infiltration. Abdullah's British-trained Arab Legion had been a decisive instrument in the Middle East for years past. Small and poor though Jordan was, the Legion and Abdullah together had given it great influence and respect in the Arab world. Whether the Legion alone could maintain the position was now to be proved.

There was a great coming and going, a flurry of diplomatic activity in the Middle East during the rest of 1951. Britain, France, America and Turkey made an abortive attempt to form a Middle East Defence Organization, inviting Middle East countries to join. It was proposed that the Suez Canal should cease to be a British base and should become the responsibility of the suggested organization. At this point, Russia took a direct hand in the game and warned any Arab state against joining under pain of losing Soviet friendship. No such warning was needed by Egypt and Syria. They had no intention of joining the proposed organization. On the contrary, their joint ambition was to see the influence of the West ended for ever in the Middle East. So deep was their hostility that they preferred to play in with Russia to some degree, dangerous though they knew that could be.

From this time on the Russian influence on Middle East affairs mounted steadily, and Egypt and Syria proved to be her most useful instruments. Egypt indeed immediately adopted a challenging attitude to Britain. In the Throne Speech, the evacuation of the British forces from the Suez Canal Zone was demanded, along with "Unity of the Nile Valley", which meant Egyptian overlordship of the Anglo-Egyptian Sudan. King Farouk cancelled the agreements under which Egypt and Britain together controlled the Sudan and actually had his title changed to "King of Egypt and the Sudan". This proved offensive in the extreme to the powerful Umma Party in the Sudan, whose aim was independence, but there was a great deal more support for union with Egypt than the British authorities cared to admit.

It was not so much that King Farouk was paying back old humiliations, or cherishing dreams of grandeur. Effete and indolent though he was, surrounded by venal advisers, he was yet aware of the rising flood of fiery nationalism among the younger, educated Egyptians, the embryo "middle class" which provided many of the officers in the army. He well knew he could not afford to be too far behind this new element in Egyptian life.

One can look back now and see how the Western world, so long accustomed to the dynastic schisms, the reactionary religious sects and the general poverty and inefficiency of the Middle East, had grossly underestimated the "Arabism" of the younger generation, that intense feeling that the Arab world had once been mighty in arms and in spirit, and that for too long it had been the despised vassal of the Europeans. Here were the makings of a 20th-century *jehad* for a political Mohammed, if he could be found.

How depressing to reflect that Britain, almost as much as any of the powers, missed the real significance of all that was happening in this great and historic area between the shores of the Mediterranean and the Persian Gulf. Despite her long and intimate knowledge of the Arab world and the real regard she had once commanded, despite the warnings from the few people such as Glubb Pasha, of the Arab Legion, who sensed what was going on, Britain suffered a diplomatic defeat of disastrous proportions. She had not been quite so thoroughly discomfited as the Americans in the Far East, but there was a distressing similarity in some aspects of the situation, not least in the fact that most of her protégés were uneasy monarchs or the representatives of the privileged classes.

To cap a year of rude shocks, the Greek Government made an official claim for the union of Cyprus with Greece. At once a jubilant Archbishop Makarios cabled Mr Sophocles Venizelos, the Prime Minister of Greece, his ardent hope that *enosis* would be achieved before 1951 was out. The Turkish Cypriot leaders immediately sent messages of protest to Britain, to the U.S.A. and to Turkey and repeated their unchanging desire to live under the British Crown. From this point on Cyprus, Britain's "aircraft carrier" off the Middle East, presented an increasingly intractable problem, and its future was to be one of blood and bitterness. Throughout the Middle East and its environs, for so long stabilized by Britain, and still a vital region to her and to the Commonwealth, there was intrigue and confusion, with every prospect of far worse days to come.

CHAPTER XXI

THE RETURN OF CHURCHILL

ON OCTOBER 25 of 1951 the six-year run of the Labour Government in Britain came to an end. Attlee was beaten in a bitterly-fought election and Winston Churchill and his Conservatives jubilantly came into office with a meagre but workable majority of twenty-six.

They had long waited their return to power. The great name of Churchill himself, the undoubted talent of his ministerial team, the fresh and eager energy of the Party itself, all these were important assets. But they could not miraculously remove the hard facts of Britain's economic plight. The payments crisis was as grave as it had been in the days of Dr Dalton in 1947. The sterling debts had reached the appalling total of £4,168 million. The dollar gap in the quarter preceding the election was 638 million dollars, and the Sterling Area reserves were down to 3,269 million dollars.

The hard fact was that the Sterling Area continued to live dangerously. If it were to survive at all, let alone play its real and most vitally important part in the world's affairs, the new government must sooner or later force Britain, and the rest of the Commonwealth, to live within their means. Events were to prove that whilst they were determined enough to halt the tide of nationalization, they were not, at the outset, very much more determined than the Socialists to curb the rapidly rising expense of running the Welfare State.

And it was not altogether true that the name of Churchill was like a rallying cry to the whole of the Commonwealth and Empire. Certainly his return to power was enthusiastically greeted by the "European" Dominions (though with some private reservations by the Government of Canada). Mr Nehru's India did not feel for Mr Churchill the same warmth as they did for Mr Attlee, and most of the Colonies believed that the pace of progress towards self-government was certain to slow down.

The British Prime Minister's choice of the men to handle Commonwealth and Colonial affairs seemed to confirm such doubts. Oliver Lyttelton was appointed as Secretary of State for the Colonies, and General Lord Ismay as Secretary of State for Commonwealth Relations. Lyttelton's reputation was that of a tough, indomitable and courageous man, an unrepentant Tory who delighted in a fight. He was an old Etonian, with a fine record as a soldier in the First World War. In the Second World War he had been a close colleague of Churchill, having been President of the Board of Trade, Minister of Production, Minister of State and a member of the War Cabinet. No man could have presented a more direct contrast to his predecessors, Creech Jones and Griffiths. To nationalist leaders in the Colonies, his accession to office seemed a straight warning that toughness would replace conciliation.

Lord Ismay's appointment seemed even more surprising. He, too, had been one of Churchill's wartime team, Chief of Staff of the Minister of Defence, and Additional Secretary (Military) to the Cabinet. After the war he had served as Chief of Staff to the Viceroy of India. He was undoubtedly a quite outstanding military administrator, and it was reasonably enough assumed that his appointment foreshadowed an emphasis on Commonwealth defence from Churchill and his government.

Another intriguing but not unexpected appointment was that of Mr Alan Lennox-Boyd as the Minister of State for Colonial Affairs. This genial and approachable giant of a man had one thing in common with Arthur Creech Jones, he was a dedicated man as far as Colonial affairs went. Michael Foot, the Socialist M.P. and writer, once said that Lennox-Boyd was "a real Tory, without prefix or suffix, qualification or mitigation". His background bore out that judgement. Lennox-Boyd was another public-school man, and a former President of the Union at Oxford. He had held minor posts in the Government just prior to and during the war, though he also spent two years in the Navy as a motor-torpedo-boat captain. During the years of Socialist Government he had been one of the Opposition's spokesmen on Colonial affairs, and had revealed an extraordinary knowledge of even the most complicated matters. Lennox-Boyd was one of Churchill's brightest young men and he was later to make a most considerable mark in his chosen field.

The Conservatives had already put on record their conviction that all the members of the Commonwealth "must stand together and help each other with all our strength both in defence and trade". But their Commonwealth and Colonial policies could not, in the nature of things, differ very markedly from those of the Socialists. They could not, any more than their predecessors, influence the other members of the Commonwealth to the same degree as before the war; nor could they halt the irresistible sweep of nationalism, the onward march towards independence in the Colonies. But there were, inherent in the Conservative approach, very real differences of emphasis and timing, and these were to become significant within a short space of time.

The older Conservatives, taking stock of the Commonwealth and Empire after six post-war years, saw changes which, in 1939, would not have appeared possible for at least half-a-century. On the economic side, Imperial Preference, which had been the great trading link, had lost much of its value. Britain could no longer act as the all-powerful provider of finance for development. Nor could she exercise anything like the former influence on the economic policies of her partners, a circumstance which was soon to have near-disastrous consequences.

On the political side, the Commonwealth was already in the process of dividing into states which paid allegiance to the Crown, and others which merely recognized it as a symbol of unity. There were now immeasurably more coloured people inside the Commonwealth than there were white, a factor which was to become steadily more significant as time went on. Already that factor had operated powerfully on the concept of Commonwealth defence. Mr Nehru was busily shaping his policy of non-alignment and neutralism. That was not altogether new to the Commonwealth; South Africa and Canada always had powerful elements who were eternally suspicious of being drawn into "British adventures". But Nehru's concept of neutralism was not a negative protest; it was a positive and dynamic policy which, as it developed, always conditioned the co-operative approach of the other members, and which could never be left out of account.

This then was the Commonwealth to which the Conservatives returned—one much more loosely linked, less coherent in its policies, and yet at the same time, in the very breadth of its interests, in the multiplicity of its viewpoints, in the extraordinary diversity of its membership, of more potential value to the world than ever. It remained the one real instrument that democracy could use against the international organization of communism.

The Commonwealth *was* the democratic answer to the Cominform. There was no other. And the Conservatives were to make, as the Socialists had done before them, the distressing discovery that this was still apparently unrecognized by the Americans, whose power and wealth made them the titular leaders of the democratic world. Here was the heralded successor to Britain, in the uniquely fortunate position of having a world-wide organization dedicated to the same principles as herself, and yet ignoring the potentialities of that organization and sometimes actively undermining it.

It was strongly felt by the Conservatives that political advance in the Colonial territories had been pushed on at a rate which invited trouble. Countries which they considered had neither the economic framework nor the means to govern efficiently were clamouring for independence. But the Gold Coast had now set the pace and would it not be more dangerous to deny it to the others than to grant it to them? What the Conservative leaders had yet to fully appreciate was that Britain could no longer wholly dictate events. It had now become more a matter of anticipating and guiding them.

The assumption that Colonial political parties were like wilful children who must feel that a firm hand would be kept on them only served to exacerbate the position. Some years later, the *Ceylon Observer*[1] was to make this famous comment, which did represent the opinion of most Colonial leaders: "How does it happen that colonial nations even after 150 years of beneficent (and 'temporary') economic development and training in the arts of civilization cannot afford their independence? . . . who delegated to Britain the divine right to judge whether a country can afford its independence or whether it has an adequate sense of 'nationhood' or not?"

Britain could answer that this was the present and not the past, that the world was a much more dangerous and complicated place than ever before and that to abandon her responsibilities before they were discharged would clearly benefit no one. But the uncomfortable truth remained that the criticism of the *Ceylon Observer* represented Colonial reaction fairly enough, and no British Government could afford to ignore that. Even so, the Conservatives were ready to be more cautious about political advancement in the Colonies, whatever the criticisms. This, of course, served to confirm various suspicions in the Colonies that they were pro-European, but the truth was that the new British Government was deeply alarmed that the rush of events was allowing no time in which to man up a satisfactory local civil service, or the semblance of opposition parties to develop. To promote the emergence of one-party states with inefficient, subservient and potentially corrupt civil services seemed to be

[1] July 1, 1957.

the best possible service to communism and an abdication of responsibility to the democratic world.

Oliver Lyttelton, as soon as he took over the Colonial Office, put two matters at the very top of his list of priorities. The first was the continuing emergency in Malaya, and the second was the suggested federation in Central Africa. Communist guerrillas had ambushed and murdered the High Commissioner for Malaya, Sir Henry Gurney, just before Lyttelton came to office. The audacity and ruthlessness of the murder had sorely struck British prestige, and in Lyttelton's view the war against the terrorists must be pursued with equal audacity and vigour, no matter what the cost. He announced that in November he would fly out to Malaya to form his opinion on the spot.

As for Central Africa, the new Secretary of State held strongly to the view that Africa and the Commonwealth needed a large-scale experiment in multi-racial co-operation, and the proposed Federation of the Rhodesias and Nyasaland offered the perfect opportunity for such an experiment. Before he left for Malaya he announced to the House of Commons that the new Government intended to press forward with the federation project on the lines laid down in the Closer Association Report, and in full agreement with the results of the Victoria Falls Conference. There would be a Conference in London in July to carry the matter forward, he said.

Lyttelton told the press that the Government considered that there was an urgent need for "a new British bloc" in Central Africa, and that this was regarded as "a great issue of imperial policy". That it most certainly was, for it went to the very heart of the modern conception of a multi-racial Commonwealth. Unhappily, this proposed experiment in Central Africa at once became a source of bitter contention. Most African leaders in all three territories exhibited a mounting resistance to the idea, and so, too, did a majority of Socialists in Britain. Lyttelton exacerbated feelings still further—though he could hardly avoid doing so now no matter what he did—when he announced that he would have preliminary discussions in London, with the Governors of Northern Rhodesia and Nyasaland and with Sir Godfrey Huggins, in January, six months before the proposed Conference. His critics argued that this was once more to shut out African opinion, although as the Governors were supposed to be the guardians of the people in their territories it was hard to follow the argument. But a great ideal, through fear and mishandling, was already becoming the subject of the first post-war split of real significance in Colonial policy.

In his approach to the problems of Malaya and Central Africa Oliver Lyttelton demonstrated his greatest gift, an ability to go to the heart of a complicated subject, to arrive at a decision based on an objective analysis of the evidence before him and to implement that decision resolutely and even ruthlessly if necessary. It was a gift peculiar to a prince of industry, and as it happened it was what was undoubtedly needed in the handling of Colonial affairs at this point of time. In the latter stages of its term of office, the Labour Government had sometimes shown a disturbing tendency to procrastinate, to temporize and to indulge in dangerous compromise rather than to court unpopularity. The jibe that they had failed to follow the "Socialist ideal" in the Colonies inhibited their actions. Decision and determination—these were now sorely needed, and Lyttelton was more than ready to demonstrate them. In the latter stages of his term, they began to lose their importance. The recognition of the hard facts of a case, the objective analysis, were not enough in the face of passionate nationalism and racialism, when emotions swamped logic.

It was not so much that Lyttelton did not clearly recognize the need for coming to terms with this racialism, but that its illogicality affronted his intelligence. There were, indeed, two extraordinary incidents, whose repercussions were still exercising the diplomacy of the British Government, which dramatically emphasized the treacherous quicksands of racialism. The first concerned a thirteen-year-old Dutch girl, Bertha Hertogh, a tragic victim of the war in the Far East. Separated from her parents during the Japanese advance, she had been brought up by a Muslim woman, and had married a Malay schoolteacher. When the fact that this child bride was a European became known, the Netherlands Government sought to have the marriage annulled, and her parents naturally claimed her. The Muslims of Singapore took the side of the bridegroom and an explosive mixture of racial and religious hatred led to major riots and world-wide publicity. An unfortunate impression arose that Britain had interfered on the grounds of European superiority, and her prestige suffered accordingly. The girl finally returned to the Netherlands, but the damage was done, and exploited in "anti-colonial" quarters.

Then there was the marriage of the Chief-Designate of the Bamangwato tribe in Bechuanaland, Seretse Khama, to a British girl, Ruth Williams. This finally led to the suspension of Seretse as Chief-Designate on the grounds that his marriage had offended tribal custom and would lead to inevitable trouble. The end result was that Seretse, not only in Africa but in many other parts of the Commonwealth, was given the status of a martyr who was suffering from Britain's obsequious desire not to offend South African racial prejudice. On the other hand, in white reactionary circles, the Seretse affair was regarded as one more instance of the folly of British "liberalism" in dealing with subject peoples.

Those were two incidents which in times past would have occupied the attention of the more popular newspapers on the grounds of "human interest". But in the new Commonwealth they became diplomatic problems of the first magnitude, causing the greatest anxiety not only to the Socialist Government of Britain, but to its successor. To millions of coloured people, the outcome of both the Hertogh and the Seretse Khama cases cast grave doubts on Britain's claim that the Commonwealth was based on the ideal of racial equality.

This reaction was one which had now increasingly to be borne in mind in the forming of Colonial policy. It was not only a problem of the haves and the have-nots, not even a straightforward problem of nationalism or racism. It was the deep and passionate emotion rising in hundreds of millions of "colonial" or "ex-colonial" people to stand up like men in their own right, to shape their own futures, to have done with the wars and diplomatic entanglements of those nations who had been their masters. This promised to be the most powerful force of the second half of the 20th century. And its most threatening aspect was that it could be so easily perverted to aid the expansion of the new communist imperialism.

As the greatest imperial power in the free world, Britain, despite the logic and sincerity of her policy, was especially exposed to the threat. Her Colonial Empire, so far-spread, so diverse as to race and religion and standard of culture, presented a bewildering complexity of problems. And so Oliver Lyttelton must have thought as he surveyed the Colonial "balance sheet" at this turn of the half-century.

The West African Colony of the Gold Coast was leading the way to negro independence, followed by its giant neighbour, Nigeria. In East Africa, the idea of federating the three territories of Kenya, Uganda and Tanganyika grew less and less realistic, and there was the complication of racial suspicion hardening into animosity. Though Lyttelton was determined to launch his "experiment in multi-racialism" in the Central African territories of Northern and Southern Rhodesia and Nyasaland, it was only too clear that it faced a stormy passage.

The shadow of communism hung darkly over the Far Eastern territories of Malaya, Singapore, Hong Kong and—to a lesser degree —North Borneo, Sarawak and Brunei. Lyttelton's immediate announcement of his journey to Malaya underlined his fear that if the communists could not be stopped there, it would only be a matter of time before they triumphed in the other adjacent territories.

At least there was peace in the Caribbean, though the proposal for a West Indian Federation was beset with suspicion and jealousy. And in the two mainland Colonies of British Guiana and British Honduras there was alarming evidence of communism or near-communism gaining an increasing hold on the ordinary people.

The remote islands of the South Pacific were well back on the road of progress, but there was a promise of an eventual closer union in the South Pacific Commission and Conference. Wherever possible, Britain was moving her Colonies on towards self-government and attempting at the same time to federate the smaller groups of territories where that was practicable. But there still remained the "island outposts" or "fortress colonies" and those smaller territories which could not by any means ever stand on their own feet. They had come into British possession during the long centuries of military and commercial expansion, meeting a strategic or trading necessity. There were many of them, such as the Gambia, Gibraltar, Malta, the Falkland Islands, Zanzibar, St Helena, Tristan da Cunha. The future of such small units and their eventual status in the Commonwealth still presented a subject for argument, but they were being steadily advanced to the point where their peoples would handle as great a part of their affairs as possible.

It could be said that all the Colonial territories had now only one thing in common—that they were held by Britain in trusteeship, not as imperial possessions. In six years, under a Socialist Government, Britain had gone far and fast towards discharging her trust. Now it was the turn of the Conservatives.

CHAPTER XXII

HOPE IN THE EAST

SHORTLY AFTER HIS return from Malaya, in January of 1952, Lyttelton appointed one of Britain's most distinguished and vigorous soldiers, General Sir Gerald Templer, as High Commissioner and Director of Operations. The Secretary of State had found the situation to be even more grave than he had anticipated, and his view was that only an over-all direction of civil and military effort, backed by a reorganized police force and a country-wide Home Guard force, would turn the tide.

But he had no intention of allowing Britain to be bogged down as the French were in Indo-China. There, despite the military successes of the brilliant General de Lattre de Tassigny, there was little local enthusiasm for the French cause. In Malaya, Lyttelton intended that the prospect of independence would be kept before the people, and that they should be brought to feel that the war was against their enemies, not only those of the British.

Templer was not long in demonstrating that he intended to fight as ruthlessly as the Communists. Those villages which withheld information, or abetted the terrorists through fear, felt the weight of his wrath. Curfew was introduced for offending communities, and the strict rationing of rice. The European community, on the other hand, were warned that they could not afford to isolate themselves in a world of their own, that they must crusade against racial discrimination and show themselves partners of the other peoples in the country. Officialdom felt the biting lash of Templer's tongue. The new High Commissioner toured the country at high speed, a dynamic and purposeful figure, brooking no excuse and no failure, visiting mines, plantations, villages, police stations, army bivouacs, government offices. They had asked for resolute leadership in Malaya, and now they were getting it. The General trod on many toes in those early days, but it could not be denied that his methods brought results. The information began to drift in, the whispered word, the anonymous note, the telephone message from the unknown. That was the decisive time. The ordinary people were beginning to back the government.

By the middle of the year, Templer was able to pay a flying visit to London to report that the number of terrorists killed each month had risen very steeply, that casualties among the security forces had dropped equally steeply. Surrenders were increasing and the terrorist attacks were quite definitely not being conducted with the old savagery and determination. Above all else, there was a new spirit of unity among the different races in combating the terrorists. Growing numbers of Chinese were joining the hitherto all-Malay police force. Not only was there a rising feeling that this war was a threat to all, there was the dawning recognition among its many races that Malaya was a prize worth fighting for.

Throughout the East, as the year drew on, the Commonwealth position at least offered some comfort. The Conference which met in Karachi to discuss the first few months' operations of the Colombo Plan heard a heartening report. No changes in the direction of the project were needed, and even at so early a stage it was proving a model for co-operation between the advanced and under-developed countries. The lack of skilled or even semi-skilled workers to "spark off" development in such countries was a major problem, and from then on the provision of technical aid assumed a steadily-growing importance in the Plan.

The death, early in the year, of D. S. Senanayake, the Prime Minister of Ceylon, was a saddening blow, but his successor was a man of equal moderation and tolerance. This was his son, the deeply-religious Dudley Senanayake, who was regarded in Ceylon with almost as much trust and affection as the father. The new Prime Minister immediately asked the electorate for a fresh mandate and won 54 of the 95 elected seats in the House of Representatives. This was a decisive setback for the Sri Lanka Freedom Party (which stood for a complete break with Britain and the Commonwealth) and also for the Trotskyist Party and the Labour Party, which had been advocating extensive "Ceylonization". Ceylon's strategic importance to the Commonwealth, and the mutually beneficial trading links with Britain, would obviously be maintained, at least as long as the younger Senanayake was in power.

India's ties with Britain and the Commonwealth grew stronger as time went on. In the April of 1952, the Governor of West Bengal, Dr Harendra Coomar Mookerjee, said in Calcutta that "The United Kingdom itself has given a lead which may in time be the foundation of the dream of one world. This is the Commonwealth, of which India is a member." The Doctor was certainly echoing a growing appreciation in India of the value of the Commonwealth. It was a remarkable fact that, five years after independence, there were more Britons in India than ever before (excluding, of course, the armed forces).

Though Pakistan had not got over her disappointment that the Commonwealth could not prise Kashmir from India, her strong sympathies with Britain were not seriously affected. The fears and suspicions inside the country which followed the assassination of Liaquat Ali Khan and the arrest of a group of high Army officers for allegedly plotting a communist coup, still persisted, but there was a growing feeling that once Pakistan could stabilize herself internally, she had a great chance to lead the Muslim world.

The self-appointed claimant to that leadership, King Farouk of Egypt, had suddenly been toppled from his throne. A group of army officers, under the nominal leadership of General Neguib, staged a lightning coup against the discredited monarchy and corrupt court. For a time, it seemed that a fresh, clean wind would blow through the Middle East. But the men behind Neguib were fanatical nationalists, and the chief of them, Colonel Nasser, cherished vaulting and dangerous ambitions which were yet to be revealed. Neguib, a man of seeming moderation, was half-Sudanese and at the outset of the Egyptian revolutionary regime there were signs of there being a new harmony of approach by Britain and Egypt to the vexed problems of "Nile Valley unity" and the Suez Canal.

Despite the clamour raised by King Farouk Britain had not deviated in any way from her policy for the Sudan. If the Egyptians refused to play their part in its development, that was no reason to halt progress. During 1952 a new constitution had been devised which assured the Sudan of self-government and a Sudanese Cabinet. The Umma Party, which stood for complete Sudanese independence, immediately laid its campaign plans. The Ashigga Party, which stood for union with Egypt, refused to recognize the plan for the new constitution and sulked the time away. General Neguib and his colleagues, however, had no desire to lose all the initiative, and they persuaded leaders of the major Sudanese political parties to come to an agreement which would enable the self-government statute to be proclaimed with the approval of Egypt as well as Britain. The revolutionary leaders did not wish to be accused of blocking the Sudan's road to freedom.

Shortly after, Egypt and the Sudan reached agreement on the use

The Queen and her Prime Ministers in London in 1956. (*Left to right*) Mr. Strijdom (South Africa), Mr. Mohammad Ali (Pakistan), Mr. Holland (New Zealand), Mr. St. Laurent (Canada), Sir Anthony Eden (The United Kingdom), Mr. Menzies (Australia), Mr. Nehru (India), Mr. Bandaranaike (Ceylon), and Sir Godfrey Huggins (Federation of Rhodesia and Nyasaland).

The Secretary of State for the Colonies, Mr. Alan Lennox-Boyd, talking with African coal miners at Enugu in Nigeria.

of the Nile waters, and for the first time in years there was a prospect of genuine friendship and co-operation between Cairo and London. Nothing was more to Britain's advantage than the prospect of a stable, democratic and honest government in Egypt. At one and the same time it would lessen anxiety about the defence of the Suez Canal, powerfully aid stability in the Middle East and dispel fears about the Sudan's future. If the Sudan were to fall under the power of men hostile to Britain, ready to traffic with her enemies, it would present a perpetual threat. For this vast and arid land was a link between Africa and the Middle East. It bordered on Kenya and Uganda, and on British Somaliland, and commanded the Nile waters.

Britain preferred to see a strong and independent Sudan emerging but she had no intention of blocking her union with Egypt, should that be her final wish. It was all the more comforting then, in case this should be the outcome, to see the appearances of an honest and moderate regime in Cairo. Britain was quite ready to see Egypt associated with her in the final emergence of the Sudan to self-government and when Neguib put forward some amendments of his own the elections were postponed until they could be discussed. Indeed, for nearly a year after this the hope of an Anglo-Egyptian friendship persisted. Had it really materialized, the course of history would have been changed, Britain would have retained much of her influence in the Arab world, and Russia would have been deprived of her subsequent power to create unrest in the Middle East. But, all the time, behind Neguib the younger revolutionaries bided their hour.

The breathing space afforded in the Middle East, and particularly in the Nile Valley, could not have come at a more fortunate time. For southwards, in Kenya, the long-prophesied storm broke at last. At first it was called a crime wave, chiefly among the able and ambitious Kikuyu people, who had long complained of "land hunger". In the interval following the retirement of Governor Sir Philip Mitchell, and the arrival of his successor Sir Evelyn Baring, there flared up a menacing outbreak of intimidation and terrorism, linked with a return to witchcraft and the dark practices of an older Africa. The slaughter of cattle on European farms, the disappearance of various Africans, and finally the murder of a Senior Chief, Waruhiu, awoke the Europeans to a realization that they faced crisis.

Mau Mau, that was the name of the terrorist movement, and it

L

was soon to ring through the world. By October, Europeans were being murdered, a state of emergency had been declared in Kenya, and Oliver Lyttelton was explaining to the House of Commons that Mau Mau was anti-Christian and anti-European. He disclosed that there had already been over forty murders and added that he intended to visit Kenya at once. The savagery of the outbreak had shocked even those discerning European settlers who had long warned of trouble with the Kikuyu, but far worse was to come.

During the first week of the emergency, Jomo Kenyatta, that distinguished Kikuyu leader who had attended the Fifth Pan-African Conference with Kwame Nkrumah and other African leaders in Manchester, some years before, was arrested. He was alleged to be the inspiration behind Mau Mau. British troops were rushed out to supplement the police force; European volunteers went on guard and on patrol, and by November over 2,000 African suspects had been convicted by the courts and some 500 were in custody. Astonishingly (in view of what was happening in Malaya) there were already foolish claims in some official quarters that the emergency was well under control. But by November the Unofficial Members of the Legislative Council (representing all races) had charged the Kenya Government with "lack of leadership, failure to co-ordinate their efforts, and subservience to the Colonial Office". And all the time, more and more of the Kikuyu took the unholy oaths of the Mau Mau, the end target of which was the elimination of the white man and all his influence. The perverted, bloody and sacrilegious means used by the Mau Mau were deplored by African leaders elsewhere, and by Asian leaders, too. But the ends they sought were not similarly condemned.

To the South Africans, far down south beyond the Limpopo River, the Kenya tragedy was the inevitable outcome of British "liberalism". Dr Malan and his supporters found a grim satisfaction in so appalling a confirmation of their warnings—for that was how they saw the matter. In this very year the South Africans were celebrating the 300th anniversary of the landing of the first white settlers on the shores of Table Bay from Jan van Riebeck's ship the *Dromedaris*. They were people of Africa, not interlopers, and whatever the great swirl and sweep of events in the outside world they believed that three centuries had taught them how to survive, and that was by maintaining their leadership of the black man. To that end, Dr Malan was determined to force through an Act transferring the

Cape Coloured voters to a separate electoral roll in defiance of his own Supreme Court ruling that it was invalid. The bitterness between white and coloured, between Briton and Afrikaner had never been deeper, and pro-British Natal even talked of seceding from the Union. Dr Malan was implacable. He threatened that he would "place the sovereignty of Parliament beyond any doubt". What he really meant was that no obstacle would be allowed to stand in the way of the implementation of *apartheid*, and that as far as was humanly possible he would ensure the perpetual triumph of Afrikanerdom.

These events in Kenya and South Africa cast into still sharper focus the attempt to establish a Federation in Central Africa based on a partnership between black and white. It is strange how the meaning of events can be perverted to prove utterly different beliefs. The African opponents of the proposed Federation and their supporters in Britain pointed to South Africa as a dreadful example of what would happen if the Federation were established. The white opponents of the project in the Rhodesias indicated that, on the contrary, it would all lead to another Kenya blood-bath. To Lyttelton, the alarming pace of events only fortified him in the belief that the experiment in partnership must be launched as soon as possible.

There were delays he had not foreseen, stemming from the unexpected strength of the opposition to the project, both in Central Africa and in Britain. The January discussions between the Secretary of State, the two Governors and Sir Godfrey Huggins went smoothly enough, and Lyttelton announced that he would now bring forward from July to April the conference "to resume consideration of the scheme for Federation in Central Africa". At once a storm burst around him. He was once more accused of trying to steam-roller the scheme through without making any real effort to gain the support of the Africans.

It could be said that even a grudging agreement on Federation was impossible from that time on. African protest campaigns were matched by church meetings of protest in Britain. The national press in Britain engaged regularly in the argument and Lyttelton himself faced continual criticism in and out of Parliament. Unmoved, he announced that, after the April discussions, another conference would be held in July to produce a final scheme. Only two Africans, from Southern Rhodesia, attended the April meetings. Those from Northern Rhodesia and Nyasaland refused to attend.

Instead they conducted their own anti-Federation campaign in London.

A draft document for a Constitution was produced by the delegates, and the final Conference was postponed until October, which gave time for a last effort to gain African support. The effort was doomed from the start. It was possibly true, as the new Minister of State, Henry Hopkinson (who had succeeded Lennox-Boyd) claimed, that in Northern Rhodesia and Nyasaland "some 90 per cent of the African population know and care nothing about Federation". The 10 per cent who presumably did understand were practically all in opposition, and they carried the bulk of the other 90 per cent with them.

There was still, also, the task of persuading the Europeans of Southern Rhodesia to approve the projected Federation. A referendum was to be held, and they could, if they so wished, turn down the scheme for all time. It was becoming clear now that if the Europeans of the three territories were in favour, the objections of the Africans would be overridden, unless so great a revulsion of feeling occurred in Britain that the Government were forced to abandon their scheme. Yet Lyttelton thought still another effort should be made to carry the Africans with them, and with that in mind he announced yet another postponement of the final Conference until the following January. Sir Godfrey Huggins and Roy Welensky, certain that they could not afford to let slip the chance they had worked so many years for, kept their eyes on what they knew to be the decisive point. They launched an unceasing campaign to muster European support in Central Africa. The major share of the task of persuading the Africans in Nyasaland and Northern Rhodesia they left to the Colonial Office.

Whilst all this turmoil and bitterness grew in the multi-racial territories, there was a refreshing change for the better in West Africa. Scarcely a year after the new and democratic constitution had been introduced into the Gold Coast, Dr Nkrumah, instead of being Leader for Government Business, became the first African Prime Minister in the Commonwealth. This was the reward of restraint and responsibility. Nkrumah and his colleagues had conducted the affairs of their country with a success which surprised their ever-ready detractors. There were formidable tasks ahead, but the determination of the African ministers to enhance the reputation of their country and their race, plus the wisdom and far-sightedness of a

Governor, Sir Charles Arden-Clarke, who was determined that the Gold Coast should lead the way, gave grounds for cautious optimism. So much so that by the end of the year Oliver Lyttelton had promised that he would examine and discuss further proposals leading to Dominion status for the Gold Coast.

In Nigeria too, under the steady hand of Sir John Macpherson, the new Council of Ministers had made a promising start, and the new Constitution—necessarily complicated for so large and diverse a territory—was working reasonably well.

Africa presented, as ever, a seemingly confused picture in the year of 1952. But it was becoming increasingly clear that a large part of the continent's problems stemmed from the clash of human aspirations and fears. No matter how shrewdly constitutions were devised or development plans conceived, their value hung on the human factor.

CHAPTER XXIII

WANTED: A PLAN

ON FEBRUARY 6 of 1952, King George the Sixth died in his sleep. He was a man of quiet and simple tastes, not personally drawn to the blaze and clamour of the world of action and great events into which a strange destiny had impelled him. By the very integrity and sincerity of his character he had won the respect and admiration of many in the Commonwealth to whom his exalted position was an anachronism, almost an affront. It was a strange coincidence that the King and his Socialist Prime Minister, Clement Attlee, who had together seen such rapid and great changes in the Commonwealth and Empire, should have exhibited similar qualities of character, not spectacular, but deep and admirably suited to the times of stress and challenge.

The Heir to the Throne, Princess Elizabeth, was far away in Kenya on one of the Commonwealth tours on which the late King had rightly placed high importance. Deeply and sincerely though the King was mourned, the accession of his young daughter in such moving and remarkable circumstances not only led to a new appreciation of the Crown's unique meaning to the Commonwealth, but to a revelation of what the Commonwealth stood for and could be. The English people recalled that another young girl, the first Queen Elizabeth of England, had ascended the throne only four centuries before to rule over a small land of four million seafaring and farming people. That small and struggling land had been beset by the might of Spain, and there was little enough to indicate that its sailors and merchants would range over the known world and build the foundations of the greatest empire in the history of man. Yet it had been so. After the grim struggle of the war and the weary disillusions of the post-war years, the British people—and many of their stock overseas—remembered all this, were heartened anew at their past and dared to hope that a new and even more spacious Elizabethan age could dawn.

In and out of Parliament, and this time emphatically, the future of the Commonwealth commanded attention. Mr Churchill himself indignantly rejected the idea that was being quietly canvassed that Britain should be integrated in a European or American federation. Speeches by members of the Government underlined the determination to find salvation within the Commonwealth. Lord Ismay, speaking in Canada, said that "the Commonwealth had a great mission to perform in providing a solid foundation for closer understanding and co-operation between East and West". In Parliament, there was a debate on a motion calling upon the Government to "pursue with fresh and vigorous determination a policy of closer co-operation and co-ordinated development of the Commonwealth and Sterling Area". On July 29, Mr Churchill told the House of Commons that during the last week in November pressing issues of financial, commercial and economic policy would be reviewed in London by a conference of the Prime Ministers and other representatives of the Dominion and Colonial territories. It was a sobering reminder that a new Elizabethan age could cost money.

But there was every reason to hope that the November meeting would produce a real co-ordination on the Commonwealth economic front. The Chancellor of the Exchequer, Mr R. A. Butler, said that the Government had decided "to embark on what they hoped would develop into the greatest effort since the war to establish with our friends and allies the conditions for a real expansion in world trade". Mr Butler added a grave warning that if the Governments of the Commonwealth did not develop a common economic strategy there was grave danger that each of them, in trying to save its own economy, might inflict lasting damage on the others.

The brave new world of free trade which was to have been ushered in under the auspices of the Americans, under the banner of the General Agreement on Tariffs and Trade (GATT), was still presumably a distant dream. It became steadily more obvious that a more direct step towards international solvency was a preliminary co-operation between groups of countries. Not only the Commonwealth came into this argument. Europe itself was moving towards economic unity and a striking start had been made with the treaty creating the Six-Power European Coal and Steel Community, which involved France, Germany, Belgium, the Netherlands, Italy and Luxembourg. There were strong arguments in favour of co-operation between the Commonwealth and a United Europe, and a group of British Members of Parliament drew up a plan to submit to the Commonwealth Conference. It was, indeed, the same plan as that adopted in September by the European Assembly at Strasbourg, visualizing economic co-operation between the Sterling Area and Europe, with a system of double trading preferences. The President of the Assembly, M. de Menthon, stated that for the sake of economic stability and the standard of living of the peoples, the European nations must tighten their economic bonds "not only among themselves, but also with the Overseas Territories and the countries of the Commonwealth".

He added: "Let me emphasize that this group of proposals, now commonly called the Strasbourg Plan ... opens up vistas of a future, when Europe, the Commonwealth, and those overseas countries having constitutional links with our European countries, will form a co-ordinated whole, maintaining close ties of friendship with the United States of America and all free nations on a scale befitting the world of today."

Here indeed was a visionary concept, which promised to end for Europe and the Commonwealth the humiliation of dollar dependence and the threat of being swallowed up by communism. It held out the fair dream of a vast "home" market on which prosperity equivalent to that of the United States could be built. And from that prosperity—so ran the argument—money would flow to help develop Britain's colonies and those of the other European powers. And in truth, on the development of those backward and underprivileged territories hung much of the hope for the survival of the

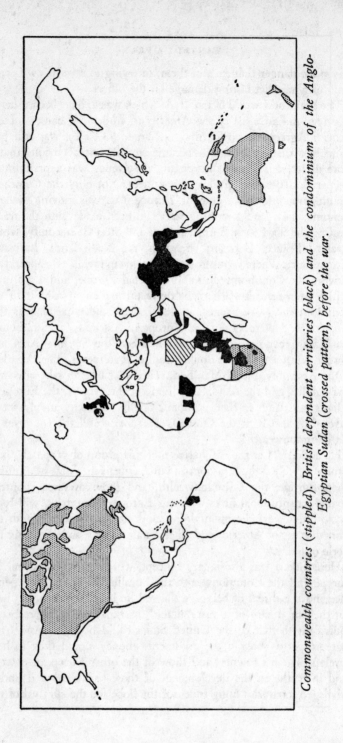

Commonwealth countries (stippled). British dependent territories (black) and the condominium of the Anglo-Egyptian Sudan (crossed pattern), before the war.

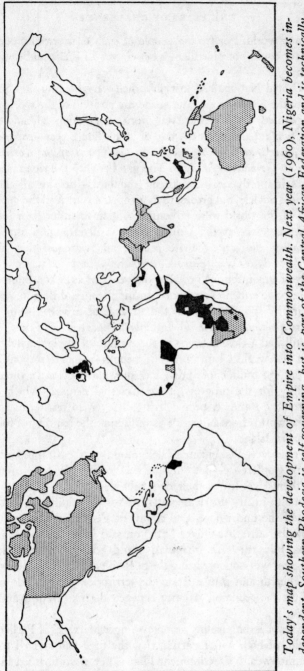

Today's map showing the development of Empire into Commonwealth. Next year (1960), Nigeria becomes independent. Southern Rhodesia is self-governing, but is part of the Central African Federation and is technically not independent. The Sudan and Burma are now independent, but outside the Commonwealth.

democratic world. For (so the people of such territories brooded) if democracy could not give them a better way of life, could not communism?

The United Nations had just published a frightening preliminary report on the general social and economic position of the world. The report pointed out that the total world population, already 2,400 million, was expanding at the rate of 22 million a year—*expanding, in fact, faster than food production in most parts of the world, particularly in the backward areas.* The gap between the rich and poor countries in production and living standards—despite all the aid given—was not less, but greater than before the war. And the deprived millions of the world were no longer content to suffer their lot like brute beasts. For—as the United Nations investigation stressed—there had spread among these peoples an awareness that higher standards of living were possible for themselves. Here was a picture not only of gloom but of growing danger. For such conditions provoked extreme remedies—such as communism. And Britain, responsible, directly or indirectly, for the advance of so vast a number of backward people, was overwhelmingly implicated.

She still had a close concern in the welfare of approximately one-third of the world's least fortunate people—a moral responsibility to aid the 450 million of India, Pakistan and Ceylon; a direct responsibility for the progress of the Colonial Empire, which comprised some 65 million people living in over 40 territories spread across the world, from Nigeria's 30 million to the handful of folk on tiny Pitcairn Island.

This then was the gigantic background to the Commonwealth Economic Conference—not only the need of the advanced countries to pull themselves up by their own economic bootstraps, but at the same time to justify the democratic process by helping forward the advance of the under-developed countries. Perhaps the one solution hung on the other. As Oliver Lyttelton said in the House of Commons on July 17: "An imaginative and bold policy of Colonial development will not only bring the possibility of much greater social services, health and prosperity to the territories, but may do much to readjust the economic balance between the Old World and the New."

There was a strong feeling among younger Members of Parliament in Britain, of both major parties, that the time had arrived for an All-Commonwealth Development Plan. They were fortified in this belief by the fact that the Americans had just published their famous Paley Report, which bluntly admitted that if the United States economy continued to expand at its current rate it would progressively depend more and more on outside sources for raw materials. This opened up the bright prospect of the Sterling Area's dollar problem being solved for good within 25 years, always supposing that the Commonwealth developed its resources to meet the predicted American shortfall.

In the event, after all these great hopes and exhortations, the Prime Ministers' Economic Conference fell far short of expectation. Halfway through the discussions, Britain's Chancellor of the Exchequer, Mr Butler, let out the uninspiring news that *if* the strict internal policies of the Commonwealth nations were adhered to, *if* the Commonwealth was helped by the terms of world trade, *if* the countries continued with the programmes they had undertaken at the previous Finance Ministers' Conference—then the Commonwealth would have a real breathing space and time to work out a better long-term position. The whole damp impression given by the Chancellor was that once more emergency salvage operations were absorbing the attention of the Prime Ministers and their advisers, while the greater aim of a long-term policy was quietly being pigeon-holed.

The all-embracing Development Plan which the more ambitious advocates of Commonwealth co-operation had hoped for did not emerge. But it is at least fair to say that there was a definite recognition by all members of the Commonwealth that they must endeavour to maintain some co-ordination of policies. The economic crisis at the beginning of the year had driven home the lesson that it was not enough to voice pious promises at economic conferences and then to go home and break them, though hoping all the time that the other countries would keep them. Indeed, without any reference back to their home governments, the Prime Ministers or their representatives agreed on these definite principles:

Internal economic policies designed to curb inflation and rises in the cost of living should be steadily followed.

Sound economic development should be encouraged with the object of increasing productive strength and competitive power, providing employment and raising the standards of life.

A multilateral trade and payments system should be extended over the widest possible area.

The nearest the Conference got to a development plan was the admission (and this was quite an advance) that "In Sterling Area countries development should be concentrated on projects which directly or indirectly contribute to the improvement of the Area's balance of payments with the rest of the world. Such projects should strengthen the economy of the countries concerned and increase their competitive power in world markets." The criticism could be made that this, too, was no more than a vague hope. Yet Britain was able to exercise some positive influence. For she undertook, at the Conference, to make a special effort to provide additional capital for Commonwealth development. But she made the provision that the schemes should be those "which will contribute to the improvement of the Sterling Area's balance of payments". And she also stipulated that she must be sure that any country getting capital "was itself devoting an adequate part of its resources to investment designed to improve the Sterling Area's balance of payments..."

There was a further significant advance towards co-ordination. The final communiqué of the Conference stated that "all Commonwealth Governments are... ready to co-operate in considering, commodity by commodity, international schemes designed to ensure stability of demand and prices at an economic level. They also recognize the need for an agreed procedure for calling together the Governments concerned to consider emergency action in the event of rapidly developing conditions of surplus or shortage of commodities entering into international trade."

On the other hand, Britain got only partial support for her proposal that all Commonwealth countries should join in seeking release from the "no new Preference" rule in GATT (the General Agreement on Tariffs and Trade).

A majority of the Commonwealth leaders maintained a stout belief in the virtues of an international outlook on economic matters. And, as the Commonwealth itself was the outcome of a world trading policy historically pursued by Britain, they were theoretically correct in their belief. But would the Americans really go in for "trade, not aid"? And was it not a little hypocritical to virtuously reject the notion that the Commonwealth should seek "the creation of a discriminatory economic bloc", when all the signs were that just such a bloc would eventually arise in Europe? If an integrated economic bloc was created in Europe, it would confront British manufacturers and Commonwealth producers alike with unpalatable problems, striking at their trading prospects, forcing them to face decisions which now the leaders of the Commonwealth seemed content to push into the background.

CHAPTER XXIV

CORONATION YEAR CRISES

DESPITE THE DISAPPOINTMENTS of the Economic Conference the year 1953 opened, in Britain, with hope stimulated and burdens seemingly lighter. The preparations for the Coronation of the young Queen Elizabeth awoke a new mood of idealism at home and overseas. But the sad irony was that this very year—despite the armistice in Korea—saw nationalism exerting its own idealistic yet blind power on a greater scale than ever in many parts of the world. Of that nationalism, the philosopher Bertrand Russell wrote that it was the greatest danger to liberty, in the present state of the world. He stressed that "what the West stands for fundamentally is the belief that governments exist for the sake of individuals, not individuals for the sake of governments".

Whatever Bertrand Russell thought, this nationalism which sprang from the fierce desire to end the control of outside interests—whether economic, as in the case of Manchu China, or political as well as economic, as with colonial territories—was the most dynamic force in the post-war world. The continuing success of the communists in directing its potential towards their own ends was frighteningly clear. Not only could they claim China as their triumph, they could discredit the free world and powerfully influence nationalist movements all over the world by pointing out that the Chinese had tried democracy for 36 years under Dr. Sun Yat-sen and Chiang Kai-shek —and it had failed. It was true. Whether it was because of consistent communist intrigue, or the agony of war against the Japanese, or lack of sufficient Western support, did not matter. To other backward countries, democracy had failed to meet China's needs, whilst communism with its new Five-Year Plan for 600 million people to all appearances was able to do so.

But these world-wide eruptions of nationalism promised to crystallize in another gigantic movement, a third doctrine which was neither communist or democratic—that of racism, the unity of new nations free from old bondage who wished to find a balance between the great, conflicting ideologies. The major development of this movement was yet to be, but it first gained reality in 1953 when the Indonesian Prime Minister, Sastroamidojo, urged that steps should be taken to achieve co-operation between the countries of the former "subject continents" Asia and Africa.

Whether this racism was to become the third great world influence remained to be seen, but clearly its prospective attitude was vitally important to both communism and democracy. The gradual development of the British Empire into the Commonwealth of Nations most certainly would have a decisive effect on the attitude of the nations of Asia and Africa and on the doctrine of racism. The success of that development was continually imperilled in the turbulent year of 1953, both in the Colonies themselves, and through Britain clashing with racism outside the Commonwealth.

In the Middle East, those explosive possibilities which had lain just below the surface when King Farouk was deposed in Egypt now began to become realities. It became increasingly apparent that the Egyptian revolution was no mere action against internal corruption and inefficiency but a determined bid to sweep away foreign power and influence and to further Egyptian ambitions of Middle East leadership. And Britain was the main target. There was irony in the fact that whilst this revulsion against Western influence grew strong in Egypt, the Persians were finding that they were doomed to disaster without it. Moussadek, desperately aware that his country had lost both prestige and markets for oil in the outside world after his quarrel with Britain, made a bid to rally the nation round him, only to end in final disgrace in prison. But that did not check the vaulting ambitions of Egypt's new men.

In February 1953 General Neguib negotiated an agreement with Britain on the future of the Sudan, which provided for early elections preceding a three-year period of self-government. At the end of that time the Sudanese would determine their own future, whether to unite with Egypt or to maintain their own complete independence. During the three years, also, British officials would, as far as that was possible and desired, be replaced by Sudanese. In effect, after fifty years in which the Sudan had been raised from bloodshed and primitive poverty, British power in the land would cease. And if General Neguib and his colleagues had their way, so too would her influence. For the General was as determined as Farouk to achieve "Unity of the Nile Valley", which in practice would mean Egyptian overlordship of the Sudan.

The Sudan elections were conducted with the maximum of rumour and intrigue, with the Egyptian Government contemptuously ignoring the provisions of the agreement with Britain and pouring money into the pockets of the pro-Egypt politicians. The National Union Party, which favoured some sort of union with Egypt, won the election in the face of all forecasts. It was a signal triumph for Neguib and a correspondingly bitter blow for Britain. But the Egyptian glee was a little premature, for it was by no means certain that even their bought men in the Sudan would sell out their own country.

Yet there was no denying the great impetus the election result gave to Egyptian prestige in the Middle East, and the corresponding slump in that of Britain. The proposed Anglo-Egyptian Suez Canal Agreement had already consolidated the position of the new Egyptian Government. The signing of the Agreement was still many months away, but there was no denying that it would, in whatever form it emerged, lead to the withdrawal of British troops from the Canal Zone. It was possible to argue that under modern conditions the Canal itself was no longer the vital lifeline of the Commonwealth that it had once been. But it was evident that the withdrawal of British troops from the Suez area would leave a dangerously attractive vacuum of power at the "crossroads of the Commonwealth" and that it would make the future of the whole Middle East still more precarious. The ominous word "scuttle" again found currency in Britain and abroad, and the Conservative Government found angry resistance to any truckling to Neguib within its own ranks.

Neguib could rest content with his year. He and his colleagues had now declared Egypt to be a Republic with Neguib as President. Not only did they present themselves as the leaders of resistance to "imperialism", but also as the new men of the Arab world who were ousting the corrupt royal leaders who (said the Egyptians) had sold that world for their own benefit. It was a beguiling rôle, and one which was to bring increasing profit to the Egyptians and a like dismay to those whom they wished to supersede—the British in particular.

There was another setback to Britain and to the Commonwealth in the Muslim world. Pakistan had decided to make itself into a republic. A militant Islamic feeling had grown within the past two years, much influenced by events in the Middle East, and no Pakistan Government could afford to exacerbate it still further by maintaining allegiance to the British Crown. At least Pakistan was remaining an Islamic democracy within the Commonwealth, said the more optimistic. But the precedent set by India had indubitably been strengthened. South African Nationalist hopes of a republic were immediately fortified. And Sir John Kotelawala, the new Prime Minister of Ceylon, made some significant references to the Queen as "Head of the Commonwealth" which underlined a strengthening desire in Ceylon also for republican status.

Sir John, Cambridge graduate and the most pro-Western in outlook and habit of all the Asian leaders, had succeeded Dudley Senanayake, and he could not afford to fall too far behind the vehement nationalism which the communists in his country were assiduously fostering. They had the best possible conditions to create trouble in the steadily rising cost of living and the parlous state of the national finances.

However, further south in Malaya communism was being contained and—happy change—nationalism was being actually used to defeat it. A clear-cut policy, pursued with determination, had effected the miraculous change. Lyttelton's qualities of decision and courage had most certainly been those needed for this particular imperial problem, and General Templer had proved himself to be far more than an iron soldier. "Shooting is only a quarter of the business," he said. "Getting at the hearts and minds of the people is the other three-quarters." On a visit to London he revealed that the battleground had been significantly transferred from the jungle to trade unions, political associations, and youth movements. This change of front was quickly countered. The promise was made by the Secretary of State for the Colonies that self-government would be given as soon as the various races were united, and the two largest political associations in the country, the United Malay National Organization and the Malayan Chinese Association, pledged themselves to strive together for federal elections. When the Malayan Indian Congress talked of joining the alliance it was hearteningly clear that Malaya was witnessing a racial *rapprochement* that it had never known for years, and which represented a major obstacle to communism.

(*Above*) Mr. Nehru's visitor. Mr. Harold Macmillan, Britain's Prime Minister, arriving at Delhi Airport with Lady Dorothy Macmillan in 1957, at the start of his Commonwealth tour.

(*Right*) Mr. Nehru's other visitor. Chou-En-lai, the Prime Minister of communist China being escorted to Parliament House, in New Delhi, by the Indian Prime Minister. There, he addressed both Houses of Parliament.

The changing faces. Compared with 1956, this group of leaders who attended the Prime Ministers' discussions in 1957 shows many changes. (Left to right) Mr. Diefenbaker (Canada), Mr. Macmillan (United Kingdom), Mr. Menzies (Australia), Mr. Louw (Minister for External Affairs, South Africa), H.M. The Queen, Mr. Suhrawardy (Pakistan), Mr. Nehru (India), Sir Roy Welensky (Rhodesia and Nyasaland), Dr. Nkrumah (Ghana), Mr. Macdonald (Minister for External Affairs, New Zealand), and Mr. de Silva (Minister of Justice, Ceylon).

But, disastrously for Britain, communism scored a most unexpected—at least in Whitehall—triumph far away in the Caribbean. To the Colony of British Guiana British warships steamed in haste and troops were landed. Out of the confusion and rumour came the revelation that a communist coup had been forestalled. The constitution was suspended and the Governor, Sir Alfred Savage, empowered to rule without the new House of Assembly.

What had happened to bring about this calamitous action? Early in the year British Guiana had been given a new constitution (following an earlier Commission of Inquiry). This constitution provided for that always potentially dangerous advance, universal suffrage. And a largely illiterate and impoverished electorate immediately returned to power the People's Progressive Party—led by Dr Cheddi Jagan and his American wife Janet. Unfortunately—and to the considerable dismay of the Colonial Office—the Jagans were devout communists. It was useless, now, to deplore their tactics in making flamboyant, unscrupulous and totally unrealistic election promises to a naïve electorate. The plain fact was that the vote had been given to backward people once too often. Universal suffrage is always a gamble, but one would have thought that the possible consequences of it in British Guiana ought to have been foreseen. It was one thing for a fervent nationalist like Nkrumah to emerge in West Africa. (He proved to be an opponent of communism, despite earlier fears.) It was quite another for devotees of Moscow to assume power on the South American mainland.

The Jagans (so ran the British allegation) had used their four months of power to foment strikes, to intimidate opponents and to lay the ground for a communist republic. It seemed to have been a somewhat clumsily-handled intrigue, but its discovery did not extricate Britain from a highly unpleasant position. Moscow had been given a splendid propaganda theme. Among colonial peoples Britain's sincerity would clearly be called in question. For on the face of it, here she was granting political advance with the one hand and withdrawing it, as soon as developments displeased her, with the other.

Luckily, the Jagans did not fill the rôle of martyrs very successfully. The Socialist Opposition in Britain did not give them much chance to achieve a vigorous lobby in Westminster. Neither did they get much comfort from Mr Nehru, who had come to be regarded as almost the patron saint of nationalism. The damage done to Britain's

M

reputation, in the outcome, was much less than had been anticipated. But, by the time the situation was retrieved and an interim constitution announced (which virtually left the Governor in full control), British politicians had plenty of time to reflect on the risks inherent in rapid constitutional advance. It was at last seen that British Colonial policy really hung upon the assumption that even an illiterate electorate would return something akin to democratic leaders. The fact that that policy also afforded communism the opportunity to exploit its most dangerous strategy, the destruction of democracies from within, had never been properly grasped. British Guiana provided a warning that was not, henceforward, to be easily disregarded.

The dangers inherent in the situation would not perhaps have been so acute if the British Caribbean as a whole had not presented a picture of continuing confusion and distrust. Yet another Conference on Federation had been held in April, this time in London. What was officially described as a large measure of agreement was apparently reached. Yet the inter-island jealousies and suspicions were only too evident. So much so that for more than a year the important post of Trade Commissioner for the Caribbean in London was left unfilled. Mr Bustamante, the ebullient Jamaican leader, declared that Jamaica would appoint its own officer, if the deadlock persisted. Then it transpired that there were strong objections in Trinidad to an over-free movement of people from one island to another, if the Federation came about. A Federation with immigration officers manning frontiers was clearly an unhappy conception, and one which would erode the idea of unity at the outset.

A sense of disquiet brooded over much of the Caribbean. There was a rising fear that Barbados might go further to the left. In Trinidad communist infiltration in trade unions was alarming both government and public. In British Honduras the People's United Party was still advocating that on self-government the Colony should withdraw from the Commonwealth and establish a republic. As for British Guiana itself Janet Jagan promised that "in the face of ruthless attacks on a Colonial people fighting for peace, national independence and better living standards the People's Progressive Party would continue to the end the struggle for liberation from imperialist oppression".

CHAPTER XXV

THE SPLIT OVER AFRICA

DESPITE THE DANGERS and the challenge to British Colonial policy in 1953, the Government and the Opposition in Britain had broadly maintained agreement in principle. Oliver Lyttelton had in a notable broadcast endorsed the words of the former Socialist Colonial Secretary, Arthur Creech Jones: "The central purpose of British Colonial policy is simple. It is to guide the Colonial territories to self-government within the Commonwealth in conditions that ensure to the people both a fair standard of living and freedom from aggression from any quarter."

Mr Lyttelton, however, went on to state four essentials without which self-government would be a mockery. Those essentials were: the assurance of law and order of the Queen's peace; the necessity to grow more food to feed the rising populations which spring from peace; the provision of capital to develop natural resources and for training and the application of new skills to new industries; and finally, above all, leadership and guidance. Practically nobody in the Socialist Party would have disagreed with the first three of the Lyttelton essentials. It was the fourth that proved to be the rock on which party agreement split. For many Socialists did not see eye to eye with the Government on either the life-span or the application of "leadership and guidance"—and particularly so in Africa.

This year was to prove one full of drama and clashing rivalries in Africa. It finally revealed in the most unmistakable way that when it came to political policies for multi-racial territories in which Europeans were settled, the Socialists were at variance with the Government. It would be fairer to say that a section of the Socialists were more or less constantly at variance—possibly no more than one-third vehemently so. But that one-third were implacable in their views and sometimes able to carry the party with them, for among the remainder there were a great many wavering, bewildered and sceptical members.

For some years past the conception of the Commonwealth as an economic partner with Britain had become deeply rooted in the Labour Party. No other than Mr Attlee himself had advocated that economic advance must go hand-in-hand with political advance in the Colonies. And it was this which contributed to the fragmented approach of the party when multi-racial problems presented themselves. More cautious and level-headed members, such as Patrick Gordon Walker (former Secretary of State for Commonwealth Relations), and ex-Ministers Maurice Webb and Stanley Evans, clearly recognized that white settlers were frequently the mainspring of a territory's economy, and that if their position of leadership was seriously undermined it could benefit nobody. But the opposite extreme was the group of members, including such ardent advocates as Fenner Brockway and Leslie Hale, who vigorously maintained that constitutional advance for the indigenous peoples was the main thing. In the centre of these two groups was yet a third, of whom the former Secretary of State for the Colonies, James Griffiths, was a chief exponent, which attempted to balance the opinions of the other two groups but was apt, in a dilemma, to sacrifice the economic case rather than come out too openly against "native" interests. The shadow of a disapproving Mr Nehru haunted the members of this third group at such moments.

Behind it all, the Labour Party practically as a whole deeply desired to preserve the fabric of the Commonwealth. But that did not prevent their internal differences, and their external disagreement with the Government, becoming apparent over African affairs in 1953, and the more particularly over Central African federation.

On New Year's Day, the delegates met in London for what was destined to be the final conference on federation. Sir Gilbert Rennie, the Governor, led the Northern Rhodesian delegation, and Sir Geoffrey Colby that of Nyasaland. Sir Godfrey Huggins, of course, led the Southern Rhodesians, his powerful ally Roy Welensky being among the Northern Rhodesians. Oliver Lyttelton and Lord Swinton (who had become Secretary of State for Commonwealth Relations) acted as joint chairmen, and Lord Salisbury was present as chairman of a committee to handle arrangements (if necessary) for federal elections and the installation of a federal government. Here was a powerful and determined group of men, all of them now believing in federation. Yet, so closely discussed was the project, so carefully designed, that it was the end of January before the conference ended. But no time was lost after that. By the beginning of February a White Paper was issued, outlining the final scheme for a Federation of Rhodesia and Nyasaland.

This final scheme maintained the Protectorate status of Northern

Rhodesia and Nyasaland and their links with the Colonial Office.
Safeguards were also provided against federal legislation which
could adversely affect African interests. But there was a passionate
resistance movement within the Labour Party on the grounds that
the Africans had not been consulted and indeed were opposed to
federation. The party—one must imagine, with some misgivings—
came out officially against federation unless it had African support.
But there was not a great deal of heart about the stand in a
number of Labour circles. When a vote of disapproval was forced in
the House of Commons, sixteen of the party's members actually
abstained.

The real decision, now, lay in the hands of the self-governing
Southern Rhodesians, who were to indicate their opinion in a referendum on April 9. The result showed that there were quite a number
of white people south of the Zambezi who were as sceptical of federation as members of the African Congress, for although 25,580 voted
in favour, there were 14,929 against.

Nevertheless, it was a great victory for Sir Godfrey Huggins and
Roy Welensky and, for the former, the crown of a long and arduous
political life. "In a year when we celebrate the centenary of the birth
of Cecil Rhodes," he said, "we will be able to take a great step
towards the realization of his vision." Not even the referendum dispelled opposition, either in Britain or Central Africa. Federation was
debated eleven times in one British Parliamentary session, but in the
final division the Labour Party, significantly, was able to muster
only a little over half of its strength.

Less than a week after the Southern Rhodesian referendum South
Africa returned Dr Malan and his Nationalists to power with twice
their previous majority. They had called out for a solid European
vote to "save White South Africa". It was a minority vote which
won them the day, but it fortified the Doctor in his belief that the
"mixture as before" was the right prescription. From this time on
not only did the Nationalists buttress European leadership, they also
worked slowly but steadily towards their ideal of an Afrikaner-style
republic. Later in the year, again emphasizing that old ambitions
had become present policies, Dr Malan repeated a demand for the
transfer to South Africa of the British High Commission Territories
of Basutoland, Bechuanaland, and Swaziland.

The victory of the South African Nationalists stiffened the resolution of all those Europeans in other African territories south of the

Sahara who believed as they did in white leadership and the policy of the races living apart. And inevitably it called forth as strong a racial response from black Africans. The feeling among literate Africans of a common cause, which had been gathering ground over the post-war years, was more apparent than ever. The trial of Jomo Kenyatta in Kenya demonstrated this in surprising fashion. One of his defending counsel was a Nigerian; another Nigerian lawyer who flew over to East Africa to offer his services was denied entry to Kenya. African newspapers gave increasing prominence to all that was happening in Africa, and especially so to events in South Africa and in Kenya.

The situation in Kenya in the first half of the year was depressing in the extreme. At the beginning of the year, Governor Sir Evelyn Baring had to issue a directive to the police and the army condemning the use of inhuman methods with Mau Mau prisonrs. At the same time, attacks by the Mau Mau, particularly on other Africans, grew more savage and numerous. Kenyatta and five of his lieutenants were sentenced to seven years' hard labour, whilst several others were sentenced to death for murder. Yet there were others to spring into their places, and with the emergency a year old, General Sir George Erskine, the Commander-in-Chief East Africa, echoed the words General Templer had used in Malaya. "Bullets alone will not finish the problem," he said.

But the Governor had no intention of depending on bullets. To the Legislative Council in Kenya he outlined a comprehensive scheme of development, particularly agricultural development for land-hungry Africans. But it would cost far more money than Kenya could find, he added. In truth, the territory was already feeling the killing drain on its resources. Perhaps the most encouraging development of the year in Kenya was the policy statement issued by the European Elected Members of the Council which clearly showed that white settler opinion was moving in a more liberal direction. The statement called for participation by all races—European, African and Indian—in the Government, for the encouragement of African efforts to grow cash crops, for equal pay for equal public service. Such compromises would have been undreamt of only twelve months before.

At the very time that this faint ray of hope was dawning in Kenya, Uganda to the north staged a drama of its own. Kabaka Mutesa II of Buganda was suddenly deposed and deported. He had consistently refused to co-operate with the Government, backing an upsurge of nationalism (or, rather, tribalism) which demanded the independence of the State of Buganda. After rejecting a final two-hour appeal from the Governor, Sir Andrew Cohen, he was whisked straight to a waiting aircraft and flown out of his country to London. At once his downfall set in train a great agitation both in Britain and in Africa. The young Kabaka at first appeared to be the champion of his people, the heroic martyr in the sacred cause of African nationalism. But the real story was nothing like so simple. It was indeed a complicated and tortuous picture of tribal politics which finally emerged.

A great deal was made of a speech delivered by Oliver Lyttelton, the Secretary of State, some months before, in which he had unwisely referred to the possibility of closer unity of the East African territories. The Secretary of State had made a sadly-wrong estimate of the political atmosphere in East Africa in ever returning to such a subject. The advance of the Gold Coast, the undeniable fact that a federation was being effected in Central Africa without African backing, had driven further away than ever the prospect of closer union in East Africa. In Uganda, and more particularly amongst the Buganda people, the assumption had grown that self-government was close at hand, and they did not want it delayed or perhaps even abandoned by any association with European-dominated Kenya.

But the Lyttelton speech was not really the major cause of the crisis. There had been a long struggle for power between several factions in Buganda—whose people had assumed that if and when self-government came to the territory they would dominate the other tribes. A progressive Governor had effected reforms which were not much to the taste of the ruling class of the Buganda, but which the younger politicians of the African Congress had attempted to use for the advancement of their own power. The Kabaka himself, the hereditary ruler, a young man of no very powerful character, had had trouble with these younger men before. Some of them had been behind the armed rebellion against him in 1949 as members of the since-proscribed Bataka Party. It is difficult, even today, to judge how far the Kabaka was impelled to his rash opposition by a genuine impulse to project the fears of his people. Certainly he was in part influenced by the desire to keep abreast of the nationalist tide, and not to let the leaders of the African Congress seize all initiative and credit. Better for him, therefore, to oppose the British Government's plans for constitutional progress and so claim the mantle of his people's martyr. Strengthening his decision there was also the undoubted fact that the Buganda did want to contract out of the Protectorate of Uganda and become a small independent state. A wholly unrealistic ambition, but one which was firmly imbedded in the minds of the people as a whole. They had never forgotten that they had formerly been the overlords of Uganda, and any outcome which did not restore them to that position was anathema to them.

Behind the whole complicated story, however, was the rising yeast of nationalism—or, once again, racialism. The key figures were the leaders of the African Congress, whose ultimate ambitions were in line with those of others of the new African leaders in West, East and Central Africa. They had no objection to joining in the general condemnation of the British for exiling the Kabaka and mourning him as the deposed head of his people. They had no desire to offend against tradition and past history, just so long as they knew present history was working for them. And indeed it was.

The Kabaka reconciled himself to a long stay in London, where he had many friends from his university days, for he was a personable and agreeable young man. And in Uganda a regency was formed of the three Chief Ministers, the Katrikiro (Prime Minister), the Omunanika (Treasurer) and the Omulamuzi (Chief Justice). They were three unhappy and apprehensive men. And they had cause to be. For they were assailed as traitors to the Kabaka on the one hand, and bitterly disliked by the African Congress on the other.

Strangely, Oliver Lyttelton came out very well in this episode. His brusque and overpowering manner in Parliament, his capacity for strong and unrelenting decision had inspired a growing opposition to him, even among some of his own party. The Labour Party, during the debate on the Kabaka, allowed themselves to be led into an ambush. Behind the Labour attack was the assumption that Mr Lyttelton would once more appear as a domineering and ruthless man, ill fitted to handle the Colonial Office in such arduous and delicate days. In the event, Lyttelton not only effectively defended the Government's action over the Kabaka, but emerged as a man of heart and feeling. His words clearly proved that his policies were inspired by the regard for African and European rights. He actually defended the Kabaka as a sincere and patriotic prince who had been misguided but nevertheless was man enough to take the consequences. His genuine and personal sorrow over the outcome was plain to see. From that time on, Lyttelton had an easier passage in Parliament and his great abilities were given recognition even by his political adversaries.

Meanwhile, in West Africa also, nationalism bubbled strongly again, this time in Nigeria. The two main parties there, the National Council for Nigeria and the Cameroons and the Action Party, were in a constant state of mutual suspicion. But neither gave pride of place to the other in the matter of extremism. The N.C.N.C. expelled three of its members, all capable Ministers in the Central Government, because they opposed the party's intention to put an end to the present constitution by any possible means. The Action Party, meanwhile, ordered a boycott of the Governor, Sir John Macpherson. Each party, in short, was determined to outdo the other in spurning co-operation with the Government. The leaders of the more backward North, who feared and disliked both Azikiwe and Awolowo, and wanted a slower pace of constitutional development for their own protection, countered by condemning the boycott and expressed public appreciation of the Governor's service to the country.

It could not be long, under such pressures, before a deadlock came. And come it did at the end of March, when a quarrel arose in the House of Representatives over a motion for "self-government by 1956". The Northern members opposed it, and asked for self-government "at the earliest possible moment". Both Eastern and Western leaders left the House in protest, and subsequently four Ministers resigned. The truth was that Mr Awolowo, leader of the Action Group, was determined to match any claim made by Dr Azikiwe of the N.C.N.C. to be recognized as leading nationalist in Nigeria. Hence the unrealistic demand for self-government, and the subsequent deadlock in Government. For a time, it looked as if Awolowo and Azikiwe might achieve co-operation in "the struggle for independence". They actually shook hands as they left the House. But the two men were so deeply opposed to each other that the *rapprochement* could not but be short-lived.

The final outcome was the inevitable conference to discuss the Constitution. It was held in London and Oliver Lyttelton's handling of it gave him a great personal success. The tensions and jealousies between the leaders of Nigeria's three Regions augured ill, but the surprising outcome was that concessions were freely made, which had the effect of lessening the rigidity of the federal framework, and giving more power to the Regions. It was agreed that the Nigerian leaders resume the discussions in the following January, but before the year was out the Eastern and Western Region leaders had broken their tenuous alliance and resumed their personal struggle for dominance.

This whole series of events in Nigeria revealed how varied and complex were the forms nationalism could take. For here were Azikiwe of the Eastern Region and Awolowo of the Western forcing the pace towards independence beyond the bounds of wisdom, simply so that neither should forge ahead of the other. And all the time, the more backward Muslim North, keenly aware that in development and education it could not yet compare with the other Regions, was putting the brake on the other two. They wanted the British to stay until they were better able to take care of themselves.

Further up the Gulf of Guinea, the Gold Coast could afford to pursue its way towards self-government at a steady pace. Nkrumah and his young men found themselves in the happy position of leading a prosperous country. Looking back, it could be said that a statue should be put up at Accra to the cocoa bean, main source of the country's wealth. Without it, the path to freedom would have been far more rocky and irksome. And human, as well as economic conditions were gratifying. Dr Nkrumah and the Governor, Sir Charles Arden-Clarke, had achieved a remarkable degree of co-operation. After three years, the growth in confidence between Africa and European officials which followed this unity at the top was better than it had been since the end of the war.

The proposals put forward at the end of the three years by Nkrumah and his colleagues for further constitutional advance revealed the Prime Minister's determination to be recognized as moderate and responsible. They asked for full independence coupled with the Commonwealth link and with a further interim period during which defence, foreign affairs and public order would still be the ultimate responsibility of the Governor. All this was reasonable enough. It was true that from time to time there were distressing stories of political intimidation and corruption which delighted the opponents of Gold Coast advancement. But the Prime Minister was determined to set his house in order. He worked to inspire confidence in the outside investor, he paid tribute to European officials, he sternly denounced communist influence inside his country. After all the tribulations of the earlier years, it did look as if the Gold Coast would provide a copy-book example of the wisdom of British Colonial policy.

The year ended with heartening news for those who believed in moderation and tolerance in Africa. In Central Africa, Huggins and Welensky, with their United Rhodesia Party, won a resounding victory in the first Federal election over the Confederate Party, whose policy appeared to rest on *apartheid*. The Confederates got one seat only. In some quarters it was said that 50,000 voters had shaped the destiny of a continent, and there was a deal of truth in that. At least the ideal of black and white partnership was off to a clear run.

CHAPTER XXVI

DIVISION IN ASIA

IF 1953 HAD been the year of tumultuous nationalism, then 1954 assuredly—as far as the Commonwealth was concerned—was that in which the threatened split in foreign policy was at last plainly manifest. In Asia, India and (rather more reluctantly) Ceylon adopted a policy which rejected that of Britain, Australia, New Zealand and Pakistan.

During the years since the partition of the Indian sub-continent, though the loosening of economic ties had been a continuing weakness, the more immediate dangers to Commonwealth unity had been the developing differences on racial and defence matters. Strangely enough the former, which had seemed the most intractable problem, had been contained. But it had its indirect, yet powerful influence on the second, as will be seen.

The year began with communism in militant mood, and China showing every sign that, despite being barred from the United Nations, she intended to emerge from her diplomatic semi-isolation and make her presence felt in the world. The unmistakable danger area at the beginning of 1954 was Indo-China, which—like Korea—suddenly threatened to become the starting-point of a third world war. The disintegration of French power which had begun after the death of General de Lattre de Tassigny in 1952 culminated in a series of disasters to French garrisons. At last, in desperation, the French determined to hold the frontier garrison town of Dien Bien Phu at whatever cost in lives and money, and thus stem the rolling tide of communism implicit in the advance of Ho Chi Minh's Viet-minh forces. So threatening now had the position become to the safety of the world that, even as the desperate and exhausting battle for the fortress town was being waged, the call went out for a meet-ing of Foreign Secretaries of the major powers .

The conference was held at Geneva, and besides Britain, Russia, the United States and France, Communist China was represented— by the redoubtable Chou En-lai himself. The delegates were barely seated round the conference table before Dien Bien Phu fell. The sullen intransigence of the United States, following this disaster to the democratic cause, was matched by the jubilant obduracy of Russia and China. But a second session was more successful. Viet-nam was partitioned. Ho Chi Minh's communist Government was securely established in northern Indo-China, and the unhappy pattern of compromise and division which had been established in Korea had been repeated.

Undoubtedly, the powerful expansion of communist imperialism which ended in Dien Bien Phu brought to a head the idea of co-operative resistance in Asia, just as it had in Europe. The Anzus Pact of 1951 between the United States, Australia and New Zealand was now seen to be only the forerunner to a far larger concept. In September, the South-East Asia Treaty Organization (SEATO) came into existence, with the expressed determination to contain communist subversion and aggression. It was optimistically talked of as being the military counterpart of the Colombo Plan, but in hard fact some of the most important participants of the Plan were fiercely opposed to SEATO.

The members of SEATO were the U.S., Britain, Australia, New Zealand, the Philippines, Pakistan, Siam, France, and a protocol covering South Vietnam, Cambodia and Laos. India, Burma, Indo-nesia, and Ceylon were the significant members of the Colombo Plan who were *not* members of the defence organization, nor had the first three the remotest intention of being so. That extraordinary character, Sir John Kotelawala, the Prime Minister of Ceylon, would certainly have liked to have drawn a little nearer to SEATO. The least Asian of all Asian Prime Ministers, with his predilection for the good things of life, his extrovert heartiness and his overpowering energy, he was too astute a politician to advocate policies which would exacerbate nationalist and religious prejudices in Ceylon. And, though there is good reason to believe that he disliked the theory of co-existence, he appreciated the danger of challenging the god-like prestige of Mr Nehru. SEATO, in short, was damned from the out-set by Nehru and had no real claim at any time to be the defence aspect of the Colombo Plan.

Indeed, SEATO stung Mr Nehru into an intensification of his campaign to buttress and expand his concept of neutralism, of co-existence with communism. The acceptance of American military aid by Pakistan had already angered India's Prime Minister, not so much because India feared Pakistan as because this intrusion of American military aid threatened Mr Nehru's developing concept of a peaceful area in Asia, secure from power politics.

Following on the first part of the Geneva conference over Indo-China, Chou En-lai had travelled to India and there signed a Sino-Indian Pact. At once there was an indignant outburst of criticism of Mr Nehru from the West. He was adjudged to have "betrayed" democracy and the Commonwealth, and to have been hoodwinked by the Chinese. The truth was that the pact fitted in perfectly with Nehru's concept of *Panchsheel*—peace among neighbours. For it embodied five principles: mutual respect for each other's territorial integrity; non-aggression; non-interference in each other's internal affairs; recognition of equality; peaceful co-existence. It could properly be said that China's invasion of Tibet and the intrigues of the Indian Communist Party mocked at least two of the principles. But Nehru was apparently willing to let bygones be bygones in the cause of *Panchsheel*.

In the April of this same year, in Ceylon, Nehru and the Prime Ministers of Indonesia, Ceylon, Burma and Pakistan had already agreed to work together in unison with African countries to safe-guard their interests. Later in the year they determined that a con-ference of Asiatic and African powers should be held at Bandung. The proposed conference was likely to help Nehru's conceptions of a peaceful area in Asia and, if possible, Africa. But it had an even greater significance. It marked the emergence of the majority of the old colonial territories on to the world stage, speaking for themselves, ready to shape their own future.

So it was that 1954 saw decisive positions being taken up in the Far East. And Mr Nehru had elected to fill the risky rôle of mediator, believing that this was in the best interests of his own country, of Asia, and indeed of the whole world. In spite of the bitter criticism of his policy in some quarters, and however much other democratic powers wished for a positive resistance to communism by India, Nehru's action did paradoxically demonstrate the value of the Commonwealth. For here was one of its leading statesmen able to deal with both worlds, able to act as an interpreter as well as a mediator.

Indeed, the whole chaos and confusion in Asia did in fact strikingly illustrate the value of the Commonwealth's links. For during the Indo-China discussions at Geneva, the Prime Ministers of India, Pakistan and Ceylon were kept informed of all that was happening by Mr Eden, the British Foreign Secretary. It was he, also, who approached them to see if they would join in a guarantee to assure the future of Indo-China. Thus, the three Commonwealth Asian members were kept intimately in touch with most vital discussions which closely concerned their own future, and yet in which they had been granted no direct part. Mr Eden had negotiated at Geneva with the interests and opinions of these three members of the Commonwealth constantly in mind.

There was comfort, too, for Britain and the Commonwealth in the consolidation of the position in Malaya. General Templer had been so brilliantly successful in repelling the armed threat of the communists that the British Government was able to announce that he would relinquish his appointment as High Commissioner in June. That clearly heralded a change of policy, with more emphasis on constitutional advance. Early in the year new proposals were made for a Federal Legislative Council with a majority of elected members—52 out of 98. That was deemed to be as large a step as was safe in the circumstances, though both Malayan and Chinese leaders argued that it was much too timid.

Their very grievances brought the Malays and the Chinese closer together. The most heartening event for years was the Alliance between the United Malaya National Organization and the Malayan Chinese Association. Obdurate and unreasoning though the Alliance leaders proved from time to time, they symbolized a racial cooperation which promised to be the salvation Malaya had sought for so long. And the inter-racial front was still further strengthened when the Malayan Indian Congress decided to fight the 1955 general election with the Alliance. What all this amounted to was a political

setback for the communists equally as significant as that achieved by
General Templer in the field.

It was striking to note how that pattern of Far East events, in 1954,
was broadly reproduced in the Middle East. For there, too, the
shadow of communist intrigue and penetration provoked a free
world reaction. But, as in the Far East, nationalism grew ever
stronger, and with it the desire of many of the Arabs to have done
with Western influence and to decide their own destiny. And Mr
Nehru, though this could hardly be claimed as his direct sphere of
influence, left no doubt that he considered the Middle East should
be part of the neutral zone which he earnestly desired. Thus, the
Middle East also reflected the divergence in Commonwealth foreign
policies. For Britain and Pakistan were hardening in their view that
only armed strength would deter the Russians.

There was no escaping the fact that the British position in the
area, already tenuous, was under repeated challenge. The Yemen
provoked continual frontier incidents with the Aden Protectorate,
which were all the more significant because of the installation of
Britain's new oil refinery. How far these incidents were encouraged
from Cairo it was difficult to assess, at that early date. But the new
Egyptian Republic was already bent on an expansionist policy. General
Neguib might have handled even this ambition with caution. But
by now he had been deposed by Colonel Nasser, who made no
secret of his ambition to build up a new and utterly independent
Arab bloc, and that without loss of time.

The Anglo-Egyptian Suez Canal Agreement had already given the
young revolutionary leaders of Egypt great prestige in the Arab
world. All British forces were pledged to leave the Canal Zone
within 20 months, and it was difficult to view the future of the
Middle East without foreboding. Britain herself had shaped no
coherent policy for the area; as for America her utter failure to
comprehend the necessity for a united free world policy was later
to have most tragic results. Nasser—and that should be remembered
now—was even then implacably resolved to break British influence
throughout the Arab world, and towards the end of the year it was
dismally clear that Egypt was positively engaged in stimulating
hatred of Britain wherever she could. The position in the Aden Protectorate grew steadily worse, and in the Sudan a campaign of vilifi-
cation of British officials, of all things British, was steadily pursued
by Egypt. Indeed, the high hopes that the Suez Canal Agreement

would inaugurate a new and cordial era of Anglo-Arab relationships were smashed within two months. Rarely in British history had such great decisions been based on such insubstantial hopes and what made it all the more difficult for Britain was that the Muslim members of the Commonwealth, whatever the clear evidence of Nasser's cynical disregard of his previous protestations of friendship, were emotionally prejudiced in favour of their co-religionists in Egypt.

Now it was that the importance of Cyprus in the scheme of things was plainly manifest. Early in 1954 Britain had attempted once more to bring peace to that vital island and to get the Greek Cypriots to accept a new constitution. But Greece herself, actively co-operating with the Cypriot leader, the priest-politician Archbishop Makarios, stood fast on the demand for *enosis*. As far as Britain was concerned, the handing over of the island to Greece was nowhere near the realm of practical politics. In the middle of the year the Ministry of Defence made the bluntest of replies to the demands from Athens by tersely announcing that Cyprus was to be the Middle East Headquarters. From that time on, the island was destined to stage a mounting tragedy, and one without apparent hope of solution.

Greece succeeded in bringing the Cyprus question before the United Nations, which decided to shelve the matter by 49 votes to nil, with 11 abstentions. In a sense, this was a victory for Britain, as it amounted to the United Nations declaring that it had no intention of interefering with the sovereign rights of member nations. But in reality it was a triumph for communism. For here were Greece and Britain, allies in N.A.T.O., parading their mutual hostility before the world. And to make matters worse, Turkey—conscious of her own people in Cyprus, and of the island's strategic importance to her own safety—chose this moment to let Greece know that if Britain abandoned Cyprus she would press her own claims. Cyprus had ceased to be merely a colonial problem.

CHAPTER XXVII

SWING OF THE PENDULUM

THE CONFUSION AND complications of the British Colonial picture continued in 1954, and it was hard to discern any coherent pattern. But, despite the diversity of secondary threads, some of the main threads were clearly visible. For some time it had been abundantly clear that the extension of the franchise had shifted the prospect of eventual power away from these Colonial leaders who had "served their time" in legislative assemblies, and towards the younger men who more closely identified themselves with the aspirations of the mass of the people.

Nkrumah had proved this beyond all doubt in the Gold Coast, and in various Colonies younger nationalist leaders had taken due note. The result of this was a continuous pressure to force the hand of the Colonial Office, an insistent demand for accelerated progress towards independence. Even the plain fact that economic viability was an essential to true independence did not hold back the ambitions of nationalist leaders. But, from 1954 on, the Colonial Office was slowly but surely able to use this economic brake to greater effect. The pendulum swung back a little. The sacred cause of nationalism was not altogether the irresistible force it had earlier seemed to be.

Another main thread in the developing Colonial pattern was the increasing evidence that leaders of nationalist movements in multi-racial territories were hardening in their tendency to reject the proposition of partnership with the Europeans. They were now thinking beyond equality to the time when political power would be theirs, and when the Europeans would be allowed to participate only as a minority. This development, obviously, was in the forefront of Oliver Lyttelton's mind when he decided to expedite the birth of the Federation of Rhodesia and Nyasaland. Looking at the increasing power of African nationalism, at the bloody strife in Kenya and the obdurate suspicions in Uganda, there was room for doubting whether the experiment in black-white partnership had come in time. At least Lyttelton could draw comfort from the overwhelming victory of Sir Godfrey Huggins and Sir Roy Welensky in the first Federal election. The nationalist leaders of the African Congress

N

were temporarily confused and divided in their aims and member-ship had declined sharply. There was a prospect that strong, liberal and imaginative leadership could make partnership something more than a convenient word.

The Secretary of State, heartened by the prospect in Central Africa, now produced his plan for another multi-racial state, this time in Kenya. There were clear signs that the Mau Mau organization was under heavy strain, and Lyttelton judged that there was a distinct chance—albeit probably the last one—of laying the foundations of real racial partnership. But his offer of a substantial instalment of responsible government was received with suspicion and doubt. His plan was based on multi-racial cabinet government, with portfolios for three Europeans, two Asians and one African. It was difficult enough to get the European Elected Members of the Legislative Council to agree, and only the dominant influence of their leader, Michael Blundell, carried the day. The African leaders rejected the plan outright on the argument that they were inadequately repre-sented, whereupon the Asians also withdrew their original support. But finally the Lyttelton Plan went through, though there were dis-turbing signs that extremist elements in all three races were more than ready to wreck it at the first opportunity.

Northwards in Uganda, the Secretary of State could claim only a small measure of success. The Kabaka had become a martyr-figure to his people, but at least other points of difference with the Buganda were satisfactorily settled, and it was made abundantly clear that Uganda would not be drawn unwillingly into an East African federation, but would follow the Gold Coast to individual indepen-dence. But though this prevented any risk of rebellions it was not enough to stabilize the country. The African Congress, at once push-ing their own cause by demanding the Kabaka's return and yet assid-uously eroding the influence of the old ruling class, showed their strength in a number of ways. They initiated a buyers' strike, whipped up anti-British feeling in the vernacular press, hamstrung the preparations for constitutional discussions and finally forced the Governor to reimpose a state of emergency. None of these things could have been accomplished if the departure of the Kabaka had not left a vacuum ideally suited to troublemakers. Indeed, it was hard to escape the suspicion that the British Government, before the year was out, would be constrained to revoke their "irrevocable" banishment of the Kabaka.

In West Africa, British policy seemed to be slowly but surely justifying itself. Dr Nkrumah and his Convention People's Party won the second general election in the Gold Coast, and so became the first all-African government put in power by that political system introduced by the white man—democracy. Nkrumah, in the intervening years, had shown himself both capable and moderate, perhaps even a world statesman in the making. The election was the final step towards independence. It was upon Nkrumah now to prove in the face of his critics that Africans could operate that democratic system and not let it be either torn apart by tribalism or eroded by nepotism.

Neighbouring Nigeria, which was even more subject than the Gold Coast to separatism and tribal feuds, looked now as if it might provide Lyttelton with yet another triumph. At the beginning of the year, the constitutional conference was resumed in Lagos, and finally effected an agreement which even the ebullient Dr Azikiwe, the Eastern Region leader, agreed would meet the Nigerian situation until 1956. Nigeria, until then, was to exist as a loose federation of three states, with a federal electorate, federal Houses and a limited but absolute authority at the centre. The jealousies of the leaders and the rivalries of the tribes had certainly been only slightly diminished, but the whole outcome represented a most considerable advance in what, considering its great size and population, was a key country of Africa for the Commonwealth.

It was at this point of time, when a majority of the great problems which had been shaking the Colonial Empire to its foundations seemed either in process of solution or at least temporarily under control, that Oliver Lyttelton resigned his office as Secretary of State for the Colonies. He had clearly driven himself to the far point of exhaustion, and the towering significance in human terms of all the decisions he had been called upon to make had taken its heavy toll on a man much more sensitive than his opponents realized. Few of the men occupying his great office had better reason to be proud of their stewardship. Lyttelton had offended and exacerbated many members of the House of Commons in his early days of office, mainly because of his lack of experience of that institution's traditions and idiosyncrasies. At his departure, he commanded the respect and confidence not only of his own party, but of a considerable section of the Labour Opposition.

The Government was more than usually fortunate in his successor.

Alan Lennox-Boyd was not merely a man with previous experience of the Colonial Office, he was utterly dedicated to Colonial affairs. Not only that, he was young, resilient and resolute, a giant of a man of great tact and considerable personal charm. Both these latter qualities were of more than ordinary importance in a field where success so often lay in personal relationships.

It was midway through 1954 when Lyttelton left, and it was clear to Lennox-Boyd that, though Buganda and Kenya were still running sores, there was a comparative breathing space in Africa. He could hardly expect this comforting condition to last for long, and he was not the man to wait for the clouds to gather again before taking action.

It was not long before he produced his solution for Uganda. Not only were far-reaching constitutional changes announced but the way was made open for the return of the Kabaka himself. The word "irrevocable" seemed destined now to end up in a communist "double talk" dictionary. Certainly the probable return of the Kabaka placed Governor Sir Andrew Cohen in a remarkably embarrassing position. Britain's prestige suffered a corresponding decline and the position of the ambitious young leaders of the African Congress was considerably strengthened. But the sad fact was that the return of the Kabaka was imperative if Uganda was to go forward. The excitement over the prospect of the Kabaka's return obscured the very great importance of the constitutional changes. They envisaged a ministerial system, three of the ministers being Africans, while half the members of the Legislative Council were also to be Africans. One more African territory was thus being advanced towards self-government by its own African leaders. There were deep misgivings about the new Uganda policy, not least inside the British Conservative Party. But there was little enough criticism, and the general opinion was that Lennox-Boyd had made a reasonable job out of a sorry, bungled business.

Two other pressing problems facing the new Secretary of State lay over in the Caribbean, in British Guiana and in British Honduras. The Report of the Constitutional Commission on British Guiana completely justified the emergency action taken in 1953, when Dr Jagan and his other "fellow traveller" ministers had been dismissed and the constitution suspended. But that was about all the comfort it did give. The Commission "reluctantly but quite firmly" came to the conclusion that a period of marking time in the advance towards self-government was still needed. In short, the certainty that another election would only result in the return of Dr Jagan to power left no alternative but direct rule.

In British Honduras the picture was markedly brighter. Britain was giving massive economic help to this backward country, and nationalist leaders like Leigh Richardson showed signs of recognizing that power entailed responsibility. But, even here, there was the suspicion that a willingness to co-operate with Britain was enough to brand men like Richardson as treacherous collaborators. Still, British Honduras had not tumbled into the chaos which had only lately seemed its unavoidable fate. That in itself was no mean gain.

The great experiment in human relations which was the Commonwealth could, indeed, be said to be showing a signal measure of success as 1954 drew to a close. The stresses inherent in all the post-war changes seemed not to be nearly as potentially disruptive as many had feared. The recognition by the self-governing states of common interests, even of a common destiny, was steadily strengthening. It was true that a sober assessment of the state of the Commonwealth underlined some distressing matters. Both Pakistan and South Africa seemed bent on republican status. The quarrel between India and Pakistan over Kashmir had reached deadlock. South Africa's native policies were a permanent irritation—at the least—to most other members of the Commonwealth.

But the very fact that self-governing nations could still continue in close consultation despite such differences was a major tribute to the continuing significance of the Commonwealth. Another meeting of the Prime Ministers was scheduled for January of 1955, and it was obvious that the economic state of the Commonwealth and an exchange of views on the international situation would be major matters on the agenda. Britain had accepted commitments in Europe which could not but have a decisive affect on her ability to defend vital Commonwealth interests. The bulk of the British Army was stationed in Europe, and a drastic reappraisal of Commonwealth strategy was overdue.

The South-East Asia Treaty Organization (SEATO) would obviously come up for further scrutiny. The value of this was increasingly suspect, and it now appeared to be little more than a belated extension of the Anzus Pact to enable Britain to participate. Only Pakistan of the three Asian signatories had any real military significance, and as meaningful Asian participation was half the battle in the current atmosphere of South-East Asia, there was no escaping the fact that SEATO was beginning to look like a last-ditch stand of the colonial powers in Asia. Mr Nehru's outright hostility to the Organization gave added strength to this particular view. Its potentialities for creating a rift in the Commonwealth were only too obvious. But how else was communist expansionism in South-East Asia to be countered?

As to the economic state of the Commonwealth the pressure for closer economic links between Britain and Europe was reaching a point where the effect on Commonwealth interests demanded detailed study. It was significant that the concept of the Commonwealth taking part in any scheme was also being increasingly supported. Not only the inherent threat to British and Colonial trade was responsible for this. The inability of Britain herself, despite great efforts, to meet the sore need for capital of the under-developed Commonwealth countries was increasingly apparent. An economic union in Europe (said its advocates) might well provide a sorely-needed alternative source of investment.

It was no easy matter to get a concrete estimate of the amount of capital needed to develop the Commonwealth's resources at the maximum practicable rate. In the preceding year of 1953 Britain had invested £120 million in the Commonwealth, plus another handsome (uncalculated) sum put in by private enterprise. The evidence was that this was not nearly enough to expand food output, to incept necessary capital works, to extract minerals which would save dollars, in short to provide for expansion on even a minimum desirable scale.

One thing that Britain could claim was that the vicious circles of poverty in many territories had been broken inside ten years by the Colonial Development and Welfare schemes. Such territories, so long accustomed to taking one step backward to every one forward, had been raised by painful effort to a point at which forward progress, however slow, was possible. The ten-year development plans drawn up under the 1945 Colonial Development and Welfare Act had given the vital impetus. It was now announced that the act was to be extended for a further five years, and that in itself was evidence of a gratifying continuity of purpose.

But was it enough that Britain should "go it alone"? There was reason enough to inquire if the other prosperous states of the Commonwealth ought not to subscribe to the welfare of their less fortunate colleagues. The Commonwealth could not survive if the greater part of it was sunk in wretched poverty, whilst the other part grew steadily richer. Political advancement and economic expansion must keep some sort of pace with each other—that lesson had been painfully learnt by the Colonial Office, and it was time for the Commonwealth as a whole to digest the same lesson, if they wished the organization to survive.

CHAPTER XXVIII

THE APPARENT ABYSS

TWO MATTERS DOMINATED the minds of the Commonwealth Prime Ministers when they met at the beginning of 1955—the H-bomb and the coming Afro-Asian Conference. For these two, between them, symbolized the growing abyss between India (and to a lesser degree Ceylon) on the one hand and Britain and the rest of the Commonwealth on the other (though Pakistan tried to stand precariously midway). Mr Nehru's neutralist and pacifist policy and the apparent reliance on arms by the British created this abyss—and it seemed impossible to bridge. But it was not really so bleakly dangerous as appeared. For India's policy, workable as it was in the current state of the world, depended in the last resort on Western military strength. And it was just as true that Western strength, at least as far as Asia and the rest of the former subject world went, was an empty beating of the wind if it lost sight of what Nehru stood for.

Yet Nehru, at the February talks of the Prime Ministers, exacerbated more feelings than he healed. His rooted tendency to didactic lecturing of others had never been more apparent. The still-dangerous state of the world, particularly in that area which he wished to dedicate to the cause of peace and neutralism, possibly sharpened his fears. And without doubt he was pinning the highest hopes on the Afro-Asian Conference in the coming April. From it, he believed, would stem such an irresistible desire for peace and development that neither of the great power blocs could ignore it. But the irony of the situation was that the Afro-Asian bloc was already fishing in the most troubled of waters. The five Asian Prime Ministers, at their preliminary meeting at Bogor, had come out in favour of Indonesia's extremely doubtful claim to Western New Guinea. They had also supported nationalist demands in Tunisia and Morocco and, to cap all, no invitation for the Bandung Conference had been sent to Israel, in case the Arab States were offended. It would be unfair to accuse the convenors of the Bandung Conference of hypocrisy, but it is not unfair to observe that, faced with complicated or delicate situations, they were forced to the same twists and deviations as those older powers whose outdated diplomacy they held to be the root of so many of the world's ills.

Pandit Nehru was the inspiring spirit of the Bandung Conference, and it is therefore significant to examine his outlook in detail. The socialist principles which conditioned much of his political thinking were not the most powerful influences in determining his international policy. His own deeply-rooted "Indianism" was chiefly responsible, and that was why he carried with him not only the great majority of his educated countrymen but the masses of the people also, who felt rather than understood the rightness of his policies.

India or rather her people, with the sea on two sides and the towering Himalayas on the third, had through the centuries inclined towards isolationism, particularly in the sense that expansionism held little appeal. When the British went, this state of mind reasserted itself. India was no longer a hub of a foreign maritime empire's defence system. For the Indians, the day had now arrived when they could look after India, establish peace and struggle towards prosperity. Their outward relations would consist in harmonious relations with their neighbours, and particularly those with age-long associations with India.

But, when this gentle world was put to the test of reality, Pandit Nehru found that he too, like the British, was impelled to establish his sphere of influence, even his concentric defence ring. In the days when India was the brightest jewel in the British Crown, her theoretical defence ring was flung round as far as Turkey and the Middle East, as far as the shores of the Horn of Africa and the coast of Borneo, as far northward as the borders of Mongolia. For Pandit Nehru, this same defence ring (sadly cut down to the north when China took Tibet) was still a necessary sphere of influence, circumscribing his longed-for area of neutrality and peace. The stark difference with the old days of the British rule lay in the fact that warlike preparations and power politics must be kept far from this hallowed region.

Pakistan's main object did not differ from that of India—to survive. But that word had a desperately more urgent ring in Pakistani
ears. India was consistently regarded as the great enemy to the survival of the new Muslim nation, and Pakistan took the hard, practical
view that its interests would best be served by alliances with the
Western world, which would at one and the same time ensure arms
to defend herself against India, and provide her with a bulwark
against the communist tide of expansion. The signing of the United
States-Pakistan Defence Assistance Agreement at once infuriated
Nehru not only because it gave arms to Pakistan, but because it
brought the breath of the Cold War into the regions which he considered his sphere. But Pakistan's predilection for Western support did not estrange her from Asia. She still worked with the
Colombo Powers, she was more than anxious to be present at Bandung. Further, she was eager to consolidate her claim as a leader of
the Muslim world, and though little reliance was placed on the states
of the Middle East, this particular concept led to a treaty of alliance
with Turkey.

The third of the Asian members of the Commonwealth, Ceylon,
hopefully pursued that dream so cherished by small territories
afflicted with strategic importance—to be fondly regarded, but to be
left alone by the great powers. Prime Minister Sir John Kotelawala
echoed this ambition in referring to Ceylon as "a potential Switzer-
land-in-Asia". A Defence Agreement with Britain, cordial relations
with other members of the Commonwealth, membership of the
Colombo Powers, were all steps designed to assure Ceylon the safe
and happy position she so much desired. Clearly the Defence Agreement with Britain was hard to reconcile with membership of the
Colombo Powers, but the ebullient Kotelawala was in no doubt that
he had found a "Middle Path" (not quite like India's, still less like
Pakistan's) which would lead on to safety.

The "white" members of the Commonwealth were of course
dedicated to resistance to communism, without qualification. But,
at the period of the current discussions of the Prime Ministers in
London, it was significant to note that Britain was especially anxious
not to let India feel isolated. There was a distinct effort in British
Government circles to present pacifism and the H-bomb as being by
no means irreconcilable. The former, in short, was not only highly
desirable but distinctly possible—with the aid of the latter.

But the two Commonwealth nations which watched the development of Mr Nehru's ideas with the most acute attention were Australia and New Zealand. The Australians had only recently sent out their largest-ever trade mission to South-East Asia, intensified their interest in the Colombo Plan and grown more sensitive about the "White Australia" policy. On the other hand, they had no doubt about the value of SEATO membership to them, they had no hesitation about sending troops to help the British in Malaya, and they refused to support the Indonesians against the Dutch over the claim to Western New Guinea. Yet it was significant that Mr Menzies, on his return from the Prime Ministers' Conference, felt it necessary to judiciously explain that while India felt that military aspects of the Manila Treaty had a provocative effect on Communist China, Mr Nehru did understand that Australia had gone into the Treaty with no thought of aggression, and with "a single eye to a security which countries like Thailand and Malaya and Australia have entirely in common".

This regard for Mr Nehru's feelings had its due recognition when, later on at the end of the Bandung Conference, Mr Nehru said: "We send our greetings to Australia and New Zealand. And indeed Australia and New Zealand are almost in our region. They certainly do not belong to Europe, much less to America. They are next to us and I should like Australia and New Zealand to come nearer to Asia. I would welcome them because I do not want what we say or do to be based on racial prejudices. We have had enough of this racialism elsewhere."

The Afro-Asian Conference at Bandung took place in the April following the Commonwealth Prime Ministers' meeting, and when both these events are surveyed in retrospect, once more the unique influence of the Commonwealth is evident. For three of the countries represented at Bandung were self-governing states of the Commonwealth—India, Pakistan and Ceylon. And Kogo Botsio, Minister of State, represented a Gold Coast that was soon to become independent Ghana. The influence of all of these countries came down on the side of moderation and tolerance, and indeed Mr Nehru played a dominant part throughout the proceedings and left his firm impression on them.

The potentialities of Bandung have, I think, been overrated. It has always been difficult to believe that 29 nations, with widely differing viewpoints and ambitions, would for long act coherently. The influence of the "Afro-Asian bloc" at the United Nations has been frequently emphasized, yet this "bloc" has just as frequently been divided in its voting on crucial matters. But there is no gainsaying the real significance of the Bandung Conference, that it dramatically demonstrated to the world the emergence of a large body of former subject races, almost all of them coloured. The danger of Bandung was that it could be turned to the most unscrupulous and dangerous account by the communists, in keeping alive "anticolonial" hates for the benefit of Russia, China and their allies.

China, as one of the delegates, had a splendid opportunity, and Chou-En-lai, the Prime Minister, made great play with it. In his major speech he attacked colonialism, America, *apartheid* and every other matter calculated to discredit the Western world. Sir John Kotelawala restored some of the balance by directing attention to "the new imperialism" of communism, Kogo Botsio stressed Britain's desire to give the Gold Coast independence, Mohammed Ali of Pakistan warned the Conference of the dangers of outside interference with sovereign states, and Pandit Nehru stated that "we mean no ill to anybody. We send our greetings to Europe and America..." Commonwealth loyalties were unquestionably a valuable stabilizing factor at Bandung.

That Prime Ministers' Conference of 1955 was the last that Sir Winston Churchill attended. Shortly after it, he announced his resignation. It was indeed the end of a political era, a colossus was departing from the world stage. Yet Churchill, strangely, had never dominated the post-war meetings of Commonwealth Prime Ministers, rarely ever had he left his own masterful impression on the deliberations. In the post-war years, Nehru and Menzies had usually been the outstanding figures. The advent of Sir Anthony Eden was warmly welcomed by the Commonwealth leaders, particularly by those from Asia. His pre-war record of integrity, his wide experience of international affairs and his known breadth of vision were great assets. And when the British electorate returned the Conservative Government to power with an increased majority in May, Eden seemed to be in a position to still further consolidate the influence and importance of the Commonwealth.

He was almost at once confronted with a crisis of a sort that must have recalled the years before 1939. For in the Middle East, the ambitious Nasser launched a series of violent radio and newspaper attacks on Israel. The object of this campaign, peculiarly similar to those of Hitler before the war, was at once to "soften up" his enemy, to maintain a constant state of suspense in the Middle East for his own expansionist plans, and to still further project himself as the great champion of the Arab and Muslim world. Carefully-staged frontier incidents and the ostentatious training of special troops fitted into a depressingly familiar pattern.

Nasser had already strongly reacted to the Baghdad Pact, earlier in this same year. The Pact was initiated by the pro-British Prime Minister of Iraq, Nuri es Said, and Iraq and Turkey were the original signatories. Nasser at once effected an alliance with Syria. He was determined not to be outbidden in his ambition to capture the leadership of the Arabs. But the Baghdad Pact, which was in reality a barrier to communist expansion, was immeasurably strengthened by the adherence first of Britain, and then of Pakistan and Persia.

But it is doubtful if Nasser, swollen as he was by his flattering reception at Bandung, would have been so continuingly belligerent if the Russians had not suddenly manipulated a really dangerous crisis in the Middle East. In September it was announced that communist Czechoslovakia would supply Egypt with arms, immediately. At once the balance of strength between Israel and the Arab countries, so carefully preserved by the free world, was shattered and a situation of great hazard created.

The last of the British forces were scheduled to leave the Canal Zone by June of 1956. There were continual reports of unrest in the British-protected sheikhdoms of Arabia, and disturbing evidence of anglophobia in Jordan. To cap all, the ambitious and intriguing Archbishop Makarios of Cyprus, strongly aided by certain circles in Greece, was creating a succession of crises. Cyprus, with its Greek and Turkish population, presented a considerable problem to Britain at any time. With the explosive possibilities now so apparent in the Middle East, it was more than ever essential that stability should be maintained in the island.

So it was that the Middle East presented another area over which the Commonwealth could be gravely split. Britain, Australia, South Africa and New Zealand could not but view Colonel Nasser's actions with the greatest alarm. And Pakistan was already committed to the Baghdad Pact, which was in essence a military pact. But India (with a reluctant Ceylon well in the rear) saw once more the threat of war on the periphery of her "peace area". And although Nasser was the potential belligerent, he was able to count on the sympathy of Pandit Nehru, simply because he could present the Baghdad Pact as a warmongers' device in an area which would be neutral if it were left to Nasser's own arrangements.

In short, the Middle East situation was not only a grave direct threat to the Commonwealth, with its effect on oil supplies and communications. It was also a potential threat to goodwill inside the Commonwealth, with India once more on the opposite side of the fence to her fellow members. And when Mr Nehru extended an invitation to visit India to Marshal Bulganin and Mr Krushchev there seemed grounds for further dismay. As it happened, the two Russian leaders overplayed their hand. The rapturous welcome extended to them by an Indian people fervently desiring a peaceful world could not disguise the plain fact that Mr Nehru himself had to correct a number of the wilder statements of the Russians. And the suspicion that the tour was arranged not simply for the sake of international friendship, but to prevent Russia being pushed out of the Asian picture by China, took a deep hold.

Nehru, who at that period—particularly when he paid a reciprocal visit to Russia—seemed to be isolating himself from his friends and from reality, actually emerged in the final reckoning as a more towering figure than ever. Previous events had proved the world's need for a great mediator, strongly placed and courted by both sides. Coming events were to prove it yet again, and the fact that the mediator was a leading figure in the Commonwealth, itself an organ of mediation, was of the utmost significance.

CHAPTER XXIX

THE COLONIAL "PARISH"

WITH THE WORLD in so uncertain a state, and dangers pressing in on all sides, Britain herself still went steadily forward with the unfolding of her Colonial policy. Lennox-Boyd at the Colonial Office had indeed taken over at a time when his predecessor, Oliver Lyttelton, had managed to at least get most of the more dangerous problems under temporary control. The position, it could be said, was being held, but no more than that. Now it was for Lennox-Boyd to produce the longer-term solutions, a manifestly more difficult proposition.

His energy, his remarkable knowledge of Colonial affairs and his genuine dedication to his office were considerable assets. And he needed to call on them all, for throughout the Colonial Empire there were pressing matters awaiting rapid decision. The Secretary of State, surveying the map of his widespread "parish", could lay his finger on a score of places, near and far, all of them demanding some degree of urgent attention.

Nearest to home was Malta, with its depressing post-war history of economic instability and political frustration. Prime Minister Dom Mintoff, having won the general election, now wanted action on the proposal for Malta's integration with Britain—but on terms which from the outset seemed likely to be unpalatable to the British Government. It was arranged that there would be preliminary talks in London in the middle of June; but it could hardly be said that Mr Mintoff was assuring the best possible atmosphere when he threatened that "Britain might lose Malta" if integration did not go through.

Amongst British politicians, particularly on the Conservative side, there were growing doubts about the wisdom of integration. The first warm glow of pride at the prospect of a colony actually wanting to become part of Britain was waning as the consequences became more apparent. Above all else, the prospect of Maltese M.P.s in the British Parliament raised uneasy memories of the former Irish members, and Mr Mintoff's talk of equivalent social benefits for Malta increasingly took on an aspect of unreality.

The significance of the Malta situation was that it appeared to offer one possible solution for some of the smaller Colonial territories, those which could never stand on their own feet. Several of these territories, such as the Bahamas, Bermuda and Hong Kong, were watching with the deepest interest to see how Malta fared. The idea that there could be some twenty or thirty Colonial M.P.s in the House of Commons, bedevilling the party balance, began to dawn on Westminster, and it was not an idea which aroused much enthusiasm.

In the outcome, the Maltese Government's request was referred to a Round Table Conference, later in the year, at which all sections of opinion in both countries were to be represented. The British Labour Party was already committed to support the integration proposition, whilst the chief opposition in Malta, the Nationalist Party, was opposed to integration and in favour of Dominion status. And in the wings was the powerful Catholic Church, studying all moves with extraordinary care, watchful that any political agreement would not strike at its privileges and influence. Even at this stage, it was obvious that Mr Mintoff had an arduous and protracted struggle ahead of him.

Apart from all other considerations, the British Government was anxious to stabilize matters in Malta because of the steady worsening of the position eastwards along the Mediterranean, in Cyprus. In an attempt to find the broadest-based of solutions for that troubled island, Britain invited Greece and Turkey to discuss the general problem of Middle East defence, including the future of Cyprus. This tripartite conference ended in complete failure, due mainly to the utter intransigence of the Greeks. Greece threatened to withdraw from N.A.T.O., there were riots in Istanbul, and the final result was that Turkey became as intractable as Greece and flatly stated that if Britain left the island it must revert to Turkey.

Britain's next move was to appoint Field-Marshal Sir John Harding, one of her great soldiers, as Governor of Cyprus. "A Field Marshal seems a heavy hammer to crack so small a nut," said one newspaper commentator. But it was an exceedingly tough nut, and Sir John was not long in discovering that. Three meetings with Archbishop Makarios came to nothing. Whereupon a £38 million development grant was announced. Cynics remarked that terrorism was the way to get money out of the British Government, but there was a great deal to be said for an attempt to try and ease political tension by going ahead with economic expansion. In any case, Harding was prepared for the worst. Troops from no less than seven distinguished British regiments were flown to the island to underpin the police force. But Makarios was still the key man. The ambitious, fanatical Archbishop, however he temporized, had in view one goal only, and that was the union of Cyprus with Greece, for the greater glory of his Church.

Further out still from Britain, Alan Lennox-Boyd had troubles to handle in the Aden Protectorate. The Yemen Government, encouraged by the support given to it at the Bandung Conference, now settled down to a purposeful and constant provocation of incidents, leading to a rebellion in the Shamsi area. There was increasing doubt among the Protectorate Sultans about Britain's ability to protect their peoples. This fear was countered by the dispatch of troops—though Britain's commitments were now so heavy that it seemed barely possible to stretch her military resources much further.

Over the sea on the other side of the Gulf of Aden, on the Horn of Africa, a hand-sized cloud was developing in the Somaliland Protectorate. This backward, sunburnt and impoverished land had largely escaped attention in the turmoil of events elsewhere, and even now it was only dimly realized that in the reshaping of the postwar world it could become of immeasurable strategic importance. Ex-Italian Somaliland, now called Somalia, had been promised independence by 1960, by the United Nations, and in that territory the militant Somali Youth League, dreaming of a United Somalia, was already intriguing to effect a leadership over all Somalis throughout the Horn of Africa.

The storm which had blown up in the British Protectorate was the direct result of the Anglo-Ethiopian Agreement whereby the Haud area on the Somaliland-Ethiopian frontier was handed back to the hated Ethiopians. This area contained important grazing grounds and, though Ethiopia's case was sound, that did not mollify the Somali tribesmen who had been in the habit of feeding their beasts there. They considered Britain had betrayed them, and the Somali Youth League, aided by Egypt, made great play with the whole matter, both in the United Nations and throughout the Horn.

Lennox-Boyd, sitting in his office in Whitehall, could look at the map, right down Africa, and reflect on the picture that consistently repeated itself—the picture of ambitious, under-developed, immature countries eager for the taste of power, while all around them the huge struggle between democracy and communism developed, a struggle which, if it stumbled into war, would take little account of the weak and small, whatever pipings rose from the halls of the United Nations. As with Lyttelton and Creech Jones before him, the one commodity that Lennox-Boyd needed most was time, and it was time which seemed always to be denied him.

South-west of the Somaliland Protectorate, in Uganda, the return of the Kabaka as a constitutional monarch was the signal for a rising activity of the African National Congress. Some of Buganda's best and most experienced leaders were being forced into the shadows, their "crime" being that they had supported the British administration during the Kabaka's exile. Lawless intimidation of chiefs, as well as officials, was the order of the day. It was a lamentable sequel, and one which served once more to remind able Colonial leaders far and wide of the dangers of over-much loyalty to Britain when a nationalist movement was rolling blindly on.

In neighbouring Kenya, the lifting of the ban on African political organizations made possible by the success of operations against Mau Mau had led to a rapid rebirth of African ambitions. With the discredited Kikuyu people too crushed and disillusioned to bid for leadership, the intelligentsia of the Luo people seized their opportunity. The African Progressive Party was formed under the chairmanship of Mr H. D. Odaba, a Luo; another political organization for the Africans of Nairobi was launched under the leadership of Mr J. Henry Gaya, another Luo. Mr B. O. Ohanga, the African Minister of Community Development in the Kenya Government, had already formed yet another body in Nyanza, and he too was a Luo. But it was in the revived African trade union movement that the most significant new leader was establishing himself, a young leader with no taint of the past to incommode him. This was Tom Mboya, a twenty-five-year-old Luo of extreme shrewdness, high intelligence and proven capacity for leadership. Mboya, as Secretary of the Federation for Labour, had played a large part in settling the Mombasa dock strike. Before long he was to emerge from the trade union movement into politics and to make his mark as one of the new African leaders not only able to come to terms with the rules of the white man's world, but to use those rules to his own purpose.

The third of the East African territories, Tanganyika, presented a more placid and comforting picture. That outstanding Governor, Sir Edward Twining, had combined a warm humanity and great administrative capacity in the exact proportions, so that Tanganyika could still claim to be a happy example to the rest of Africa. At the end of 1955, Sir Edward promised a plan for the country's first general elections, albeit only within certain areas. The principle of equal representation on the Legislative Council, he emphasized, would stay, with 10 African Representative Members, 10 Europeans and 10 Asians. "There are some who are impatient," he observed. "Perhaps that is quite natural, but any thinking person who reflects on the facts of the situation must know that it is folly to press for a quicker tempo than we can take."

One of those who was impatient was Julius Kambarage Nyerere, a thirty-four-year-old schoolteacher from one of Tanganyika's smallest tribes, the Zanaki. His father, indeed, was the Chief but Nyerere

o

was ambitious to be the heir of a newer world. After studying at Makerere College in Uganda and later at Edinburgh University (on a Colonial Development and Welfare Fund Scholarship) he had returned to his own land to receive a lower salary than Europeans with equivalent qualifications. It was the old story of frustration. Nyerere responded by turning the Tanganyika African Association into the politically militant African National Union, with himself as President.

Like Nkrumah, Nyerere was a natural orator, and his meetings drew large and enthusiastic crowds. Two visits to the United Nations headquarters in New York to press for African self-government built up his political appeal still further. Nyerere seemed set to be yet another of Africa's "impatient young men". But he was more cautious than most, and less inflexible than Mboya proved to be. And the far-sighted political planning of Sir Edward Twining left him with only a few openings. Yet he turned those openings to good account. His goal was clearly power for the Africans, under his leadership, and he was astute enough to manœuvre himself into that rôle which, as Nkrumah had shown, led to power—the rôle of the national martyr. But there was little that was violent or menacing in Nyerere's progress.

Even in somnolent Zanzibar, lying off the east coast of Africa, the signal was up for advancement. For forty-four years the Sultan, Seyyid Sir Khalifa bin Harub, had calmly observed the political upheavals on the mainland, once the territory of his forebears, and the hunting ground of their slavers. Now he too (and his protector, Britain) could not ignore the pressure of the younger Arab leaders, clamouring for a greater share of government. Changes were announced in the Executive and Legislative Councils, but an unofficial majority was still denied, and so too was elected representation. This was far from satisfactory for the younger men, but at least the Sultan withdrew from the Presidency of the Executive Council, which meant that Zanzibar ceased, even in outward form, to be a monarchy. Democracy had gained a toehold.

Far down in Central Africa, the Federation of Rhodesia and Nyasaland had entered its third year. The economic advance was gratifying in the extreme, but the political situation was beginning to worry the advocates of partnership. Garfield Todd, the handsome and energetic New Zealander who was Premier of Southern Rhodesia, claimed that the liberal forces in the Federation were

becoming divided in their loyalties because of faltering leadership at
the centre. This could only be taken as a criticism of Sir Godfrey
Huggins for hanging on as Federal Prime Minister instead of
making way for Sir Roy Welensky. Huggins, stung for once from
his imperturbability, retorted that "If and when I choose to retire
from political life, it will be when I judge it to be unharmful to the
national interest . . . it is a case where only I can be the judge." But
it did remain true that Sir Roy Welensky was going to be short of
time for a reorganization of the administration and a preparation
for the next vital election if his ageing fellow-architect of the Federation stayed in office. Todd's warning was underlined when in a by-
election in Northern Rhodesia G. F. M. van Eeden, a racial segregation advocate, soundly defeated Sir Roy's own protégé, Geoffrey
Beckett.

From this time on, the rift between the conservative and radical
sections of the pro-partnership section in the Federation became
steadily more apparent, despite the frequent attempts at reconcilia-
tion. Garfield Todd continued to urge a quicker rate of progress
towards partnership, feeling that week by week the prospect of en-
listing African support for the policy was slipping away. In the end,
this was a campaign which led to his political downfall.

But if the partnership policy in Central Africa was facing trying
times, the policy of independence for African territories in the West
was no less under fire. In the Gold Coast, Dr Nkrumah was faced
with a rising tide of discontent, particularly in Ashanti. The cocoa
farmers of Ashanti felt that they were being exploited, and many
people in Ashanti were convinced that Nkrumah's significant State
Councils (Ashanti) Ordinance was nothing less than a determined
effort to break up "the great Ashanti nation" and to reduce the
Asantehene to a mere divisional chief. Nkrumah himself left no
doubt of his intentions to meet tribalism and destroy it as quickly as
he could. "The Convention People's Party is not going to tolerate
kingship in the Gold Coast," he told a public meeting in Accra.
"We are determined that sovereignty rests with the people." The
response was a wave of violence and murder in Ashanti.

The National Liberation Movement, which had sprung up in the
previous year to resist Nkrumah and his party, gathered considerable
strength from all this. Many people flocked to support its demand
for a federal constitution. It particularly had the blessing of the chiefs
and sub-chiefs—naturally, for Nkrumah meant to cut down their

power. In the end, the Prime Minister was forced to recognize the persistent strength of tribal and regional loyalties. He asked Sir Frederick Bourne, a British Constitutional expert, to visit the country and to advise the Gold Coast Government on regional devolution of powers. Sir Frederick's advice was a sore blow to the N.L.M.'s ambition for a federation, but he did suggest a substantial transfer of power from the central government to the regions, through the formation of regional assemblies which would have considerable responsibility for development and social services. Sir Frederick also suggested that no measures should be taken to affect the position, traditional functions and privileges of the chiefs without consulting the state councils.

All that was happening in the Gold Coast clearly illustrated the major threats to the fulfilment of British colonial policy in African territories. On the one hand was the danger that the new, elected leaders would turn towards dictatorship or autocracy, whether by choice or by force of circumstance; on the other hand was the equal danger that the old traditional wielders of power, the chiefs, would destroy democracy before it had a chance, through appeals to tribalism to preserve their own position. Nkrumah had had to give ground, but his opponents could not but be aware that they had only halted the tide for the time being.

In Nigeria, another variation of the same problem was still defying solution, though here it was not tribalism under the chiefs versus the new heirs of Western democracy but tribe versus tribe, each paying homage to democracy, but still unwilling to really use it as the basis of national unity. Political feelings still persisted in being local and the Federation's bonds were of the lightest. This was not surprising, for Nigeria had not been a single unit at all until 1914. The real hope lay in the economic interdependence of the coast and the hinterland, but there was little enough time left for the politicians to compose their major differences before the decisive conference on self-government in 1956. There was a deep significance in the declaration made at Ibadan by Chief Obafemi Awolowo: "We on our part are resolved to have one Nigeria or no Nigeria at all. If for any reason the North is annoyed out of the Federation, Western Nigeria will have nothing to do with Dr Azikiwe's Southern Dominion."

Far away in Malaya, Britain's experiment in colonial democracy was encountering yet another test. During July, the country held its

first general election, in which the Alliance of the Malay and Chinese
parties (U.M.N.O. and M.C.A.) was confronted by the Party Negara,
a fairly uncompromising Malayan nationalist party, whose direct appeal was to the Malay fear of being engulfed by the Chinese. It
also installed itself as the champion of the Malay Sultans. In short,
Malaya was not simply a land of tribal animosities, but of potential,
indeed actual, racial antagonism.

Led by Tungku Abdul Rahman, a great friend of Britain, the Alliance surprised even the most astute political observers by winning 51
out of 52 elected seats. The Party Negara did not even win the odd
seat, that went to the Malayan Islamic Party. Whitehall could take
considerable comfort from the dramatic victory of an organization
pledged to co-operation between Malay, Chinese and Indian, and
that in a land which not long before had seemed the certain prey of
communism.

But all was not so heartening in Singapore. The volatile, mercurial
David Marshall, Chief Minister under the new constitution, was
already calling for a much more rapid advance towards self-government, and stigmatizing the new constitution as a "hand of death
clutching at the brake of progress". Marshall's gift for the colourful
phrase only hid the apprehensions of a man who knew himself to
be merely the temporary leader in Singapore. He had no intention
of being (in his own words) "a gold-plated shock absorber for
colonialism". Indeed he never was that, but he most certainly was
the shock absorber for a militant and left-wing nationalism, whether
he knew it or not. On his heels the more resolute and dedicated men
of the People's Action Party pressed. David Marshall's theatrical and
flamboyant defiance of the Governor, his sustained quarrel with the
Colonial Office, was but a shadowy play.

Lennox-Boyd himself visited Singapore to see how matters were
shaping, and gave an assurance that it was H.M. Government's
policy to prepare and help the Colony towards self-government. It
was also announced that the U.K. Government was prepared to
receive a comprehensive delegation in London in the following April
to review the working of the constitution. But before the year of 1955
was out Marshall himself was in London having exploratory talks,
demonstrating to all who cared to listen that no man, not even the
leaders of the P.A.P., was more determined than he to win freedom
for Singapore. Clearly it would be more comforting for Britain if
Marshall could be sustained in power, for he was a man of moderate

political outlook, despite his emotional outbursts. But it was the old story. The people of Singapore would soon decide where the power should be, not the Government of Britain. What was certain was that Singapore and Malaya were drifting dangerously apart, and that was not a good thing, particularly for Singapore.

CHAPTER XXX

THE AMERICAN AWAKENING

ELEVEN YEARS AFTER the end of the war, in spite of all the hazards which had attended the development of British colonial policy, there were grounds for cautious hope. The Commonwealth, though some of its links were apparently dangerously fragile, did seem to be shaping into the democratic instrument the free world so desperately needed. Both major political parties in Britain had played their part in this outcome. The aim of both had been the gradual transformation of Empire into Commonwealth, however much they differed on timing and method.

At this point of time two men of exceptional value held key posts in the British Government—Lennox-Boyd at the Colonial Office and Lord Home at the Commonwealth Relations Office. Both men drove themselves hard, were continually visiting Commonwealth countries, and pursued positive ends. Lennox-Boyd did not see his job as merely to provide a finishing school in self-government. He kept before himself the ideal of an ever-growing Commonwealth of free nations, and dedicated himself to that end. Lord Home was no "postmaster-general" at the Commonwealth Relations Office. He kept before the British Cabinet a strong Commonwealth viewpoint and he and Lennox-Boyd effected an important liaison, particularly over Colonial territories approaching independence. The practice had developed of making arrangements well ahead of independence to ensure a smooth transition of any territory from Colonial Office to Commonwealth Relations Office. One example of this procedure was the appointment of an Assistant-Secretary in the C.R.O. to the post of Adviser on External Affairs to the Governor of the Gold Coast. Again, at the end of 1955 Gold Coast and Malayan officials began training as diplomatic officers under arrangements made by the Colonial Office with the co-operation of the C.R.O. and the Foreign Office.

But by far the most significant development as 1956 opened was the growing, if sometimes reluctant, recognition by the United States that the Commonwealth could be a valuable influence in the world. This recognition still clashed with the inherent American opposition to "colonialism", but there was no denying that Britain was steadily leading her charges to independence. And there was also no denying that as territories attained or approached independence they became of paramount concern to the United States. Under British rule they had been stable and dependable, and it was vital to American foreign policy that they should continue to be so.

The plain truth of the matter was that the Americans had been bitterly disillusioned, as leaders of the free world, at the reception given their policies. Neither arms nor wealth had been enough to ensure loyal allies. It appeared to many a critical U.S. citizen that Krushchev and Bulganin could do more towards influencing Asia with one barnstorming tour of India than all the costly aid schemes and defence pacts of Washington.

Bandung underlined the missing factor in American policy. Not all the gold in Fort Knox could buy an admission ticket. The Americans had no voice there. But the Commonwealth had. What was now apparent to America's leaders was that the Commonwealth had influence in all international groupings and associations. It was, indeed, the only international organization in the non-communist world. It would have been grossly misleading to say that the Americans, as yet, either understood the Commonwealth or realized that it offered the best possible means of implementing their own foreign policy. They regarded it as a stabilizing factor, and that was a considerable advance on the irritated embarrassment with which they formerly viewed British "imperialism". The generally accepted view was that the Commonwealth survived by courtesy of the United States. The possibility that the United States might yet itself survive by alliance with the Commonwealth had not entered the realms of practical political thought.

Yet even this cautious approach to the Commonwealth by the Americans, this belated recognition of its stabilizing value, drew them inevitably closer to it. When, early in 1956, Sir John Kotelawala suffered a crushing defeat in the Ceylon elections, there was as much consternation in the U.S.A. as in Britain. For Kotelawala had been a champion of the free world at Bandung, he had been fêted in the U.S.A., he had been regarded as a staunch and dependable ally. It was this excessive identification with the West that brought about his downfall. Sir John was a singularly astute politician who had never completely committed his country to any power. But he had made the extraordinary error of forgetting to be an Asian.

Mr Bandaranaike, who defeated him, was a clever and forceful leader much closer to the Asian spiritual tradition. He had already declared his intention of nationalizing the tea and rubber estates, declaring Ceylon a republic and getting rid of the British bases. But he was a friend of Nehru, and Nehru was still a friend of Britain. Moreover, though Bandaranaike was a shade condescending towards the Commonwealth, he gave no sign of leaving it.

If a general election had fortified Western hopes in Ceylon, the lack of one was the trouble in Pakistan. That country lurched from crisis to crisis. Three months after the enforcement of the constitution, the President was compelled to suspend it in East Pakistan and take over direct administration. An appalling mixture of jobbery and corruption and sheer inefficiency afflicted both wings of Pakistan, and the continual postponing of elections made a cynical mockery of democracy. The Americans had pinned great faith in Pakistan as a bastion against communism and as a powerful democratic pillar of the Muslim world. But here was the strongest evidence that it was not equal to either rôle.

There was, on the other hand, a tragic irony in America's continuing suspicion and dislike of India and above all of Mr Nehru. India's continuing economic struggles could not obscure the evidence of her basic stability. An extremely carefully wrought constitution provided a powerful framework for the country's political progress. The process of consolidating a nation out of the innumerable sects and races of India went fitfully but resolutely forward, though not without much torment and agony, as the demonstrations against the States Reorganization Commission's Report showed. Yet India was demonstrably succeeding so far as the world's largest democracy.

Southward in the seas where the U.S. had made such desperate endeavours for victory in the war there was also cause for American disquiet. The Conference called to discuss Singapore's future had broken down, on the decisive question of internal security. The British Government had rightly decided that Mr Marshall's Government was not strong enough to take risks with the security of what was still an island fortress, not simply for the Commonwealth but for the free world. For his part, Marshall felt he was being offered only the shadow of independence and not the substance. Britain's dilemma was that Marshall's party, uncertainly placed though it was, was the only one in Singapore with which they could reach a satisfactory agreement. There was more hope in the situation when the flamboyant Marshall was replaced as Chief Minister by the much more discreet and canny Lim Yew Hock.

But the question of defence arrangements for not only Singapore but Malaya continued to trouble the British Government. The political outlook in the Federation was promising. Tengku Abdul Rahman returned to Malaya from his triumphant talks in London which virtually made his country self-governing and provided for independence within the Commonwealth by the following year. The Chief Minister was so sure now of his position that he could tell the leader of the communist terrorists, Ching Peng, that he would only meet him again to receive his surrender. What a miraculous transformation that was from the days when the communists seemed to be tearing the country asunder ready for its final conquest. But even Tengku Abdul Rahman had to be cautious about his external connections. He was not able to carry his colleagues with him over membership of SEATO. It was known that he was strongly in favour of Malaya joining but some of his ministers were equally determined that Nehru's policy should be their guide.

The U.S. Government could take comfort from the continuing success of one of their most trusted friends in another Commonwealth country, Australia. There, Mr Menzies had led his party to victory in the Federal elections for the fourth time, and with an increased majority at that. His Labour opponents were torn and riven by internal dissensions and were beaten before they started. But it was problematical whether even a united Labour front would have carried the day. What was happening in Singapore, Malaya and Ceylon did not make for public confidence in Dr Evatt's placatory foreign policy.

The major area in which the policies of Britain and the United States were in dangerous contrast was the Middle East. Here, U.S. commercial interest and dislike of "colonialism" obscured the perils of a vacuum that the departure of the British would inevitably leave. The Russians had their instrument to hand in Nasser, and that vain and ambitious man made no secret of his intention to crush Israel in the near future. Crisis followed crisis in the Middle East and still Britain and America were at odds. Glubb Pasha was dismissed from Jordan, the last of the British troops left the Suez Zone, and the fires of insurrection lit by Egypt and Saudi Arabia threatened to run through the Aden Protectorate. The Arab rulers of the Protectorate were suspicious that British attempts to establish a federation of their territories were merely the prelude to a new British overlordship. To add to the perils of the situation there was the unseemly and provocative "oil war" between Britain and American interests, each trying to outbid the other. Over all this scene of pending chaos in the Middle East a jubilant Nasser gloated. And behind him stood the men of the Kremlin.

There could be no surprise that Britain's determination to stabilize Cyprus and stay there was fortified by the rapid deterioration of her influence in the Middle East. Apart altogether from British and Commonwealth interest, Cyprus was essential to the democratic world. This the Americans appreciated, but their belief was that Britain's handling of the Cyprus problem was more likely to lose the island than to retain it. The strong Greek element in the American population, acting as a pressure group for the Greek Cypriots, made matters worse. But Britain was largely to blame for her predicament. Her own case over Cyprus had gone largely by default in the U.S.

Much nearer home, the Americans had a totally different worry, and in this instance they themselves were the criticized party. Across the border, a Government blue-book dramatically revealed to the people of Canada the alarming extent to which American capital controlled their economy. The trend was well enough known, but its astonishing growth in the post-war years came as a considerable shock to Canadians. The blue-book in question—*Canada's International Investment Position, 1926–1954*—showed that Canada now controlled only half of its own manufacturing industry and about 40 per cent of mining. British investment had shown a steady decline since 1926 whilst that of America had almost trebled. It quickly became clear that the alleged "Americanization" of Canada would develop into a major issue in the next general election. And from this point on a decided anxiety about American influence became steadily more apparent in the Dominion.

All these events, in so many parts of the world where their national interests now indubitably lay, directed American attention to the next meeting of the Commonwealth Prime Ministers, due to be held in London in June. The U.S. press gave it an attention never known before, and there was a great deal of speculation as to the subjects the Prime Ministers would discuss. Coupled with this there was a general satisfaction in the U.S. that sterling, at long last, was showing signs of recovery. It was beginning to be appreciated that Britain herself had greatly strengthened her productive capacity (though sometimes running a grave risk of inflation), and that she would soon be able to release greater resources for the other countries of the Commonwealth.

Altogether, even though there were great problems still to be solved, this turning of the economic tide, this slowly growing sympathy for the Commonwealth in America, and the undoubted diplomatic successes of the Commonwealth all induced an invigorating atmosphere that promised well for the meeting of the Prime Ministers. But, at this very time, events in the Middle East were moving with a deadly certainty towards an upheaval which threatened to tear the Commonwealth apart and indeed destroy it.

CHAPTER XXXI

THE HOUR OF TRIAL

A LONG LIST of subjects awaited the attention of the Prime Ministers. And apart from the urgencies of the international situation (particularly in the Middle East) all of them except possibly Mr St Laurent of Canada had the same priority question in mind: *How could they get capital for development?* It was known that Britain's Chancellor of the Exchequer, Harold Macmillan, was determined to make more intensive efforts to produce a balance of payments surplus which would provide money for Commonwealth development. On the other hand, previous modest surpluses had been consumed by British industry and, despite eighteen months of the credit squeeze, there was little sign of home industry slackening its demands.

The proposed European Common Market was also clearly destined to occupy a prominent place in the minds of the Prime Ministers. The British Government were applying themselves to a close study of this project, aware that events were moving fast and that Britain must decide what sort of association she could effect, if any, with the Common Market. The Commonwealth was, of course, most vitally concerned, and all of its members were anxious that their own interests would be fully protected. And there was some suspicion among the Asian members that it was a device to keep "white" influence in the ascendant in the Commonwealth. Proposals being urged by the Expanding Commonwealth group in the British Parliament sharpened such suspicions, for the group argued that new members, particularly from Europe, would greatly strengthen the influence of the Commonwealth.

The fear that was shared by all of the Prime Ministers was that their inter-Commonwealth trade might suffer. This clashed with the equal hope that a European Common Market could become so powerful an economic bloc that it would amass solid surpluses of capital which could be made available for overseas development. It was true that such a market would embrace nearly 250 million people, an economic unit comparable with Russia and the U.S.A. And it was equally true that the Sterling Area's own reserves, which represented a mere eight per cent of the annual turnover of the Area's trade with the non-sterling world, were quite insufficient to finance Commonwealth development.

In the outcome, the official statement issued after the meeting of the Prime Ministers gave away as little information as ever as to the real play of opinion. For "ten days the Commonwealth Prime Ministers have together reviewed the current state of international affairs", said the statement. Mr Krushchev's remarkable denunciation of Stalin and the temporary wave of liberalism in the communist world which succeeded it excited the particular interest of the Prime Ministers. They reviewed the situation in the Far East and South-East Asia, they were happy to note the progress of the Gold Coast and Malaya towards independence, and were suitably sympathetic about Britain's efforts to find a solution for Cyprus. Mr Bandaranaike, during the meeting, informed his fellow Prime Ministers that though Ceylon proposed in due course to introduce a republican constitution she intended to remain in the Commonwealth.

The problem that darkly overshadowed all else was vigorously discussed, but discreetly dealt with in the official statement: "The

Prime Ministers considered the situation in the Middle East. They reaffirmed their interest in the peace and stability of the area. They welcomed the efforts of the Secretary-General of the United Nations to ensure observance of the terms of the armistice agreements between Israel and the neighbouring Arab States. They agreed that all practicable steps should be urgently taken to consolidate the progress thus made and to seek a lasting settlement of this dispute."

Even as the Prime Ministers agreed to this optimistic effusion, Nasser had set alight a fuse that was destined to fire the most disastrous explosion in the Middle East. Daily he was provoking the maritime nations by his autocratic handling of the organization of the Suez Canal. Inflated to grotesque proportions by his success in getting rid of the last of the British troops, by his dictatorial powers as President, and by his conferences with the "neutralist" leaders in the world, Nehru and Tito, he was more than ready for any adventure to further his cause. Then came a devastating blow to his pride. On July 26, the Americans, precipitately and in a curiously humiliating way, withdrew their offer of financial aid for the building of Nasser's pet project, the Aswan High Dam. Britain followed suit. Within a week Nasser dramatically countered by announcing the immediate nationalization of the Suez Canal, although the Canal Company's concession had twelve years to run. The stage was now set for trouble on an appalling scale.

Nasser had seized Britain, and Western Europe for that matter, by the throat. Over one-quarter of Britain's trade flowed through the Canal and 85 per cent of her total oil requirements. This, now, was at the mercy of a man who had become her implacable enemy. Sir Anthony Eden announced that "no arrangements for the future of this great international waterway would be acceptable to Her Majesty's Government which would leave it in the unfettered control of a single power which could, as recent events have shown, exploit it purely for purposes of national policy". The Leader of the Opposition, Mr Gaitskell, went further and said: "This episode must be recognized as part of the struggle for the mastery of the Middle East. It is all very familiar. It is exactly the same that we encountered from Hitler and Mussolini in the years before the war."

Eden himself had the memory of pre-war dictators and the follies of appeasement heavily in his mind, and from this time on that memory seemed to control all his actions. He called a meeting of the principal users of the Canal in London, including Egypt. Eighteen of them agreed that there should be some sort of international control, and a mission headed by Mr Menzies went to Cairo to meet Nasser. The Egyptian President rejected the plan, arrogantly and finally. The response of the eighteen powers was to set up a Canal Users' Association. Canal payments were withheld from Egypt, and the matter was taken to the United Nations.

What was disturbing was that India, Pakistan and Ceylon (apparently conscious of the bonds of comradeship of the Bandung Conference) remained neutral, which meant in hard fact that they sympathized with the Egyptian case. Pakistan qualified her position later by letting it be known that whilst she recognized the sovereign right of Egypt to nationalize the Canal she would also like to ensure that it was maintained as a free international highway. This was an obvious attempt to balance her Bandung principles with her dislike of Nasser's arrogant assumption of leadership in the Muslim world. The unpalatable truth remained: there was already a split in the Commonwealth over Suez which could well become a dangerous abyss.

As far as India was concerned, the Bandung spirit was overwhelmingly apparent. And it must be remembered that, to India, the Middle East was West Asia. After his early irritation at Nasser's precipitate action Mr Nehru arrived at the surprising conclusion that Nasser was the underdog threatened by Britain and her backers. Though 70 per cent of India's desperately-needed imports passed through the Canal, he and his ministers were still able to convince themselves that the withholding of the Canal fees from Nasser was little better than the old "gunboat diplomacy". To many of the British people, this was a classic example of Mr Nehru's unfortunate habit of adopting the rôle of "unco' guid". If Mr Nehru was irritated and disappointed with Sir Anthony Eden, the mass of the British public were angered and embittered at what they considered to be Indian hypocrisy.

As the dispute went on, with Nasser growing still more obdurate, India's Prime Minister swung over to a more "middle of the road" viewpoint. Mr Krishna Menon, India's spokesman at the London conference, had so bungled matters as to give the impression that India was in the Russian camp. Nothing could have been less to Mr Nehru's liking. His cherished "neutrality" status was endangered and he was driven into making several statements in an effort to correct the position. "The Egyptian way is not India's way," he now announced. There was, at this point, a clear rift developing between

Nasser and Nehru. The Indian Prime Minister was not only concerned about his own position; he now believed that the Egyptian leader had wilfully pushed aside the opportunity of compromise and had endangered that peace to which Mr Nehru was so passionately devoted.

Even as the danger to Commonwealth unity seemed thus to be slowly receding the long-threatened storm broke. Nasser's campaign of intimidation recoiled on his own head. The Israelis, in the conviction that he who strikes first strikes best, waited no longer for the Egyptian dictator's threats to materialize. On October 29, hard and fast their tough citizen army struck at Egypt. With astonishing speed they rolled back the enemy forces, took vast numbers of prisoners and masses of equipment.

The day after Israel launched her attack, Britain and France issued an ultimatum to the combatants to stop fighting. Israel was ready to listen, but Nasser, wounded and humiliated by his crushing defeat, ignored it. Two days later, on November 1, Britain and France intervened in strength, with the declared objective of stopping the war and preserving the safety of the Suez Canal. Port Said was captured, the Egyptian airfields were rendered harmless and Nasser was on the verge of extinction as a power in the Middle East. But the Anglo-French operation was bungled, was hopelessly slow. Triumph within 48 hours would have presented the world with a *fait accompli* that would have put Britain and France in a much stronger position to withstand the avalanche of criticism which descended upon them. As it was, both countries stood in the international dock, not as virtuous policemen safeguarding the peace of the world, but as criminals returning to their bad old "imperial" ways—and inefficient criminals at that.

The rising in Hungary and its brutal suppression by Russia complicated the whole situation. It was possible to argue that the Russians would never have dared to so arrogantly flout world opinion if Britain and France had not given them a lead in Egypt. Yet their murderous campaign in Hungary did prevent the Russians gaining a massive propaganda advantage from the Egyptian crisis. And ironically enough it also helped to save Commonwealth unity. For the Bandung spirit dominated the reactions of the Asian members of the Commonwealth. Here was Britain leading an attack on a Bandung nation, and whatever the reasons there was no excusing that. Nehru could hardly have held the weight of public opinion in

India against Britain, particularly with the communists skilfully manipulating the situation, if Hungary had not diverted the full force of that opinion.

It is possible to argue that not only the Hungarian tragedy, but the very inept bungling of the Suez operation, worked towards the salvation of the Commonwealth. The Asian powers could never have forgiven the humiliation to the Bandung concept of a triumphant Britain standing over a prostrate Egypt. As it was, the partial failure of the operation, the time lag, allowed for wider considerations of the whole Middle East problem, instead of permitting racial and emotional reactions to be the ultimate guide.

True enough, Britain's humiliation seemed all too clear in the eyes of many people. Not only had she returned to the use of force, but she had also been revealed as apparently too weak to stage a war without the permission and aid of the Americans. The truth was that this was almost as great a setback for the Americans as for their two allies, for the Suez episode was the inevitable outcome of Mr Dulles' own inept performance in the Middle East.

Even accepting the fact of Britain's humiliation it is fair to say that there was a good deal of force behind Sir Anthony Eden's belief that Nasser was a dangerous dictator who must be stopped in his stride before he plunged the whole world into war. There was force, too, in his belief that if Israel had been allowed to go on with her war other Arab nations would have gone to the aid of Egypt, with the distinct possibility of Russian intervention as the final outcome. There was the somewhat illusory gain of a United Nations "police force" being at last established, and the Americans launched the "Eisenhower Doctrine" in the Middle East. But Nasser emerged more firmly established than ever and his opportunities for provoking trouble for the West were only too depressingly evident.

During the storm over the Suez operation, Australia, New Zealand and the Federation of Rhodesia and Nyasaland stood by the British action. But the two former did so with some foreboding, for they were acutely conscious of the necessity of retaining their Asian friends. South Africa's Nationalist leaders, though by no means displeased that Nasser was humiliated at the beginning, found it as difficult as ever not to feel some satisfaction that Britain had suffered a setback. Their view was that having got herself into an awkward situation, Britain could get out of it as best she could. Besides, the whole Suez crisis had redounded to South Africa's benefit, for the diversion of shipping from the Canal to the Cape route provided handsome profits at South African ports. However, in the last analysis, the South African leaders would undoubtedly have dropped their isolationist attitude and come out on the British side, had it proved necessary.

Pakistan, much though she disliked Nasser and, even more, being forced on to the same side as Mr Nehru, could not condone the British action. As a Muslim power, she could not reject Egypt's case, although her leaders saw clearly enough that Nasser was dangerous, and that his seizure of the Canal endangered Pakistan's development plans. It was this latter point which enabled Mr Ali, the Prime Minister, to counter the anti-British demonstrations incited by the mullahs, and at least to keep the hard facts of the Canal issue from being swamped by religious fanaticism.

It was hardly to be thought that Ceylon, under Bandaranaike, would sympathize with Britain's use of armed force. But even Ceylon's hostility was conditioned by her heavy dependence on the Canal as a waterway. Almost every aspect of the country's economy became affected; prices shot up, development plans were endangered, government requisitioning and rationing were inevitable.

In India, the feeling against British policy which had been losing its force now hardened into outright anger and hostility. It was even solemnly declared in the press that Britain's moral leadership in India was passing to America. Indian faith in British diplomacy and, above all, in Sir Anthony Eden, collapsed temporarily. Mr Nehru himself lost a great deal of face with his own people by seeming to evade condemnation of the Russian action in Hungary whilst at the same time condemning Britain outright. Why did he do this? The Anglo-French action in accepting a "cease fire" in Egypt and their handing over to the U.N. forces contrasted favourably with the Russian rejection of U.N. "interference" in Hungary. Undoubtedly it eased the heavy pressure on Nehru to break the Commonwealth link. There are those near him who claim that this was what he was working for—the preservation of that link. It could explain the baffling intricacies of his actions.

The reaction of the Canadian Government was wounding in the extreme to Eden, though Mr St Laurent and Lester Pearson, Minister of External Affairs, had their own fierce pro-British critics inside Canada itself. To the Canadian leaders, the chief sin of the British was that they had endangered the very structure of the United

P

Nations, and it was on the U.N. that Pearson's foreign policy really rested. Further, the split between Britain and the U.S. was most alarming to the Canadians—"a spectacle which we never hope to see repeated", said Mr St Laurent. In the end, Lester Pearson garnered great credit for his country when the U.N. accepted his suggestion for the U.N. force in the Suez. But many of his own countrymen still did not forgive his strictures on Britain.

The links of the Commonwealth had been strained as far as even "invisible" links could have been expected to go. The paradox of the situation was that the strain served to strengthen them. For those, throughout the Commonwealth, who most violently opposed Sir Anthony Eden's action, particularly emphasized the alleged harm done to the Commonwealth. Suez, in short, inspired a feeling that it was "our" Commonwealth and not the British Commonwealth that was in danger of disintegrating. That was precisely the reaction for which the more far-sighted protagonists of the Commonwealth ideal had awaited since 1945.

Another benefit which stemmed from Suez was the realization that Commonwealth liaison and consultation were inadequate. The airy claims that the Commonwealth Prime Ministers were in each other's confidence were seen to be grossly misleading, as everyone but complacent officialdom had long deduced. It was hardly to be expected that Britain, having committed herself to military action, would destroy its hoped-for effect by spreading news of her intention, even to her best friends. But the utter dismay and astonishment of her colleagues in the Commonwealth underlined how far from their thoughts had been the possibility of military intervention. The British outlook had most clearly been under-estimated by them. No less had Britain erred in her estimates of Commonwealth reactions. All that happened pointed to the fact that the British Government had assumed they would have the understanding, if not the support, of their partners.

All the members of the Commonwealth were shocked into a realization that its functioning was far from satisfactory. Even more important, a new sense of their common responsibility for its survival was brought home. For Sir Anthony Eden, broken and humiliated after all his great work in the cause of world peace, this may well have been a solitary, if bitter-sweet, consolation. Mr Nehru himself confessed that he had had second thoughts about India remaining in the Commonwealth. "To leave it at the moment would solve nothing," he told those in his country who called for the link to be broken. "We have thought it good for us and, if I may say so with all respect, to the Government of England too, that we have this connection."

If any tribute to the powerful prospect for good that the Commonwealth offered were needed it lay in the action of the Russians. For the watered-down "Titoism" reluctantly accepted by the Russians in Eastern Europe after the terror of Hungary was simply a fake promotion from "colonial" to "dominion" status, an imitation of the Commonwealth. The true face of communism was revealed in the bloody streets of Budapest, and the brutal domination of the Kremlin was the prospect for its satellites, whatever temporary concessions they imagined themselves to have won. In the Soviet empire, there was the voice of Krushchev, and none other. Not even the most bitter critics of Britain could avoid the admission, after Suez, that all were equal in the Commonwealth, including Britain.

Historians of the future may well indicate 1956 as the most fateful year in the history of the British Empire and the Commonwealth. On the short view, and to the more pessimistic, 1956 was the year in which Britain finally accepted the dismal fact that she was a second-rate power and that her Commonwealth was nothing more than a pious aspiration, ending in a whimper. But, out of the chaos, it was possible to command a bolder vision, of a Commonwealth whose members were at last awakening to the knowledge that on all of them depended the survival of a unique experiment in human relationships, forged out of the triumphs and the errors of the centuries.

CHAPTER XXXII

THE MAN AND THE HOUR

IF BRITAIN WAS expected to continue kneeling at the penitent form she gave little sign of it. As the new year got under way the picture presented was again that of a resilient and seasoned people going unshakeably forward with their declared intention of transforming an Empire into a Commonwealth.

There were several reasons for this heartening transformation. One was the heavy-handed manner in which the United States continued to handle the post-Suez situation, making an awkward attempt to draw India away from Britain and closer to herself, and also attempting to end British influence in the Middle East for good. The reaction to this, inside the Commonwealth, ranged from foreboding to outright resentment, and served to strengthen loyalty towards Britain. Secondly, Nasser's blocking of the Suez Canal during the fighting had cost (and was still costing) many of the Commonwealth countries and the Colonies a great deal of money, not to mention frustration. Sterling, indeed, had been under heavy pressure and there was a common desire to rectify the position. Thirdly, Sir Anthony Eden had resigned and Harold Macmillan had succeeded him. There was a deep anger among a large number of British people that Eden had been sacrificed. And all that followed in the two years after his going only served to emphasize that he was at least correct in claiming that Nasser's ambitions were a continual threat to the world. Eden's departure, the calamitous fall from his high place, subdued criticism from the rest of the Commonwealth.

To cap all, two of Britain's dependent territories, Ghana (the new name for the Gold Coast) and Malaya, were due to attain full independence in this year of 1957, Singapore was to reach self-government, and the final arrangements for the launching of the West Indian Federation were nearing completion. All this contrasted impressively with Mr Krushchev's return to an iron imperialism in Eastern Europe. And it also made nonsense of Mr Dulles drawing a grandmotherly skirt away from the taint of British "colonialism". Mr Macmillan addressed himself at once to repairing the breach in Anglo-American relationships, but he had a long way to go before he could hope to dispel the sorry reversion to an outdated "anti-colonialism" in the American State Department.

Ghana's approach to independence was marked by all the drama and flamboyance which had characterized the whole career of Dr Nkrumah. During 1956, he had once again been returned to power by the people of Ghana, though he had lost a little of his support. No man could have been asked to prove himself more. Yet the Opposition still demanded a federal form of government, not trusting Nkrumah to handle the power a unitary state would allow. But Lennox-Boyd declared that on March 6, 1957, the new Ghana would become independent. There were dark threats of secession and even

of civil war, particularly from Ashanti. A deadlock over the Constitution for independent Ghana ensued. At this stage, Lennox-Boyd
himself visited the country at the invitation of Nkrumah and once
more added to his already considerable reputation by bringing the
parties together and convincing the Opposition that the Constitution
did provide reasonable safeguards against abuse. As the trusteeship
territory of British Togoland had already voted in favour of joining
the new state of Ghana, Dr Nkrumah had clearly not only found the
"political kingdom" of his early vision, but was entering into it with
all the trumpets blowing. A sum of £600,000 was set on one side
for celebrations, and 56 nations were invited to send representatives
on March 6 including, very fittingly, Fernando Po, from which the
first cocoa bean had been brought to Ghana to found the greater part
of the country's wealth.

The emergence of Ghana to independence was an event of major
significance to Africa, to the Commonwealth and to the whole
world. No honest observer could disregard the possible hazards
facing a new state which had yet to prove whether it could implant
democracy in the face of a still resistant tribalism. But it undoubtedly stood as a symbol to nationalist leaders throughout Africa,
and the consequences of that could not but be profound. Both Dr
Nkrumah and the Leader of the Opposition, Dr K. A. Busia, had
stated their desire that Ghana should be a member of the Commonwealth. Nkrumah, though he was clearly devoted to the ideals
enunciated at Bandung, was very much aware that ideals were not
enough, and that the close friendship and assistance of stable and
powerful states was a considerable comfort in a dangerous world.
And likewise, an authentic African voice in the counsels of the
Commonwealth was an asset of remarkable importance.

Surprisingly, whilst considerable criticism had been directed at
Britain from some quarters for hastening the progress of Ghana, it
had largely been forgotten that Malaya, the second territory approaching independence, had even less experience of the democratic process. Until 1951, that country had not seen any form of election, and
moreover the six years of hastened tutelage had been conducted
under the shadow of a communist terror. And an independent
Malaya had not merely the threat of tribalism to meet, but the much
stronger one of racialism. The Reid Commission, set up to make
constitutional proposals, tried to provide something for everybody;
citizenship, after meeting certain requirements, for the Chinese and

Indians, a short-term safeguarding of their special privileges as the indigenous population for the Malays. What was especially significant about the Commission was its membership. Lord Reid of Britain, Sir William McKnell of Australia, Mr Justice Malik of India, Mr Justice Abdul Hamid of Pakistan and Sir Ivor Jennings of Britain. This was indeed a "Commonwealth operation" and gave the Commission's Report a prestige and authority which, considering the various racial suspicions, was distinctly helpful.

It was obvious that the new Federation of Malaya would have been the gainer if Britain had been given more time to draw the races more closely together, particularly as Communist China was so near and unpredictable a neighbour. But the agreement on the constitution finally reached between the British Government, the Government of the Federation and the Conference of Rulers did represent an intelligent compromise which held out a reasonable prospect of a stable future for Malaya. Once more Britain had no alternative but to take some risk. It was clearly going to be difficult to make democratic Malayans out of 3,100,000 Malays, 2,500,000 Chinese and 800,000 Indians. But the running tide of events could not be denied, and an independent and democratic Malaya was the best—indeed the only—answer to the communist challenge.

One fortunate circumstance was the personality of the Malayan Prime Minister, Tungku Abdul Rahman. A sincere, resolute and tolerant leader, with a strong faith in the Commonwealth, he was a flat contrast to the more usual type of flamboyant, erratically brilliant national leader. But his more mundane and dependable qualities were precisely what his country needed at this time and in her especial circumstances. He, more than any other one man, had brought to Malaya a realization that racialism is not enough. On August 31 the Federation of Malaya embarked on its independence, having attained this coveted state quietly and with the minimum of bother. For all its tragedies and trials it had probably the highest living standards in Asia. That, its military agreement with Britain and its membership of the Commonwealth gave the new state some hope of becoming the stable bastion of democracy which was sadly needed in the troubled area around it. As Tungku Abdul Rahman said: "For us, with an active communist enemy in our midst, there can be no neutrality. We have made our choice. That choice is with the Commonwealth and it is irrevocable. We will float or sink with our British friends and the great Commonwealth which their leader-

ship has inspired." After the abasement of Suez those words had a
doubly happy sound in faraway Westminster.

In neighbouring Singapore, Chief Minister Lim Yew Hock had
successfully steered the Colony close to self-government. Differences
with the British Government over security had been amicably settled,
but the Singapore leaders were dismayed (or perhaps they just appeared to be) by Lennox-Boyd's decision that anyone judged to have
engaged in subversive activities should be barred from contesting the
first "self-government elections". It was hinted in Singapore that
Lim Yew Hock and his colleagues, during the constitutional talks
in London early in the year, had themselves asked for the veto to be
inserted, and that the British Government had elected to bear the
odium. In any event, the Legislative Assembly approved the London
agreement (stipulating that Lennox-Boyd's veto be taken up again
later) and the stage was set for self-government in the year following.

But it was far from Whitehall or the Far East that circumstance
was now producing a man whose impact on the Commonwealth was
to be of supreme significance. In Canada the 22nd Parliament was
on the eve of dissolution, and in June Prime Minister St Laurent
had determined to go to the electorate for what all the political fore-
casters agreed would be an inevitable victory. Since 1935 the Liberal
Party had repeatedly won, and it was confidently stated that only the
size of the majority would be in doubt. The Liberals, it was said,
were the only truly national party in Canada, their opponents were
scattered, and the French-Canadians always voted Liberal. Of 61-
year-old John Diefenbaker, the new leader of the Conservatives, it
was patronizingly observed that his only hope was to slightly reduce
the large majority of Louis St Laurent.

Nearly every Canadian, including the great majority of Conservatives, believed this. One of the massive, outstanding exceptions was
Diefenbaker himself. This brilliant and dedicated man, a successful
criminal lawyer, was at the height of his powers. A staunch believer
in Britain and passionately devoted to the Commonwealth ideal, he
had an instinct that victory was not only possible, but there for the
asking for the bold and the resolute. He was right. Many Canadians
felt that, after 22 years, it was time for a change of Government.
Others still felt resentment at the lukewarm attitude of the Liberals
to London, especially after Suez. The feeling that the St Laurent
Government had given too much economic power to the Americans
was another great grievance. And the Government had certainly

been showing definite signs of that arrogance which comes from too long a term of power. Diefenbaker not only hammered away at all these things in his campaign, but launched his own evangelistic crusade for a stronger Commonwealth, calling for a Commonwealth Trade Conference as a first step.

The election result provided one of the greatest shocks in Canadian history. The Conservatives won 110 seats in a House of 265, while the Liberals dropped from 170 to 103. Diefenbaker had not won a clear majority. But with the aid of the Co-operative Commonwealth Federation and the Social Credit Party he could govern and he had the chance before him of quickly calling another election whilst the Liberals were still shattered. The very day he was sworn in as Prime Minister he flew off to London to attend the meetings of the Commonwealth Prime Ministers.

Canada's new Prime Minister was certainly not anti-American. But he believed that Canada could not rise to her full stature if she continued to lean so heavily on U.S. aid. He believed that Canada should get nearer the middle of the road again, so that she could truly claim to be the bridge between the U.S. and the Commonwealth. Over and above that he had his own inspiring vision of a Commonwealth growing ever more powerful in influencing the rest of the world. And he was prepared, even with his precarious majority, to add a decisive element of Canadian leadership to that of Britain. He was prepared not merely to talk, but to act. It was this which made Diefenbaker a figure of incalculable significance, that he was eager to be actively responsible for the development of the Commonwealth. This was precisely what had long been needed—a leader from the Commonwealth who was prepared to make it the cornerstone in the development of his own policies, and not relegate it to a subsidiary position. In brief, it was not nearly enough to remove the word "British" from in front of "Commonwealth" to demonstrate that all were equal. It was for the members of the Commonwealth thenceforward to put as much into its development as Britain had done. Diefenbaker saw that. And he was prepared to do something about it.

His impact on the other Prime Ministers at the London meetings was not so dramatic as his admirers anticipated. He was, after all, the "new boy" and it was not to be expected that other statesmen who had been handling the gigantic intricacies of world affairs for years past were going to be swept off their feet by personal dynamism or dramatic speeches. But Diefenbaker pressed home his suggestion for an economic conference. It was illuminating to see how circumspectly it was dealt with in the official statement after the meeting: "The Commonwealth Ministers noted that the Annual Meeting of the International Monetary Fund and the International Bank for Reconstruction and Development will be held in Washington in September. The normal practice is for this meeting to be followed by a meeting of Commonwealth Finance Ministers. The Prime Minister of Canada extended an invitation that this meeting of Finance Ministers should be held this year in Ottawa."

There was nothing revolutionary about that, and its chilly caution might have daunted a lesser man. But to Diefenbaker it was at least a first step. He followed it up, after the Prime Ministers' meetings, with the startling proposal that 15 per cent of Canada's purchases in the U.S. should be switched to Britain. At once he was accused of "electioneering" and of setting a target he well knew could not be reached. Diefenbaker's belief was that the switch would not only save Canada from becoming a mere satellite of the U.S. but it would do more towards strengthening the unity of the Commonwealth than any proposal put forward in the post-war years.

In September, it was clear that Diefenbaker was making headway. The Finance Ministers of the Commonwealth, meeting at Mont Tremblant, agreed that there should be a trade and economic conference of the Commonwealth in the following year. Peter Thorneycorft, the British Chancellor of the Exchequer, said: "We have laid the foundation for another step in the future for the building up still further of this Commonwealth as a vital and moral force in world affairs." And even the City of London agreed that not only was it high time for a ruthless reappraisal, but that the coming conference might well produce startling results.

Mr Diefenbaker's other proposal for a shifting of Canadian trade to Britain drew a suggestion from the U.K. Government for a "free trade area" between Britain and Canada. This appeared to be a somewhat cynical spiking of Diefenbaker's guns, and deeply alarmed Canada's industrialists. But what was undeniable was that the Canadian Prime Minister had shown a hopeful road. From this time on, the efforts to increase Canada-U.K. trade rapidly intensified. In the latter part of the year, a most powerful Canadian trade mission came to Britain led by Minister of Trade Mr Gordon Churchill. It was an extraordinarily stimulating and successful tour for the mission, and its members frankly admitted their pleased astonishment at the post-war performance of British industry. The seeds for the promised trade expansion were being sown. Mr Diefenbaker, despite the criticisms and the caution he had encountered, had already accomplished much of what he set out to do.

To return to the Commonwealth Prime Ministers' meetings in London, it was clearly evident that the wounds of Suez were already healing fast. The presence of Dr Nkrumah, the first African Prime Minister to attend the meetings, spoke more loudly than any words in Britain's favour. Here was warm and living evidence of her integrity of purpose, of her success in her Colonial policy. Nkrumah himself was deeply impressed by the experience, and was particularly drawn to Mr Menzies, the Australian Prime Minister.

Another aspect of Commonwealth co-operation was mentioned in the official statement—the use of nuclear energy for civil purposes. The Prime Ministers "recognized the growing importance of the contribution which nuclear energy can make to the peaceful development of their countries and the rest of the world and the value of close collaboration between members of the Commonwealth in this field". It was stated that nuclear scientists would be invited to an informal meeting in Britain in 1958. One more link was being strengthened. But how remarkable it was to recall that exactly 60 years before, to the month, Queen Victoria's Diamond Jubilee had been celebrated, and the first Imperial Conference in London held.

CHAPTER XXXIII

"THE MOST EFFECTIVE ANTI-COLONIALIST"

AFTER THE Prime Ministers' meeting, there was evidence of a slow but sure change in the American attitude towards Britain. Mr Adlai Stevenson, President Eisenhower's Democratic opponent in the Presidential election, declared at the University of Oxford ceremony that "Britain has been the most effective anti-colonist of all time." Mr Stevenson had long had a shrewder and broader view of international events than many other leading Americans, and it was certain that his views commanded great respect in some of the more informed quarters of the U.S. Mr Eisenhower himself was clearly aware that his previous strictures on Britain had gone far beyond either wisdom or fairness.

During his Oxford speech, Mr Stevenson had much cheered the hearts of those who knew that the rift between the U.S. and Britain was dangerous in the highest degree. He spoke of "some of the great achievements of British imperialism—stable administrative order in Asia and Africa, world-wide economic advance and a high measure of international security". And when one looked back over 1957 these words of a great American did not overstate the case. Ghana and Malaya had captured the greatest attention, with their final emergence to independence, but all along the line there was the indisputable evidence of actual or intended advance.

The Nigerian leaders at their conference in London had cleared up many of the problems delaying their attainment of independence. True, Britain had refused to be stampeded into a firm date, but it was widely recognized that the Nigerians would be in full control within the next three years. And this space of time was necessary if the prickly fears of minority peoples were to be resolved. These fears had led to the demand for still more states in the Nigerian Federation. What was too often forgotten was that Nigeria was not a natural state, but a British creation, formerly consisting of colonies and protected states. It was for the "Big Three" of Nigeria to demonstrate within the next three years that they had the stuff of statesmen in them, and that they could between them forge a sense of Nigerian patriotism.

It was intriguing to note that whilst the Nigerian national leaders were facing up to the problems of democracy, leaders of some other Colonial territories, much further back on the road, were imitating the earlier extravagances of the Nigerian leaders and trying to force the pace against the dictates of reason.

In Zanzibar, for example, Arab nationalism had overreached itself and had been overtaken by an African nationalism which now threatened to engulf the Protectorate. The Arab Nationalist Party's leader, Sheikh Ali Muhsin, had pressed home a demand for a common electoral roll, and won. But when the elections were held they resulted in a complete defeat of the Arabs and a total victory for the African-Shirazi candidates. The Arabs found themselves in the embarrassing position of being a minority group, like the Europeans in Kenya. What had happened was that the Africans wanted slower, not faster, constitutional advancement so that they could look after their own interests, and prevent the Arabs from seizing the power.

On the further rim of faraway South-East Asia an even more ironical position had arisen. The people of the small but oil-wealthy British-protected state of Brunei actually turned down the chance of playing a much larger part in government. Their enlightened ruler, Sultan Sir Omar Ali Saifuddin, had announced a plan two years before to democratize Brunei's feudal-pattern government. He wanted to grant a written constitution, leading eventually to State Council Members being elected, and to set up urban and rural councils. In reply to this the new People's Party agitated for "freedom from colonialism" and opposed the plan. The majority of the ordinary people were certainly against the Sultan's proposed changes, though some observers said that this was because of the People's Party misrepresenting the Sultan's intentions. The truth was that the People's Party wanted their own plan adopted—free elections everywhere, apparently for a central legislature. His Highness expressed himself as "deeply disappointed that such an important step should not have received the welcome which was confidently expected", and there the matter sadly lay.

The leader of the People's Party, Sheikh Azahari bin Sheikh Mahmoud, a Brunei Malay, was a man of considerable ambition. He aimed at bringing Sarawak and North Borneo into union with Brunei, and then linking all three with Malaya in "one great Malay homeland". Despite accusations of communism, Azahari and his party openly paid tribute to Britain's work, and showed no desire to break away from the Commonwealth, still less from the Shell Company. Their first aim was to break the "autocratic power" of the Sultan, even though that ruler was rapidly turning Brunei into the first welfare state in Asia.

In the end, it was announced that it was hoped to bring a new constitution into effect in 1958. Details of the Sultan's draft proposals, amplified by the British Resident, stated that district councils would be elected by secret ballot, and that there would be a Privy Council, an Executive Council and a Legislative Council which would have 15 unofficial members out of 28. But the Sultan was still to remain head of the executive and all executive authority was to be vested in his name. Azahari had apparently gained some points, but he was a long way short of his objective.

Neighbouring Sarawak was also given a majority of unofficial members on its Council Negri (Legislative Council) and election arrangements were in hand. This corner of the Commonwealth in South-East Asia was now markedly on the move after years of what seemed to be self-induced somnolence, for war-shattered North Borneo was also to be given a majority of unofficial members. As for Azahari's plan for a union of the three territories, all the evidence was that Whitehall wanted to encourage just such an outcome.

Complicated but hopeful developments were evident in many parts of the Colonial Empire. But what of those enduring problems— British Guiana, British Honduras, Cyprus and Malta? All four of them had been the subject of alternate hopes and fears through the post-war years; "solutions" had disintegrated time and again, and between them they added up to a major setback in the British record.

For a time it had seemed as if the way ahead was clear for British Honduras, with Leigh Richardson showing every sign of having become a responsible and intelligent leader. Alas, he was heavily defeated by his old colleague and present enemy, 37-year-old George Price of the extremist programme and anti-British views. History had repeated itself, and the country was back where it had been in 1954, possessing a popular government opposed to Britain, the Commonwealth and the West Indies Federation.

British Guiana was in slightly better shape. That country had again been given the democratic privilege of free elections and immediately returned the unpredictable Dr Jagan to power. His pro-communist party secured an absolute majority of votes, winning nine out of fourteen seats. Some of his pre-election speeches gave little hope that he had learned the lesson of 1953, when the constitutional crisis he provoked ended in a postponement of the democratic experiment. But this time there was a brake to hand to check the Doctor if need be. The new interim constitution gave the Governor power to appoint up to eleven members to the Legislative Council. These, with the three official members, could match the fourteen unofficial, and the government itself was in the hands of an Executive Council— appointed by the Governor, who also possessed a casting vote.

It was as well that the Governor was that same able Sir Patrick Renison who had handled matters so wisely in British Honduras on a previous occasion. He could block any further attempt by Jagan to introduce a communist state, but he was not the man to use his powers so ruthlessly as to put compromise out of court. As it happened, Jagan himself chose the path of discretion and bent his early efforts as the new Minister for Trade and Industry towards developing British Guiana's prosperity. Even on federation (which previously he had resolutely opposed) he intimated that he had an open mind. But he deftly sidestepped any questions as to whether he had forsworn his Marxist ambitions.

Both the problem islands in the Mediterranean were causing the British Government acute concern, but Cyprus the more so because terrorism had neither been discredited nor destroyed. The Radcliffe constitutional proposals, accepted by H.M. Government, provided for a period of self-government under British sovereignty, as a prelude to self-determination. They looked reasonable enough, for anywhere else but Cyprus. The Greek Cypriots thought nothing of the proposals, and the Turks started to demand partition. But some relief came to the island when Britain released Makarios from the Seychelles—to go anywhere but Cyprus. Eoka, the terrorist organization, thereupon proclaimed a temporary suspension of violence.

Towards the end of the year, it was felt that conditions now allowed for an attempt at a political approach, and Sir Hugh Foot, an experienced and resolute Colonial Governor, succeeded Sir John Harding as Britain's man in Cyprus. Harding, for all his critics, had done what was required of him in the circumstances, blunting the power of Eoka even before the truce. Now it was for Foot to see if constitutional progress was possible. He made a good start, touring the island, meeting all kinds of people, establishing a reputation as a good and sincere man. But it was not to be long before Foot's conciliatory approach was answered with blood and tears.

As for Malta, the talks on integration went on and on, through postponement and crisis to eventual deadlock. Finally, the economic conditions of Malta began to overshadow the constitutional prospects. British defence cuts were clearly going to affect the Malta naval dockyard, which was the mainstay of the island's economy. Britain set up an industrial advisory committee to "foster and encourage industrial development and promote tourism", but that did not allay the fears of severe unemployment in Malta. Premier Mintoff grew steadily more inflexible in his viewpoints, and all the signs were that he was ready to make the issue of the dockyard a test of the British Government's faith.

In Africa, it was Kenya which was now entering a new and delicate stage. Sir Evelyn Baring, the Governor, had gone to the territory when the bloody "panga politics" of the Mau Mau were challenging the very existence of Kenya. Now, his term of office having been extended, he faced a different sort of challenge. Led by Tom Mboya, the African nationalist leaders declared their opposition to the Lyttelton Constitution, which was based on a system of racial quotas in the council of ministers. They refused, also, to take any part in government. It was Baring's task and duty to hold Kenya on to a multi-racial course, but the racial antagonisms—not to mention the antagonisms within the races—faced him with a daunting test.

For the first time in history, the Africans of Kenya had voted their own representatives into a legislature. But only about 126,000 had used the vote at all, out of half-a-million who had been expected to register. To the vast bulk of Kenya's six million Africans the apparatus of democracy was still unknown. Yet Mboya from this time on regarded himself as the voice of the Africans, and indeed there was no denying that his power among his people mounted steadily. He demanded increased African representation in the government of the country, and both the Asian and European political groups agreed in principle. What they did not agree with was the sweeping nature of Mboya's demands. Mboya was a young man in a hurry, and he wanted equal rights and opportunities for all races in Kenya in quick time, whatever the risks.

It was all too obvious that the Africans of Kenya could not provide more than a minute percentage of the men to man a modern system of government, or with the managerial and technical skills needed to operate a national economy in the modern world. If ever a country needed a policy of *gradual* transition from Colonial Office control with local white dominance to racial parity with equal rights for all it was Kenya. Mboya must have recognized this. The unavoidable conclusion is that he felt he must play his hand strongly in the present, in case fortune turned against him in the future. And that could well happen. For the Kikuyu might recover their self-belief and want none of Mboya. And the parlous state of "democratic" government in a number of newly-independent territories outside the Commonwealth had certainly strengthened Britain's hand if she wanted to return to more cautious political advancement in her Colonies.

In November, Lennox-Boyd (who had visited Kenya in an attempt to find what agreement there was between the races over political advancement) said that local agreement was not in sight. The European and Asian Elected Ministers had resigned, in the belief that "the best interests of Kenya would be served" by the Secretary of State himself taking the initiative. Lennox-Boyd announced that he had decided that there should be six additional seats in the Legislative Council for African elected members. There would also be twelve other new seats, four for each race, which would be filled through election by the whole Legislative Council sitting as an electoral college. Two Ministers would be selected from the African members, and there would not be less than three and not more than six Parliamentary Secretaries, whose office would be changed to that of Assistant Minister. Two of these were to be Africans, one an Asian and one an Arab.

Mboya rejected Lennox-Boyd's solution, and it was clear that he intended to block any step that involved the development of Kenya as a multi-racial country. The risk now arose of a government operating in a vacuum of its own, divorced from the mass of the people. And that would mean one more deadlock for democracy. Perhaps it was what Mboya wanted. His ears seemed deaf to the blunt warning of Lennox-Boyd: "I do not see any prospect in the foreseeable future of the holder of the office in the United Kingdom which I now hold being able to abandon his responsibilities in respect of Kenya".

It was a sorry outcome for those who had believed that out of the travail of the Mau Mau terror a new spirit of racial amity had been Kenya."

CHAPTER XXXIV

"APPOINTMENT WITH DESTINY"

To a great and enthusiastic audience in London's Albert Hall in November of 1958, Prime Minister Diefenbaker of Canada, his peculiarly piercing, light blue eyes shining with fervour, raised his hands in a commanding gesture: "The Commonwealth has an appointment with destiny!" he cried.

A trite enough phrase, one of a hundred such which have too often in the past served to wrap the Commonwealth in a platitudinous fog. But there was a difference this time. The difference lay not only in the sincerity but in the purpose of the man who uttered those words, and in the remarkable response of the people who listened to him. Led by the Prime Minister of the United Kingdom, Harold Macmillan, they stood to their feet, clapping for minutes on end. They sensed that the Commonwealth was indeed reaching a stage in its development that would decide how great an instrument for the welfare of man it would be.

If humanism is to survive in the world through the triumph of democracy, then the Commonwealth still stands as the chief instrument for that triumph. One by one nations of Britain's Empire have emerged to independence, all of them except Burma and Eire as members of the Commonwealth, all of them taking over a democratic system of government. And there lies one of the chief anxieties. Among the African and Asian nations of the Commonwealth, how deep has democracy been planted? Will it wither because of feeble roots? Has communism only to wait for the inevitable?

The year 1958 has given a new urgency to those questions. For Pakistan, stumbling from one desperate expedient to another, is under military dictatorship as these words are written. However benevolent the early intentions of that dictatorship, history shows how difficult it is to return to ordered and elected government after rule by force. Pakistan has been a disaster for democracy. Yet it is still linked with democracy through the Commonwealth, and in that lies its chief hope.

In Ceylon, "rule by emergency decree" could steadily slide into suppression of opposition and a totalitarian one-party government. Mr Bandaranaike has had a desperate struggle to keep the struggling factions of his government together, a government in which Buddhists and communists are strange bedfellows. Furthermore, he has the intractable problem of the Tamils on his hands, plus an undoubted recrudescence of corruption and inefficiency inside Ceylon. Bandaranaike, an aristocrat buttressed by left-wingers, does not appear to have either the dominant character or the wide-ranging tolerance which could bring a proper conception of nationhood to the Sinhalese. And if he fails, the present odds are on Ceylon moving still further left, possibly to a milk-and-water (but none the less dangerous) communism.

The Federation of Malaya has already met the full fury of communist imperialism and—at least for the present—defeated it. That single accomplishment represents a considerable victory for

Q

democracy. But let us not blind ourselves to the fact that the menace of China is still near at hand, that communism may come again and this time triumph by way of Chinese-dominated Singapore. Yet if Malaya, Singapore, Brunei, North Borneo and Sarawak could be brought together in a democratic federation, there could be a new morning of hope for freedom in those far seas.

All this leaves India as the one towering bastion of democracy in Asia. And it can be said at once that Pandit Nehru stands as one of the most important men to the Commonwealth, and to the whole free world at the present time. Whatever his detractors say, and whatever his errors of judgement, the monolithic fact remains that Nehru is running the only true and stable democracy in all Asia. Let there be no mistake, he has not hesitated to deal with the communists ruthlessly and efficiently inside India, whatever his wooing of them outside. His extension of the Preventive Detention Bill demonstrated his resolve to safeguard democracy. Yet even Nehru has to face the fact of Kerala, that communist-dominated state inside his own borders which may prove the Trojan horse.

What will happen when Nehru goes? That is the question of almost frightening importance to the free world. The strength of the Indian Communist Party has risen from 50,000 to a quarter of a million inside five years. It wages a resolute and adroit war against Nehru, and cleverly works to steal the all-powerful cloak of patriotism from the Congress. A return to despair, a halting of the slow, grim advance to a better way of life for India would let in the communists. India must not be allowed to fail, and that is probably the most vital task facing the Commonwealth today.

If Pandit Nehru, with his enormous personal prestige throughout not only India but all Asia, leaves the scene the present talk is that Finance Minister Morarji Desai would succeed him. He, too, is a man of complete integrity and remarkable prestige. Yet he is also one of the last of the Ghandians of the great years, and time is not on his side. But with the most powerful and unwavering help of her friends, India could so continue to buttress her democratic way of life as to make it impregnable. The survival of democracy in Asia, and in all the undeveloped countries of the world, depends overwhelmingly on India.

What of Africa? Ghana, first of the "black Africa" territories to reach independence, remains an enigma. From the beginning, Britain was taking a calculated risk in handing over the reins of power to Dr Nkrumah. He has survived several hazards, and Ghana has not fallen into the chaos so gleefully predicted by its doubting critics, and especially by malevolent and short-sighted enemies. Yet tribalism is still rampant, and so is that African tendency to autocracy, even despotism. Circumstance and tradition may yet make a dictator out of Dr Nkrumah, and it would be self-delusion not to recognize that.

The Nigerians, next door, will take over their own country completely in 1960. And that means that Britain's imperial mission will have come within sight of completion, for roughly half the population of the Colonial Empire is in Nigeria. The affairs of only some 35 million people will remain the business of the Colonial Office, as compared with around 650 million people in the free nations of the Commonwealth.

After the final conference in London, in October of last year, it was clear that the preservation of democratic government and membership of the Commonwealth were genuinely regarded by the Nigerian leaders as basic to their very existence. There was a determination to avoid some of Nkrumah's errors, even a ridicule of his concept of "an African way of doing things". The Nigerian leaders settled for democracy, without subterfuge or qualification. But intention is never enough, particularly for young and unskilled countries, and the ever-present threat of tribal and religious fissures in Nigeria is only too apparent. Yet the beginning has been good, and a tolerance has developed that few would have thought possible. If Nigeria succeeds in not only establishing democracy but resolutely practising it, its influence in "black Africa" will certainly be predominant.

In Africa, that other concept on which the Commonwealth rests, partnership between race and creed, will meet its decisive test. Dr Nkrumah's outlook has most certainly influenced the post-war generation of African leaders in East and Central Africa, even if the Nigerians are suspicious of his pan-African ambition and post-Bandung effervescence. It may be that the more cautious and realistic approach by Nigeria will lead to amity between white and black in "Commonwealth Africa". But at present Nkrumah is the guide and from his feet, burning to spread a gospel of Africa for the Africans, have come Dr Hastings Banda of Nyasaland and Tom Mboya of Kenya. Between them, these two could harden all black Africa south of the Sud swamps and north of the Limpopo into complete non-compromise. For their policy is that of "multi-racial democracy" for East and Central Africa, which in short means an overwhelming black predominance in government, with European and Indian tolerated on African terms.

Against this stands the partnership experiment in the Federation of Rhodesia and Nyasaland. Sir Roy Welensky has just won another term of power in the Federation. He has five years in which to offer something that will triumph over the heady promises of Mboya and Banda, and it is going to be fierce going for him. If, in these five years, Welensky cannot rally to his side able and imaginative leaders (the word "moderate" has become too tainted to use in an African context) then partnership will be crushed between the pressure of black nationalism and the equal pressure of South Africa's "white supremacy" policy. Banda, the older man, knows this and he aims to hasten the process. Mboya, young and impatient, is forcing the issue up in Kenya. Ironically, he could overplay his hand and give partnership a better chance of succeeding.

Tanganyika will bear watching. There, Julius Nyerere is already in a unique position. In the first general election in Tanganyika's history, the successful Indian and European candidates were those given Nyerere's blessing. Only with that could they get the African votes necessary for their election. In effect, Nyerere is the first African in a multi-racial territory whose goodwill is a condition of survival for European politicians. It will be intriguing to see how it works out, whether Nyerere continues to act as a Tanganyikan (as in the early days of his success) or whether he acts as an African.

The real answer to Africa's problem—and what would be the triumph for the Commonwealth—is that men should cease to base their actions on the colour of their skins, and be Rhodesians, or Kenyans, or Tanganyikans. Inevitably, there will eventually be more African voters than European or Indian in the multi-racial lands. But that day must be delayed until the African contribution to the welfare and progress of their country entitles them to that dominance. And once they have reached that stage, the hope must be that dominance would not enter into it at all, but that the mass of Africans would so far have advanced as to recognize the incalculable value of the European and Indian contributions, out of all proportion to their numbers.

To give unlimited power now to Africans in East and Central Africa would lead to economic collapse, civil war and the almost certain emergence of a black dictatorship. Those dangers have so far been averted in Ghana, but by no considerable margin. How real and inevitable they would be in multi-racial territories. All this is not to say that the Europeans must not face up to the real implications of partnership, and its inevitable outcome. But between their fears and the ambitions of the Africans the way must be found, and no other realistic solution has been advanced except that of partnership.

South Africa—or rather her leaders—believe they have found an answer. But Dr Verwoerd and his lieutenants pursue a policy which, to practically all outside observers (even the most sympathetic), seems utterly unrealistic in the light of modern events. That, in short, is the trouble: the *apartheid* policy seems to have been conceived by men who believe that South Africa can be insulated from the mighty flow of forces in the outside world. Furthermore they seem to believe that South Africa is not subject to ordinary politico-economic laws, and that you can launch an industrial revolution without dynamic changes. Mr Strijdom's crushing electoral victory in 1958 only demonstrated how really barren and full of despair is the South African political scene. When Dr Verwoerd succeeded Strijdom, it went without saying that *apartheid* would have thenceforward an even more implacable prophet.

For the Commonwealth, the danger of South Africa lies in its distortions of democracy, and in its utter rejection of racial partnership. There have been clamorous voices for the "sacking" of South Africa from the Commonwealth. On the contrary, membership of the Commonwealth offers the best hope for both white and black in South Africa. For the Commonwealth remains the only liberal influence which can to any degree bring influence to bear on the Union's vast and daunting problems.

Even if the will and the experience to practise democracy are present, the battle will be still lost if communism can offer better standards of living and a more efficient system of development. In Asia and in Africa, ideals do not fill bellies, and for hundreds of millions of underfed, under-privileged and under-educated people the first conditions of survival are food and medicine and shelter. This battle, too, the Commonwealth must face and win, and that was abundantly recognized at the Commonwealth Economic Conference in Montreal at the end of September 1958.

Mr Diefenbaker set in train greater things that perhaps even he had dreamed of when he pressed for a Commonwealth conference.

For out of Montreal there evolved the idea of a joint attack on poverty by a free world. This had of course been dealt with in a million words before, even tackled on a moderate scale, piecemeal. But now there was clear the pattern of a grand design, and that pattern became clearer soon after the World Bank meetings in New Delhi. Briefly, it came down to this: the richer nations of the Commonwealth (led by Canada and Britain), the United States and the wealthier countries of democratic Europe were pledged to raise the living standards of less fortunate lands. The grim and unremitting war between the two great political creeds of the world, democracy and communism, was to be fought out on the economic as well as the ideological front, and victory there was the first essential.

This unqualified recognition of a common cause, leading to co-operation between the Commonwealth, the United States and Europe, is clearly the ideal for the preservation of all three. That is why the proposal for a European Free Trade Area, to link up with the already-established European Common Market, was so important. A Europe divided, a Britain torn between Europe and the Commonwealth—these things would be disastrous. As this is written, negotiations in Europe are bogged down, and it is difficult to see how French requirements can be met without making the proposed Common Market farcical. The Commonwealth has recognized the desirability of such a Market and sees in it the prospect of great benefits for all parties concerned. Clearly, the aim of Britain must continue to be the link between the Commonwealth and Europe.

A constant theme of this book has been the powerful necessity for a closer understanding and liaison between the United States and the Commonwealth. The passage of events serves continually to underline that theme—the downfall of the "old guard" in Iraq, the perpetual threat to Jordan and the Aden Protectorate, the whole menace of Nasser's vaulting ambitions in the Middle East; the constant challenge of China in South-East Asia; the deep and dark stirrings of the uncommitted African giant; the troubled discontents in a Europe whose unity is perilously strained and weak.

It is for the Commonwealth countries to realize now exactly what their responsibilities are, as Britain's colonial policy is gradually fulfilled. A study of the map shows how comparatively near that fulfilment is. Over in the West Indies, with the Federation launched, only the future of British Honduras and British Guiana remains to be decided. It is in Africa that the major work remains to be done, and even that may be completed more quickly than we think. If the Federation of Rhodesia and Nyasaland attains Dominion status, Kenya will remain the outstanding problem, for the road ahead for both Uganda and Tanganyika is now clear. What is there left? A number of smaller or less-developed territories and islands—Aden, Bermuda, the Bahamas, Gibraltar, the Falklands, the Gambia, Hong Kong, St Helena, the Seychelles, Fiji, the islands of the Western Pacific, Zanzibar, Malta and Cyprus, Mauritius, Sierra Leone.

Their very names light up the long and complicated story of a maritime empire, and certainly their future will be equally complicated. A few may stand, if not by themselves then in league with their neighbours—Sierra Leone, the Somaliland Protectorate, the Aden Protectorate. Others will surely remain the perpetual charges of Britain with a degree of self-government, and still others will become international problems, as stricken, bloody Cyprus has been. The other Commonwealth powers can sometimes be the guardians, as for example in the Pacific with Australia and New Zealand and a federation of Oceania. The confusion and bitterness which have arisen over Malta show how little prospect there is of integration of smaller territories with Britain herself.

Clearly, there is still much work and many problems ahead for the present Secretary of State for the Colonies and for his successors, but it remains true that the time has arrived for the independent nations themselves to come in with Britain with all their strength and conviction in the shaping of the Commonwealth. Diefenbaker of Canada has given a great lead in associated leadership, Nehru of India is the champion of democracy in Asia, to Sir Roy Welensky falls the burden and perhaps the honour of establishing multi-racial nationhood, Menzies of Australia bridges Europe and Asia ten thousand miles away from Britain.

It is such positive acceptance of a leading rôle, plus the unswerving determination on the part of each member that the Commonwealth must succeed, which will count more than any number of words, more even than meetings or committees or missions.

There are so many ways in which the member nations can strengthen their responsibility, instead of still leaving so much to Britain. For a modest start, the more powerful nations should have a Commonwealth Relations minister inside the government. And attached to his department should be a Commonwealth information department. However excellent the work of the British Council, the information services of the British Commonwealth Relations Office, or the British Central Office of Information, it is not good that everything about the Commonwealth should be stamped with the word "British".

As Mr Bernard Braine, M.P., said in a debate in the House of Commons on Commonwealth development: "We are in the last stages of transition from a centrally directed Empire to a loose partnership of equal and independent States. The idea of tutelage is fast giving way to the concept of partnership."

The Commonwealth, despite its weaknesses and imperfections, is what the United Nations should be, but is not, a genuine brotherhood of man. It can provide the inspiration and the means for a better world, a prosperous and peaceful world, but only if those who belong to it are prepared to recognize that it is no longer the British Commonwealth but "Our Commonwealth".

BIBLIOGRAPHY

AMAMOO, J. G., *The New Ghana,* 1958

AMERY, LEOPOLD, *The Forward View,* 1935

BAILEY, S. D., *Parliamentary Government in the Commonwealth,* 1951

BELSHAW, HORACE, Ed., *New Zealand,* 1947

BROWN, G. W., *Canada,* 1950

BURNS, SIR A. C., *History of Nigeria,* 1942
         Colonial Civil Servant, 1949

CALVOCORESSI, P. AND WINT, GUY, *Middle East Crisis,* 1957

CARRINGTON, C. E., *The British Overseas,* 1950

CHATTERJEE, SIR ATUL CHANDRA, *The New India,* 1948

COATMAN, JOHN, *The British Family of Nations,* 1950

CRAWFORD, R. M., *Australia,* 1952

DULLES, F. R., *America's Rise to World Power,* 1955

EMERSON, RUPERT, *Malaysia,* 1937

FRANKS, SIR OLIVER, *Britain and the Tide of World Affairs,* 1955

GRIFFITHS, SIR PERCIVAL, *The British Impact on India,* 1952

HAILEY, LORD, *Place of the Colonies in the Commonwealth,* 1941
         An African Survey, Reprinted 1957

HALL, D. G. E., *History of South East Asia,* 1955

HANCOCK, W. K., *Survey of British Commonwealth Affairs,* Two volumes—1937 and 1942

HARVEY, HEATHER, *Consultation and Co-operation in the Commonwealth,* 1952

HEWITT, A. R., *Guide to Resources for Commonwealth Studies in London, Oxford and Cambridge,* 1957

HILL, SIR GEORGE, *A History of Cyprus,* 1940

HINDEN, RITA, *Empire and After,* 1949

HOLDEN, LORD, *Ceylon,* 1939

HUXLEY, ELSPETH, *East Africa,* 1941

JENNINGS, SIR WM., *The British Commonwealth of Nations,* 1948

KENYATTA, J., *Facing Mount Kenya,* 1938

KIRK, G. E., *Short History of the Middle East,* 1948

KNAPLUND, PAUL, *The British Empire, 1815–1939*, 1941

LOW, SIR FRANCIS, *Struggle for Asia*, 1955

LUMB, S. V., *A Short History of Central and Southern Africa*, 1954

MAITLAND, P., *Task for Giants*, 1957

MANSERGH, NICHOLAS, *Survey of British Commonwealth Affairs*, 1952 and 1958

Documents and Speeches on British Commonwealth Affairs, 1931–1952, 1953

The Multi-Racial Commonwealth, 1955

PANNIKAR, K. M., *Asia and Western Dominance*, 1953

PARKINSON, SIR COSMO, *The Colonial Office from Within*, 1945

ST CLARE GRONDONA, L., *Commonwealth Stocktaking*, 1953

SIMNETT, W. R., *The British Colonial Empire*, 1942

THOMSON, IAN, *The Rise of Modern Asia*, 1957

UNDERHILL, F. R., *The British Commonwealth*, 1956

WALKER, ERIC A., *A History of South Africa*, Reprinted 1940

WEI, HENRY, *China and Soviet Russia*, 1956

WINT, GUY, *The British in Asia*, 1954

Spotlight on Asia, 1955

WOLFSON, FREDA, *Pageant of Ghana*, 1958

ZINKIN, M., *Development for Free Asia*, 1958

Crown Colonist, Vols. 1 to 20 (1939–Sept. 1950)

New Commonwealth, Vols. 21 to 36 (Oct. 1950–Dec. 1958)

Material was also gathered for this book from a vast number of newspapers, periodicals and reports from many countries of the Commonwealth, too numerous to mention in detail. British Government White Papers, the various editions of the Commonwealth Relations Office List and the Colonial Office List, the Annual Reports of the various Colonies, publications of the Reference Division of the Central Office of Information, texts of speeches etc made by the Prime Minister, the Rt. Hon. Harold Macmillan, M.P., on his Commonwealth Tour of January-February 1958, *The United States and Africa* published by the American Assembly, Columbia University; the Communiqués of the Meetings of the Commonwealth Prime Ministers have been of particular and constant assistance.

INDEX

Date Due

NOV 1 '62			
MAR 6 '69			
	PRINTED	IN U. S. A.	